'Nepal' in China's Foreign Policy

'Nepal' in China's Foreign Policy

Mukesh Kumar Singh

PRASHANT PUBLISHING HOUSE
DELHI-110094

Published by :
Prashant Publishing House
C-34, 28 Foota Road, Gali-3,
West Karwal Nagar, Delhi-110094
Phone : 011-22963970, Mob. : 9810396373
e-mail.: prashantpublishinghouse@gmail.com

'Nepal' in China's Foreign Policy
Reserved
First Published **2014**

ISBN 978-93-80565-41-5

PRINTED IN INDIA
Published by Mr. R.K. Jha M/s Prashant Publishing House and Published at H.S. Offset House Press, Delhi.

Preface

On foreign policy front, Nepal's achievement is considerable. Nepal successfully organized the eleventh South Asian Association for Regional Cooperation (SAARC) summit in Kathmandu on January 5-6, 2002 after the hiatus of three and a half-year. President of Sri Lanka Chandrika Bandaranaike Kumaratunga handed the chairmanship of SAARC to Premier Sher Bahadur Deuba. The SAARC leaders signed the Convention on Preventing and Combating Trafficking in Women and Children for Prostitution and Convention on Regional Arrangements for the Promotion of Child Welfare in South Asia.

There has been a major shift in China's foreign policy towards Nepal since the Maoist ascendance to power. China had earlier adopted a policy of 'non-intervention' in the internal matters of Nepal and largely stayed out of Nepalese internal politics. However, the demise of the monarchy and the ascendance of political parties have forced China to reshape its Nepal policy. Moreover, frequent protests by Tibetans in recent months alerted the Chinese to the possibility of the China-Tibet border being misused. Consequently, China has sought to engage Nepalese political actors at all levels, primarily to secure the border with Nepal. With the Maoists in power, China also hopes to use its ideological commonalities to suppress the Tibetan movement in Nepal.

As the book addresses this crucial issue quite deftly, it is hoped that it would prove to be a source of great information for the reader.

—Editor

Contents

1

Foreign Policy and Nepal's Achievement

On foreign policy front, Nepal's achievement is considerable. Nepal successfully organized the eleventh South Asian Association for Regional Cooperation (SAARC) summit in Kathmandu on January 5-6, 2002 after the hiatus of three and a half-year. President of Sri Lanka Chandrika Bandaranaike Kumaratunga handed the chairmanship of SAARC to Premier Sher Bahadur Deuba.

The SAARC leaders signed the Convention on Preventing and Combating Trafficking in Women and Children for Prostitution and Convention on Regional Arrangements for the Promotion of Child Welfare in South Asia.

They committed to the SAARC economic union as the common long-term goal of SAARC and to frame South Asian Free Trade Area (SAFTA) by the end of this year; endorsed the reports of the Council of Ministers and decided to address terrorism in a holistic manner; directed to expedite some specific programs such as the completion of SAARC social charter; discussed about making a common position on various international issues, especially related to the WTO; and ended with the release of Kathmandu Declaration in which they agreed to commit themselves to 56 points of various issues including poverty alleviation, terrorism and cooperation in the economic sectors and agreeing to meet in Pakistan which, unfortunately has been cancelled.

On August 19, the SAARC Standing Committee comprising the foreign secretaries agreed that the member states' domestic laws on terrorism had to be made compatible with international laws on terrorism. In its meeting on January 1 in Kathmandu, the Committee had recommended that the UN Resolution 1373 (on combating terrorism) be implemented in the region. The Committee took up several other issues, such as SAARC Integrated Program of Action, narcotics and drugs, intra-regional economic co-operation, inter-government group on trade liberalization, SAARC network of researchers on global financing and the finalization of the SAARC Social Charter. On August 28-29 SAARC Conference on Cooperation in police matters, a meet of police chiefs in this region to control crime and terrorism in South Asia took place in Kathmandu. Information sharing and intelligence gathering were two basic hallmarks of fighting terrorism and drug trafficking. The formation of SAARCPOL, a regional police body, to fight drug trafficking, terrorism and crimes has been endorsed, in line with the Interpol.

Bi-Lateral Relations

Nepal-India Relations: Nepal and India are historically close neighbours. Nepal's geophysical exposure towards south, circulation patters, transport and communication, transit, tourism, open border and treaty obligations make cordial ties with India a necessity. In February 6, Nepal and India simplified travel procedures for the nationals of both countries visiting by air. The immigration authorities recognize passports and voters ID cards as valid travel documents.

Nepal-India Trade Treaty 1996 was renewed and came into effect from March 6, 2002. Officials of both sides agreed to impose a mandatory 25 percent value addition slab on material and labour content on Nepali goods to gain duty free market access to India in the first year, and 30 percent from the second year onwards. The percentage of value addition would be calculated taking the export price at the base. They also agreed to include provisions relating to safeguard measures in case of surge in export from any of the countries. Similarly, four Nepali items—vegetable ghee, acrylic yarn, copper products and zinc oxide— that India claimed to have surged will now be allowed to enter free of basis customs duty into Indian market on a fixed quota basis. The exports of these four items constitute almost 20 percent of the total Nepali exports to India.

During his six-day goodwill visit to India on March 19 Premier Deuba sought Indian assistance in curbing the Maoist terrorism, review of the treaty of peace and friendship 1950, inundation problem due to Laxmanpur bund, border demarcation, implementation of Mahakali Agreement, enforcement of Nepal-India trade treaty, Indian cooperation in development projects, etc. During his meeting with his counterpart Atal Behari Bajpayee, both the countries decided to work closely in fighting terrorism. The two governments agreed, "not to allow their respective territories to be used for activities inimical to the interest of the other," "intensify their cooperation and continue to work closely with each other," and "an early conclusion of the agreement for mutual legal assistance and updating the extradition treaty."

They agreed to set up an Institute of Technology in Nepal, conduct survey on East-West Railway feasibility, hold negotiations on the operationalization of Raxaul-Birgunj rail link, cooperation in science and technology, tapping of hydropower, border demarcation, etc. The two sides should hold negotiations and conclude the bilateral agreement on the operation of the Birgunj-Raxaul rail-link and the Inland Container Depot (ICD or dry port at Birgunj). On April 12 India extended grant assistance to the tune of Rs. 1344 million to Nepal for setting up optical fibre cable based 1,000 km long information superhighway.

During his four-day visit to Nepal on May 13, Indian Army Chief General S. Padmanabhan said, "India would provide Nepal more military hardware including an armed helicopter. There is quite a lot in the pipeline. Weapons such as small arms, armaments of various types like mortars, ammunition for smaller arms, some other vehicles, couple of helicopters, including an armed one are part of the package." India has already provided Nepal with two Cheetah helicopters, 20 military vehicles and arms and ammunition to fight Maoist insurgency.

On June 23, King Gyanendra and Queen Komal made their first six-day official visit to India at the friendly invitation of Indian President K. R. Narayan and Usha Narayan. The king said, "in recent years, Nepal has been afflicted with the menace of terrorism. Terrorists have launched a series of destructive and disruptive activities against society and the very roots of democracy. Nepal is prepared to extend all necessary assistance to industrialists, businessman and entrepreneurs from India to invest in Nepal. " On June 28 Indian Prime Minister A. B. Vajpayee pledged to help Nepal in its fight against Maoist rebels. He, however, also told that the "problem was an internal matter of Nepal and therefore must be solved by its government."

On July 5 the border demarcation joint team of experts of Nepal and India came to a halt as they found that India unilaterally built 300-meter long a dam over Bakraha river inside Nepal causing inundation in some border villages of Morang district and submerging about 400 meters of Nepali land. Jagadish Prasad, Indian team member representing Nepal-Indian Joint Demarcation Team claimed the Indian government's ignorance over the already built dam. Similarly, in the hill town of Pashupatinagar, Ilam, six houses of Nepalese and a government custom office have now fallen on Indian territory after the India side unilaterally erected four subsidiary border pillars in the eastern border of Nepal.

On August 16 in a secretary level meeting of Nepal-India Inter-Governmental Committee (IGC) in Delhi, the Indian side pledged to support the Nepali industries by removing all the additional taxes its federal states have been imposing on the Nepali exports to India and agreed in principle to wave Special Additional Duty (SAD) soon while it assured the immediate waiver of the Luxury Tax on Nepali exports. The Indian side had been imposing 4 percent SAD on all Nepali goods, which had hard hit the major Nepali exports. It also agreed to remove 40 percent Anti-Dumping Duty (ADD) imposed on acrylic yarn and zinc and decided to establish quarantine checkposts at

Indian bordering cities of Sunauli, Jogbani and Banbassa in November 1 and lower down the existing quarantine fees. The Indian side also agreed to raise the quota fixed for Nepali copper wire exports by further 2, 500 tons.

On August 30 Nepal and India signed the Program of Cooperation and agreed to create viable atmosphere for exchanging scientific and technological support for the mutual benefit of the people of both countries. On September 15 forest officials conservationists from Nepal and India agreed to set up a joint trans-border committee to monitor progress related to landscape conservation.

The committee will hold quarterly field level meetings to discuss protection measures for endangered wildlife species in a globally important eco-region.

Bhutanese Refugees: More than 100 thousand Bhutanese refugees are languishing at seven UNHCR-administered camps in the eastern part of Nepal. The Joint Verification Team manned by the officials of Bhutan and Nepal since 2001 has already verified about 1,300 refugees. Nepal has been awaiting Bhutan's approval for the dates to hold the 12th round of ministerial level meeting where they would discuss who of the verified refugees should be repatriated. The Bhutanese Refugees Support Group (BRSG) a non-governmental organization in Kathmandu called upon the government, the Bhutanese government and the international community to intensify their efforts to end the refugee crisis.

On July 3 European Union Ambassadors in Nepal who inspected one of the refugees camps expressed concern over the delay in the verification of refugees and called for immediate declaration of the results of the identification in the Khundunbari camp, "The delay in the verification process has made us worried and alert," said Gent Meinceke, Denmark's ambassador to Nepal. "We believe that there has to be long-term solution to the refugee problem as the refugees cannot remain dependent on aid." The visiting German Ambassador Rudiger Lemp said, "The results of verification must be declared immediately." He called for the immediate repatriation of refugees and conducting of the verification process in the other six camps.

On October 6 feeling frustration over the intransigent attitude of Bhutanese government on the solution of refugees Foreign Ministry of Nepal revealed its "last ditch attempt " to hold 12th round of negotiation. Said a Foreign Ministry official, "we will have no option but raise the issue at the international level since we cannot afford to let the issue linger any longer."

Nepal-China Relations: China is Nepal's another friendly neighbor providing it an alternative route for trade, tourism, foreign aid for development and the diversification in international relations. On April 16 in an effort to boost trans-Himalayan trade, China scrapped the provision of licenses for importing Nepalese goods aiming to reduce trade deficit between the two neighbours. On June 17 the agreement on bilateral cooperation signed by the central banks of both countries allowed the Chinese currency Yuan convertible in Nepal aiming to boost bilateral trade, tourism, and economic cooperation.

On July 9, King Gyanendra and Queen Komal made a ten-day state visit to China at the invitation of Chinese President Jiang Zemin. King Gynanedra and President Zemin held talks on matters of mutual interests and letters were exchanged on the opening of an honorary Nepalese consulate general in Shanghai, aside from its existing consulate generals in Tibet and Hong Kong. Agreements were signed on an annual grant of Rs. 780 million aid to Nepal and the renewal of trade treaty with Tibet which is done in every 10 years. The grant is utilized to construct an 18-km road between Rasuwa and Syaphrubeshi, to open a civil servant hospital and a polytechnic institute at Banepa. China's underbelly, Tibet, shares about 1,000 kilometers of border with Nepal. About 35,000 Tibetan exiles have settled in Nepal, forming an ongoing concern for Beijing. Chinese president also condemned "terrorists" action taking place in Nepal. Chinese premier Zhu Rongji indicated that China would help construct the Baglung-Beni-Jomsom road once Rasuwa-Syaphrubesi road is completed. On July 24 a

Memorandum of Understanding was signed between the Federation of Nepalese Chambers of Commerce and Industries (FNCCI) and the All-China Federation of Industries and Commerce (ACFIC) hoping to reduce the annual trade deficit of Rs 12 million with China. Both the groups agreed to expand Nepal-China Non-Governmental Cooperation Forum.

In September the seven-member team led by Deputy Commander of the Lanzhou Military Region Command of the People's Liberation Army of China Lieutenant General Zhou Gengren returned home on completion of their six-day visit to Nepal. On March 24 as part of exchange of visits between high level army teams, a seven-member Nepali army team, led by Lt. General Pyar Jung Thapa, visited China and discussed about the matters of mutual interests.

Nepal-Germany Relations: On April 17 the Federal Republic of Germany committed 28.95 million Euro in grant to the Kingdom of Nepal for the next two years. Three agreed priority areas of cooperation in the year 2002-2003 are health and family planning, promotion of local self-governance and civil society and the promotion of renewal energy. Germany also supports Nepal through its contribution to non-governmental organizations and multi-lateral institutions. Nepal-US Relations: On January 18 American Secretary of State Colin Powell visited to Nepal and met King Gynendra, premier Deuba, and Commander in Chief of the Army Prajwolla S. Rana. Powell condemned the Maoists saying that "there is no place for violence for bringing about a change in a democracy" but he also indicated to the deep-rooted causes of turmoil referring to the disaffected youth who have lost hope and are being attracted to radical cause. He pointed three measures—good governance, economic development and an end to corruption and assured the government of the continuity of American cooperation in Nepal's development including support to military exchange, training of military officers and equipment.

The US government announced US $ 4 million grant to Nepal for the betterment of children rescued from the child labour market and its Embassy has announced humanitarian assistance to the tune of $100 thousand to fund programs targeted at victims of the Maoist insurgency. On June 6 it showed readiness to end worldwide trafficking in humans including in Nepal by means of penalties which involve votes against loans from the World Bank and International Monetary Fund.

On April 24 State Department Spokesman Richard Boucher reported "We are assessing Nepal's needs and reviewing several options for military assistance to Nepal. We have asked Congress for a supplemental appropriation of $20 million in foreign military financing for Nepal."

On May 5 premier Deuba left Kathmandu for a visit in the US and UK seeking support for war against terrorism. On May 7 while talking to premier Deuba, the US president George W. Bush referred about global terrorism, regional security situation and Nepal-US cooperation.

On September 22 the US government agreed to provide Nepal a grant of $ 14.3 million for promoting peace through improved governance and incomes in targeted areas. It also disbursed $3.6 million this year while rest will be delivered over a period of four years. On December 12 the visiting US Assistant Secretary of the State for South Asia, Christina Rocca, discussed about security situation in Nepal and possible US Cooperation to support the government in the context of escalating Maoist violence, about Nepal's entry into WTO, Bhutanese refugee stalemate and possibility of increased economic assistance to Nepal.

While meting the party leaders of main political parties, especially G. P. Koirala, Madhav Kumar Nepal and Sher B Deuba, she suggested them to forge unity with the king to fight against Maoists. The source close to Koirala revealed that "while the US wanted to end insurgency militarily, the parties on the other hand want to resolve the problem through dialogue. On December 31 Nepal and the US signed an agreement agreeing not to surrender each other's nationals to any international tribunal or in third country without the expressed consent of the other.

Nepal-UK Relations: On February 19 British Parliamentary Under Secretary of State for Foreign and Commonwealth Affairs responsible for South Asia, Ben Bradshaw, said, "We are worried about Nepal's security situation and our cooperation in this regard will be continued."

Upon completing his visit to USA, premier Deuba reached London on May 12 and held talks with British Prime Minister Tony Blair. Blair pledged strong support to Nepal's fight against terrorism and assured the British government's support to Nepal's economic development. They also discussed about the pensions of ex-British Gorkha soldiers.

On May 19 General Sir Michael Boyce, Chief of Britain's Defense Staff, visited Nepal to discuss on the potential British military and development assistance to the Royal Nepal Army in fighting against the Maoist rebels. A team of senior British army officials would draw up a list of requirements of the Nepalese army. Boyce visited Maoist-hit areas and met ex-Gurkhas in Pokhara, Dharan and Okhaldhunga. About 3,000 Nepalese are still serving in the British army.

On November 27, ex-Gurkha soldiers have won the right to compensation from the British government after more than 50 years they were taken as prisoner by the Japanese. Ex-Gurkhas PoWs have won the right to compensation. Each of 343 surviving PoWs will receive 10,000Pound as compensation.

The UK organized Nepal Aid Meet in London on June 18 to discuss on the ways of international cooperation to Nepal to cope with the development problem as well as Maoist insurgency. It announced an increase of its financial assistance to Nepal from 20 to 27 million sterling pound annually including an increase of military support from 0.7 to 7 million sterling pound annually as it is concerned about the security situation in Nepal. British government also urged other donor countries such as United States, Japan, China, Australia, India, Russia and EU members, UNDP, UNDPA and the World Bank to increase aid to Nepal. On July 24 the British Embassy in Kathmandu revealed that the UK government announced an aid package of 650 million to tackle the Maoist insurgency and two transport aircraft to Royal Nepalese Army. The UK Foreign Office Minister Mike O' Brian visited Nepal on October 9 to chair the first follow up meeting to the international conference of friendly countries on Nepal held in London in June. He said, "Nepal's struggle against Maoist insurgents should be seen as a part of the wider war against terrorism." All the donor community were concerned about the status of democracy, human rights and good governance and wanted the effective implementation of anti-corruption measures.

Nepal and Asian Development Bank (ADB): The ADB has been focusing on programs aimed at poverty reduction, gender and development, good governance, water supply and environment preservation. It agreed to provide Nepal $ 15.58 million aimed at training primary school teachers and building capacity of National Centre for Educational Development and teachers' training centres. The loan carries an interest rate of one percent to be repaid within 50 years. On March 28 the visiting high-level mission of the Bank revealed that its proposed lending for 2002-2004 totals $300 million, an average of $102 million per year. The Bank can charge the amount depending on the performance of the beneficiary. The Bank agreed to provide technical assistance to Nepal amounting to Rs. 58 million (750,000 US dollars) for the purpose of preparing the community based water supply and sanitation projects and $20 million as an additional support for public expenditure management in Nepal over a period of one year. So far ADB provided 6 loans for US $ 75.7 million and 11 Technical Assistance for 5.1 million for education sector in Nepal. The Bank has approved a loan of US$30 million for improving essential infrastructure and services in nine urban areas of Nepal.

World Bank and IMF: Under the World Bank (WB) pressure, the Finance Ministry decided to hand over the management of the country's two largest commercial banks—Rastriya Banijya Bank and Nepal Bank Ltd. to private company. The WB warned that it would retract the promised loan of Rs. 830 million if the process were not completed by February 15. The WB agreed to extend a loan assistance of US $ 22.56 million to Nepal for the implementation of Telecommunication Sector Reform Project. Nepal has been trying to enter into IMF-sponsored Poverty Reduction and Growth Facility (PRGF). With its entry, Nepal will get US $ 20 million annually for the next three years, which would be spent on programs related to poverty reduction and pursuing reform measures.

On December 2, the WB scrapped nine irrigation projects in mid-western Nepal due to the lack of explosives. The security forces have tightened their grip on explosives used in development projects due to security reasons. On December 22 the WB approved a credit of US $ 16 million in support of Financial Sector Assistance Project. The current credit of US $ 16 million from the International Development Association (IDA), the concessionary lending arm of the World Bank Group, is part of a financing plan totaling US$30.1 million. The Department for International Development (DFID) will finance US$10 million and the government of Nepal will fund US $4.1 million. Discussing the progress report of the Bank's Country Assistance Strategy (CAS) for Nepal the WB Board of Executive Directors in Washington agreed that availability of resources would be parallel to Nepal's performance on reforms. Slow progress in addressing poor governance resulted in a sharp decline in the Bank's lending to Nepal.

Nepal-Japan Cooperation: Nepal-Japan relations have always remained friction-free. It is one of the biggest donors for Nepal's development. The Japanese government extended a grant assistance of Rs.5, 791,000 to the Nepalese government for the Emergency Disaster Rehabilitation Project and its Embassy offered a grant assistance of US$82,500 to Milan Club Nepal to buy educational equipment to the primary schools in Kathmandu. Similarly, Japanese government provided a grant assistance of $897000 to Nepal as the Debt Relief Measures, $680,000 for the promotion of UNESCO's Education for All Programs in Nepal and US$10,667,000 as non-project grants aid. The latter grant was meant to aid Nepal's social and economic development. On July 25 the government of the US and Japan signed a memorandum on "Joint Japan-US Project Formulation Mission" to help Nepal in population and health, child and maternal health, tuberculosis and HIV/AIDS.

UN Cooperation: Kathmandu-based office of UNICEF provided Nepal a grant assistance of approximately Rs. 5624.65 million to enhance the need of children and women. The International Fund for Agricultural Development (IFAD) provided a loan assistance of $ 20.11 million and technical grant assistance worth US $ 37,358 for the Western Uplands Poverty Alleviation Project (WUPAP). The project covers 11 upland districts of Far and Mid-western Development Regions, which are remotest and characterized by a high incidence of poverty, low human development indicators and deprivation.

Other countries and Organizations: On June 25 the Danish International Cooperation Agency (DANIDA) provided US $ 30 million grant for the development of a secondary education program and 20 million Danish corner to help Bhutanese refugees. Norway promised to extend financial assistance of Rs. 200 million for the reconstruction of the Jhimruck Hydropower project, which was destroyed by the Maoists. On July 4, the Swiss government extended Rs.73.7 million grant for the fourth phase of a program to rehabilitate the Arniko Highway, the only highway linking Nepal and Tibet and Rs. 576.3 million for the implementation of Trial Bridge Sub-Sector Projects.

EU: On August 19 the European Union approved a Rs. 46.5 million (Euro 615,000) assistance package to Nepal to help it reduce the impact of the current conflict on long-term EU assistance programs. The new package is financed under the EU 's Rapid Reaction Mechanism and forms the first stage of a revised strategy for EU assistance that is under discussion with Nepali authorities. Canada: On October 9 the government announced the launch of Local Development Facility (LDF), which is five years project from 2002-2007 with a budget of 4.3 million Canadian dollar to support timely and innovative initiatives which address basic human needs and build socio-economic infrastructure and capacities of both government and civil society at local levels. Dutch Grant: The government of the Netherlands provided Euro 14.6 million technical grant assistance for the implementation of biodiversity project in Nepal. The money will be spent on poverty alleviation, and productive bio-diversity conservation through forestry sector development in Tarai and Siwalik.

RELATIONS WITH OTHER COUNTRIES

China is landlocked Nepal's next door neighbor in the north. Nepal's relations with China are based on pragmatic grounds. Relations with China are determined by security, economic and political considerations. Nepal wants to diversify its relations and China offers one alternative. Before 1990 China and former Soviet Unions were the two major countries supporting Nepal's industrialization, expansion in road, electricity, communication and education.

Tibet Autonomous Region of China provides a small outlet for its trade and transit diversification and tourism expansion. Nepal has also requested China to open four more passes besides the traditional passes and the modern 113Km long Kodari (Arniko) Highway links Nepal with Tibet. Chinese and Nepalese officials are working to speed up the Syabrubensi-Rasuwagadi highway project. If constructed, the highway will link Nepal with Tibet's Kerung, which lies next to Rasuwagadhi. China has agreed to provide necessary financial assistance for the project. Experts say that only 19-kilometers long road need to be constructed in the central mountainous district of Rasuwa.

China constructed a Buddhist temple in Lumbini, the birthplace of Lord Buddha in the year 2000. It has also agreed to support equipment maintenance facilities in BP Koirala Cancer Memorial Hospital as well as to provide six Chinese technicians for a period of two years to the development of Nepal Television. Chinese motivation to support Nepal is only to turn Nepal into an independent state, rather than becoming a conduit for anti-Chinese activities through free Tibet movements and succumbing to anti-Chinese pressures.

On August 27 Foreign minister Chakra Prasad Banstola upon returning from his week-long visit to China said that Nepal and China had agreed in principle to add two more routes in the Nepal-Tibet border to facilitate increased trade between the two countries. The two new transit points are Kimathanka and Lizi, besides the existing Tatopani, Yari, Kerong and Olanchungola. He also raised the issue of trade imbalance between Nepal and China. Chinese also showed interest to cooperate in Nepal's hydropower resources and trade expansion through the avoidance of double taxation. Nepal's relations with Bangaldesh remained cordial as usual. Bangaldesh provides Nepal transit facilities in Chittagong and Khulna-Chalna Ports. Both the countries are exploring to utilize Kakarbhita-Fulbari transit route (a land route that links Nepal with Bangladesh through India) to expand trade, commerce and investment opportunities.

Japan is the largest donor country in Nepal, which provides aid in the field of road, hospital, community development, agriculture, education and tourism. Each year over fifty thousand Japanese tourists visit Lumbini, the birthplace of Lord Buddha. Japanese interest in Nepal lies in economic development, market expansion and protection of heritage, environment and culture of Nepal. On August 25 Prime Minister of Japan Yoshiro Mori made a one-day goodwill visit to Nepal and discussed the matters of mutual interests with the Nepalese premier G. P. Koirala. Prime minister of Japan urged premier Koirala to provide security to 300 Japanese volunteers working in Maoist-infested areas and improve law and order situation in the country. His visit highlighted IT sector and 50 Nepalese youth would be provided IT training in Japan under Mori Fellowship. Besides, five thousand youths would also be invited under educational and cultural exchange program from the South Asian region. Japan also pledged a number of economic assistance for Nepal, according to which Nepal will get a grant of Rs 1.14 billion rupees during the Japanese fiscal year for the construction of primary schools and debt relief measures and 300 thousand US dollars for the relief of flood victims.

German cooperation to Nepal is based on the promotion of "rule of law, democracy, human rights, political participation and development orientation of state action." On February 17, a three-day bilateral meeting between Nepal and Germany took place in Kathmandu. The German delegation was led by Dr. Karl Kirchhof, Director of South Asia, Federal Ministry of Economic Cooperation and Development. Germany agreed to provide a total of DM 59 million during 2000-2001 period, including DM 33 million under financial cooperation and DM 26 million under technical cooperation. On July 12 the government of the Federal Republic of Germany agreed to provide Nepal a grant assistance of DM 42.0 million. The assistance will be used to support four different project activities: biogas support program, town development program, the renewable energies development program and the upgrading of the Makalu-Dhadingbesi road. On November 21, the government of Germany informed the Nepalese government that in addition of funds for financial cooperation for the two-year period 2000-2001 committed (totaling DM 33.0 million) a further amount of DM 12.0 million would be made available to implement a medium-sized-run-of-the river hydropower station (DM 8.0 Million) within the framework of the project "Renewable Energy" and the establishment of small hydro-power plants (DM 4.0 million). On November 29, German Development Bank, KFW, acting on behalf of the German government, agreed to provide grant assistance of DM 31 million for three development projects-biogas projects, Urban development program and upgrading of road between Malekhu and Dhadingbesi road.

Nepal-International Monetary Fund Enter Into Crucial Negotiation

On November 29, Nepal concluded a crucial negotiation with the International Monetary Fund (IMF) sponsored Poverty Reduction Growth Framework (PRGF), that will guide the country's economic decision-making, including social spending for the next three years. Nepal's entry into PRGF will particularly expedite the pace of economic reform initiated by

Nepali Congress government in 1992 but slackened due to ensuing political uncertainty in the second half of 1990s. PRGF mainly focuses on macro-economic stability (low fiscal deficit, low inflation and comfortable foreign exchange reserve), structural reform (privatization of public enterprises, civil service reform and restructuring of financial sector among others) and poverty reduction. Though the IMF mission and high-level government officials concluded, it will have to be endorsed by the cabinet and IMF Board of Directors before Nepal enters into PRGF, possibly by April 2001. Besides, Nepal should pass through three crucial requirements to qualify for the entry: it should award the management contract of Rastriya Banijya Bank and Nepal Bank Ltd; conclude the mid-term Budget review and finalize Poverty Reduction Strategy Paper before April. With the entry into PRGF, IMF will extend Nepal an annual assistance of US $ 20million for the next three years, which will be spent in reducing poverty and pursuing reforms.

NEPAL'S DETERIORATING HOME, DEFENSE AND FOREIGN POLICY

Since 1990, Nepali congress government has been trying to change Nepalese foreign policy to one sided, though previously it was quite balanced. After the popular movement of 2005, the home, defence and foreign policy of Nepal has completely failed.

The Pro-Indian foreign policy has caused a crisis on the existence of Nepal. Bhutan borders with China and India has always been against the friendly bilateral relationship between China and Bhutan. Bhutan is protected by India. Nepal also borders with China. India does not wish there to be a friendly bilateral relationship between Nepal and China. Indian leaders frequently visit Nepal. But if any Chinese leader visits Nepal, it becomes a headache for India. India wants Nepal under its control.

After the establishment of democracy in Nepal, nationalists protested against unequal treaty of 1950 (made by India) and the Delhi agreement. Nepalese people protesting against Delhi Agreement were accused of being communists. The Communist

Party was also banned with same issue. Later in 1956, King Mahendra lifted the ban on the Communist Party. Even after the general election of 1958-59, India did not abandon exhibiting its bad intensions towards Nepal. As the existence of Nepal was endangered, King Mahendra dissolved the Parliament in 1960 and safeguarded the Nepalese nationality. If the King was not there, Nepal may have ceased to exist.

On the initiation of King Mahendra, Indian army check posts that were kept for security after Delhi Agreement were sent back from northern Nepal. India could not speak because Nepal had very good relationships with China and other world powers. Indeed, Nepalese monarch and northern neighbour China have contributed to saving Nepal. Initially, India was afraid of communists. Due to Chinese terror, India started to use communists. Nepalese communists, being whatever revolutionary, could not get rid of India game. It is said former premier Man Mohan Adhikari was being paid on the name of freedom fighter of India.

India understood that Nepali communists can be used in favour of India. After 1990's popular movement, as Congress and UML rose to government, India found a way to interfere in Nepal. But only leader Madan Bhandari of UML protested the Indian imposition. India thought him a barrier and after his murder, India was happy again.

Still as India could not do as it wanted with Congress and UML, then in 2005 India convinced the Maoists and now India is free for naked interference. The intensions of RAW and CIA were unified to destroy United China in the name of Free Tibet since the beginning of 2000. In between, Nepal is entrapped. India always tries to maintain its supremacy either in non-aligned foreign policy or in SAARC. So, Nepal needs to resign from non-aligned policy and SAARC.

Chinese are simple and they understand things slowly. Due to this delayed understanding by China, Nepal is in a difficult situation. The strategic unification of RAW and CIA in this region is a dangerous indicator for China and Nepal.

Therefore China should openly come out to protest the conspiracy of imperialists against Nepal. Chinese communist leader Mao Ze Dong, never took the confidence of Nepali communists. He was in favour of the Nepalese monarch because the monarch always fought against imperialists.

Now India is trying to capture Nepal by behaving like an Ostrich with China, being broker of US and UN, and using so-called Nepalese political parties. Even in 1989, India tried to capture Nepalese foreign, defence and home policies by terrorizing then King Birendra with popular movements. India tried to confuse King Gyanendra with expectation to control the movement of 2005.

However India was unsuccessful in doing so. Apart from surrendering to foreigners, King Gyanendra happily handed over power to the Nepalese people. India constructed a 40 km long tunnel investing billions of rupees between Jammu and Srinagar valley. But Kashmiris did not favour India. We know, India has invested huge aid in every field but because of the ill-intentions of the Indians, anti-Indian sentiment is increasing day by day.

If Indian interests in Nepal are like that of Bhutan and Sikkim, India won't be safe. It is because terrorism can be institutionalized in this situation which will be harmful to India. Therefore we warn India to correct itself from such blunders. The Indian interest is to make Nepalese defence and foreign policy in accordance with India's needs. Since 2006, Nepal has been guided by pro-India party leaders.

After the downfall of the Maoist led government in May 2009, two women, defence minister (UML) and foreign minister (daughter of Girija), who have no diplomatic capabilities, both are pro-Indian. It seems this could be a strategy to surrender Nepalese foreign and defence policy to India. If you see a list of ambassadors of Nepal to be sent to friend country, you will find smugglers, murderers and criminals who have no idea of foreign affairs. Therefore Nepalese foreign policy is at a shameful status at the international level.

After 1990, Nepalese people never became free, although they were called sovereign. As the King was separated from sovereignty, in 1974 in Sikkim, under the leadership of Lendup Dorji, Sikkim parliament decided to unify with India on 10 April 1975. Similarly in Nepal, using Girija Prasad (former PM), Madhav nepal (PM) and a few Maoists, India is trying to capture Nepal.

The factors behind failed foreign policy of Nepal are betrayer leaders of Nepal and ever continuing interference by India. India is always involved in a conspiracy to shrink Nepal. Nepal is situated in between China in the north and India in the south, east and west, with a 1880 km border. The border is open.

Due to this, India is always engaged in attacking Nepalese territory and also some Indian citizens commit crime in Nepal and hide in India. Indians enter Nepal with small and large scale business and ultimately demand Nepalese citizenship.

In 2006, 4 million Indians succeed in taking Nepalese citizenship. Being landlocked country Nepal must have transportation facility in accordance to international treaties and traditions. But India violated it and wants to control over Nepal. The Late King Prithvi Narayan Shah is a creator of Nepal. The Nepalese monarch established fighting against imperialist power. In order to remain protected in between China and India, even in those times Prithvi Narayan Shah preached (1768) - 'Nepal is just like a Yam (tuber) between the two stones'.

We are sandwiched between giant India and China. So, we are bound to have a balanced understanding between them. The nation builder had preached us the same fact. "Establish good and amicable relations with China, have relations with the emperor of south understanding well that he is very clever. If the investors from foreign (India) come to Nepal, they will make our people poorer.

Indeed, the ideology of Prithvi Narayan Shah is immortal. Therefore the monarch of Nepal made an incredible contribution to save the country. India was being destroyed by Muslims for some 800 years. For 200 years, India was attacked by English imperialism in the name of East India Company. They had clear intension to demolish Hinduism and establish imperialism in this region. Communists do not believe in religion. JNU is popular for producing Extreme Leftists.

It was Indian Congress government and policy makers like SD Muni who not only assisted but funded Nepal Maoists to wage a war against Hinduism. However Prithvi Narayan was only one who protested it.

He raised the Nepalese flag, maintained originality of Himbatkhand and unified the great Nepal. From the beginning of the Prithvi Narayan Shah Regime in 1868, the balanced Nepalese relationship with China and India was maintained by every King till 2005.

NEPAL: FOREIGN POLICY IN THE DOLDRUMS

A country's foreign policy is "a set of political goals that seeks to outline how that particular country will interact with other countries of the world and, to a lesser extent, non-state actors." Foreign policy is generally designed "to help protect a country's national interests, national security, ideological goals, and economic prosperity." For a small country like Nepal sandwiched between the Asian giants, this can only occur as a result of peaceful cooperation.

Eight months after the introduction of Loktantra (total democracy), Nepal's foreign policy lies in shambles. There can be no doubt that foreign policy lacks direction and that it is not transparent. It is not only uni-dimensional, i.e. only directed towards India or reacting only to impulses from that country. It can even be said that India dictates policy as in the heydays of the Nineteen-Fifties. The Indian Embassy in Kathmandu is the focal and power point for all domestic and (the minimalist) foreign activities. The Ministry of Foreign Affairs (MoFA) at Shital Niwas could easily be re-named 'the Ministry of Indian Affairs'!

Let us set out the instrumental criteria in terms of which we can attempt a dispassionate evaluation of Nepal's foreign relations since the success of the violent political agitation of April and the dismantling of the Royal regime. In the first instance, we must attempt to analyse the situation arising out of the events leading up to and after the said change of regime. The massive international pressure and funding of the opposition was, no doubt, instrumental in the collapse of the King's administration, which was neither repressive nor dictatorial. India and its strategic partner, the United States played the defining role. India, in fact, brought together the seven opposition parties and the Maoist terrorists (India now denies this characterization). The Indian Communist parties also interfered in the domestic affairs of the country. In these circumstances, the hands of the new policy-makers were bound tight-they and their Maoist partners had no choice but to toe the Indian line. As one commentator put it, they have been degraded into the 'running dogs of Indian neo-imperialist policy in South Asia.'

Next, let us attempt to assess the flow of information and intelligence that would influence the formation of the perception of the new power elites. Eight months on into the 'new Nepal' the career diplomats in Shital Niwas and former envoys have not been taken into confidence; neither have any think tanks or foreign policy experts. MoFA's own Institute of Foreign Affairs is lying idle since the power take-over. The foreign minister is a novice in the realm of foreign affairs, and the PM's own advisers are all amateurs (with neither the experience, nor the education and know-how in international affairs). Who has been providing facts and figures is anybody's guess. Whether the sources are in the national interest is another vital question.

One of the government negotiators with the Maoists, the minister for Tourism and Civil Aviation, Pradip Gyanwali (who has proven himself most incompetent and out of place in his chosen portfolio) has now gone out of his way to propagate the politics of 'dis-information'. He lately accused "foreign powers" in attempting to disrupt the elections to the Constituent

Assembly" and the United Nations for the delay in promulgating the so-called "Interim Constitution". To divert widespread dissatisfaction with the government's domestic and foreign policies, Gyanwali has been sent to the forefront to intensify the "blame game" (also against the King and the "Monarchists") and to underscore the role of the "foreign hand" (but pointing in the wrong direction!)

The dismal state of affairs is reflected in the indubitable fact that the current government foolishly recalled the ambassadors from nearly a dozen countries and has not yet been able to fill the vacant posts, among them Washington, Tokyo, London, Paris and Brussels (European Union). A significant flow of information has dried up and demonstrates the government's dilettantish conduct of foreign affairs.

Forget about the 'democratic' conduct of external relations; this government is so emasculated that it is unable to reach a consensus on major issues, let alone appoint ambassadors to key countries. Kathmandu is rife with rumours that the main political parties are having a tussle with regard to appointing their own hangers-on and favourites to these lucrative posts. The politics of nepotism is in full swing.

In any modern state, it is possible to identify the government units most responsible for handling and managing external relations. Moreover, the responsibility of coping with the predicaments of foreign affairs, therefore, falls within the jurisdiction of the several units.

There exist clear-cut rules, practices and conventions for inter-governmental and inter-unit arrangements to allow for concerted action. In the case of Nepal, there is a manifest lack of coordination between the PM's office, Shital Niwas, the Defence Ministry, the National Defence Council and the relevant committee(s) of the parliament. Only a small coterie of power-elites (with little or no knowledge of the conduct of foreign policy) is deciding the fate of the nation. Both the parliament which has in a ridiculous manner declared itself 'sovereign' and the MoFA are only mute spectators in the country's external relations. The principle of checks and balances-a must in any functioning government-is prominent by its absence! So much, too, for 'good governance'.

It stands to reason that when even the major actors are unclear about the nature and conduct of foreign policy, their perceptions of any predicament in our external relations must of necessity be hazy and incomplete. This can only lead to hazardous situations and disgrace. Future repercussions were not thought out when recalling our envoys. This interim government failed to do its home-work when canvassing for the non-permanent Asian seat in the UN Security Council, resulting in a fiasco. Without considering the history of the problem of Bhutanese refugees and the Indian interests involved, the foreign minister foolishly announced the immanent solution of this cancerous and long drawn-out stumbling block in the multilateral relations of South Asia. The present care-taker government has also failed miserably to set priorities for goals ranging from the imperative, through the desirable to the least-expected, but simply hoped for targets. Its dependence on India has made it muddle-headed and its capacity to act in the national interest circumscribed. The Indians, on the other hand, have cleverly and diabolically manipulated the Maoist insurgency to further their own interests. To sum up: Nepal has become a prey to the Indo-American grand design of containing China and is on the way to becoming a satellite state in all but name.

NEPAL: PRAGMATIC APPROACH TO FOREIGN POLICY

Apparently the political change in Nepal demands for a fresh look at the substantial style of the conduct of foreign policy. The change itself should not be just a matter perceived but it should reflect a reality experienced all around the national life. It needs to be followed by the changed behavior and attitude. We understand that as Arnold Bennett has said; "Any change, even a change for the better is always accompanied by drawbacks and discomforts" Leaderships, therefore, should be highly aware of the defective sides of the change and work relentlessly toward eliminating them for the better prospect. Alongside the domestic change, the global scenario has also passed through the stage of change from the uni-polar world to that of the multi-polar one in recent years.

Eminent experts on international affairs including Stephen Brooks and William Wohlforth have now predicted the evolving of the world system as a "1+x world" with the United States as the lone super power with a variable number of other major powers playing their respective role with their interests and concerns taken into their hearts.

Coincidently, the domestic change in Nepal and the change in the international atmosphere insist us to adopt new approach in our conduct of foreign policy. Evidently, re-adjustment to the changing environment has now become not only a desirable thing but also a compelling element. Addiction to and indulgence in the old setting and mindset of the bygone era have to be minutely re-examined to enable Nepal to meet new challenges thrown up by the emerging situation.

Surprisingly, Nepal is still exhibiting its weakened ability to see new regional and global situation in their right perspectives, because the country is now plunged into the political turmoil with political fragmentation at its apex and with no genuine democratic consolidation in sight in the foreseeable future. Vividly, experiences gained from the earlier period insist on the leadership to have farfetched vision and take right actions for the appropriate conduct of foreign policy in the situation prevalent now. Unmistakably, adamant and indifferent work culture would not serve the national and people's aspirations and needs that are sky rocketing at the moment.

Today, people's awareness and their concern have assumed greater magnitude and value in the formulation and implementation of not just domestic policy but also of foreign policy in the national life. In reality, people's era and dominance is on rise irresistibly in these early years of the 21 century. Nepal is no exception to this development. Naturally, people's confidence and opinions have to be noted perceptibly, while pursuing the trajectory of foreign policy, if a democratic consolidation is to be ensured in Nepal. As an implementing tool of foreign policy the conduct of diplomacy itself has become more and more open and predictable with the speed of time and situation. The tall wall of the secret diplomatic move has almost been torn apart by the exerting pressure of the fundamental and democratic right to information as demanded by the people.

New Touchstone of Diplomatic Efforts

To accommodate the people's say manifestly, the increased importance of public interest in the handling of foreign policy calls for the conduct of public diplomacy to resolve any major problem or issue with any country, which would have bearing on the people's life.

Public diplomacy is an appropriately developed tool that searches the feels and pulse of the people on any foreign policy question at home. This would ensure the public support in managing diplomatic concerns. Similarly, efforts should be made to win "hearts" of foreign people for favourable opinion by reaching out to them through contacts and communications by use of the media. An eminent person William Cecil Burleigh says; ""Win hearts and you have men's hands and purses". Personal touch with concerned important individuals and groups are far more significant than any other means. Public diplomacy thus addresses people both at home and abroad with the appropriate program chalked out and capability shown by the executers of foreign policy and diplomacy.

Nepal's diplomacy at the official level and contact is,as of yet, considered inadequate to meet greater needs and challenges, nor is the diplomacy at the level of people-to people enough to take it to a greater height. In the present context of Nepal, both these Track I (official) and Track II (people's level) diplomacy seem not sufficiently capable to move ahead on the proper track. To cope with intractable issues and irritants with other countries efficiently and effectively, the blending of both appears advisable and pragmatic in every sense. Nepal, therefore, needs to encourage and prod the one and a half diplomacy- a right mix of the official as well as people's diplomacy that can go a long way to ensure the public support to the government policy. One supplements and compliments the other.

As a weaker country, especially in terms of economy, technology and resources, Nepal can hardly be able to own hard power to impress upon other countries for several decades to come. This concern is undeniable from every consideration. However, given the ongoing situation and the appropriate context developing in the country most recently, Nepal can muster soft power at home.

Soft power is nothing but a much valued point of attraction to make good impression on others. This magnetic power can be augmented by Nepal with the consociational democracy developed satisfactorily and equitable social justice dispensed virtuously. Although the task ahead seems formidable in an underdeveloped Nepal, the reach is within our ability provided the Nepali political leadership moves on with vision, understanding and tolerance. Certainly, such steps would enhance Nepal's image abroad with points of attraction gained for the country, which in turn greatly facilitates to conduct of foreign policy with the useful tool of soft power on hand.

If pursued with consistency and coherence in its dealings with the external world, Nepal can showcase its new ability to update the marshalling of its foreign policy sensibly with the people's favour and appreciation won for the foreign policy concerns and questions.

The bastion of popular support and consent would largely strengthen national and democratic forces to preserve and promote the freewheeling journey of Nepal in the world in a visible way. If the political leaderships move on untiringly and warily, Nepal can, to a greater extent, gain on the foreign policy front. For all this to achieve, appropriate mechanisms and preparedness are highly needed. If not, we cannot go beyond where we are now. Reflective thinking indeed turns experience into insight to beneficially conduct foreign policy for advancement of the country. We need to see the situation around us in its proper and comprehensive perspective.

CHANGING PARADIGMS IN INDIA-NEPAL RELATIONS

Today Nepal stands at the crossroads amidst the swiftly changing political tracts and it becomes a scarce to found a closer understanding over the core issues among all the political parties. Such political opportunism truly missing the plight of democracy besides pulling down the national priorities in crucial matters; indeed it's an outcome of internal political strife instead from an imposed international pressure.

Stability is very crucial for India in the case of Nepal where India hasn't any option except to see a sovereign Nepal; concerned authority in India's External Affairs Ministry has been consistently showing similar concern and landed all possible support to assist in Nepal's integration. Through an honest introspection it's easily revealed that India never resolute any action in past against the national interest of Nepal, further India never obstruct the formation of any democratic government even including the Maoist government and send their foreign secretary just three days before the government formation.

India-Nepal relations are so strong that it's very hard to shape in mere words because these two neighbouring nation has a history of deep ties and shared concern from ancient times. Quality of relationship between these two countries shouldn't be seen in terms of treaty; having faith in each other's role any dispute can be solved and consensus could be formed between these two friendly nations.

Indeed there are no reasons among the peoples of the both side of border to involved in any sort of hate campaign against each other; any development in this regard would be ended with an impractical and unviable consequences. So, it must realized that that interest of India wouldn't affect the any move of peace process in Nepal; it's need of hour to end the causes of political insecurity among the diasporas on the both side of borders.

State of Nepal's internal security possessed as much concern as her own existential safety for India, so any anti Indian move will jeopardize the friendly terms and left alarming ramifications for both the country. India's concern over the presence of ISI's agents inside the territory of Nepal must be seen in genuine light by the Nepalese government since it could be highly disturbing in long term for Nepal's own sake as well. Indian government is very serious towards tackling the terrorist network with wrenched resoluteness and would keep affirming on Nepalese government to check their activities from their sovereign territory.

With more meticulous action some unfortunate developments may be easily avoided; that would required a consensus based approach in top notch Nepalese political circle and within their civil society towards the India's plight for security. India never felt any sort of discontents with the democratic proceedings in Nepal; of course Maoist should stay and play active role within their national political framework.

Indian government would remains very keen for strengthening of democracy in Nepal and issues like human rights would be a key priority for them with putting finest efforts to see it in universal way beyond the geographical boundaries. In recent past Gorkha's role in Indian Arm Forces has gained some critical applauds from a reactionary section in Nepal which is quite unfortunate and is an effort to dampen the historic and marvelous symbolic ties between these two friendly nation.

The word consensus has been largely misused in Nepal consequently ultra nationalism in Nepal largely seen in the context of anti-Indian sentiment; a very lucid approach would be needed from Nepalese side over such relentless unfortunate developments. In international affairs domain Nepal needs to play more matured role and must develop a sense of its own best interest; mutual integrated relationship with India paves way for safe passages of trust between them which is quite symmetric to the actual requirements and should remain a foremost concern for both the countries to keep intact these flame of spirits; any constructive solution of joint interest would be emerged from mutual effort instead through isolatory stances.

In changing circumstances it's quite essential for both the countries to make immediate revisions in bilateral treaties and shaping them as per the suitability of present time. Infrastructures are major issues that needs to look on in such active manner since perennial floods is a major impediment for socio-economic structure of Terain region in Nepal and entire north Bihar. A radical shift in policy towards the existing infrastructure of water management is the first step that required to be taken by the governments of both countries. Water management possessed very crucial and strategic place in the sphere of India-Nepal relations as their catchments are very productive for the vast agricultural areas as well an alternative source of energy; projects like Pancheswar, Saptakosi, Naumure etc. needs rational handling as they are immensely crucial for the sake of both countries energy requirements. Border management is another issue that needs more regulated treatment though it should remain open as even before because prevalence of open border is the biggest asset of India-Nepal relation and it has potential to be framed as an ideal border of south Asia. Indeed open border plays utmost significance in the lives of population adjacent to border; since time immemorial they have been sharing the ties of Roti (Bread) and Beti (Matrimonial ties) which even creates complexities of identity.

In present state Nepal is coping with the difficulties of constitution making besides having to win the trust of peoples in democratic institution which shown severe fluctuation in immediate past. In this situation grooming of an idea of ethnic federalism and other major issues wouldn't be less than a fatal as handling of such major issues depends upon the state of stability which is completely out of seen in present circumstances. Terain's plight and refugee's problems are some other rudimentary issues that need proper concern and action from the governments of both the side as law and order situation is a matter that requires the co-operation of other side due to geographical nature and open borders. In decade long civil war like situation, the Terai region faced adverse setbacks and witnessed the losses of human lives, infrastructure, ecology, law and order etc. Even in last few months toll of losses in Terai is quite frightening, almost 1200 peoples has been killed and more than 3600 were abducted; situation is still very grim inside the Terai region and peoples have some distraught feeling as they used to feel during the bloody strife phase. Glorifications of Terain Armed groups are caused by the political affiliations and patronage that's making situation worse in any effort to contain and disband their growing role; catchments areas of North Bihar or Mithilanchal region becomes a hideout place for these groups in the absence of a specified and clear set of mechanism on joint level; a strategic move in this regard is immediately required.

Till today Nepal is missing the actual taste of democracy and whatever has been represented on the name of democracy that never touched the ground of actual aspiration of its citizen. Maoists short stint in government couldn't materialized their own professed goals instead they turn up to attack on religious identities, authoritarianism, non-pluralism, against right of property besides showing very immature stand on Nepalese Armed Force chief Rukmangad Kotwal; such bad conflict management with Arm force deciphered the feeble understanding of realpolitik in Maoist camp.

Before that incident Nepali Army has history of passive presence and following the civil supremacy which was very conducive with the expectation of Nepalese intelligentsias. But now stands humiliated, Nepalese Army becomes more powerful and strategic which may played crucial roles in further phage of development. India too witnessed some implications after this incident as the role of India felt prominent by a section of reactionaries in Nepalese politics; former Prime Minister Prachanda's remarks as "Promped by Prabhu" to present Prime Minister Madhav Kumar Nepal was clearly referred towards the India which was completely unjustifiable. India maintains silence over such rambling propositions even the Indian side never downbeat with the growing Chinese influence in Maoists rule and regarded it just as lacking immune system. India has utmost concern with Nepalese state of affairs in similar manner; Nepal too has immense benefits from a stronger India, so despite some ups and down in events it would be compatible to remains in same strong bond of sharing forever' Brotherhood always remains a great idea as in such set of relationship every member has some specific roles to play irrespective of identities like big brother and small brother; being sanguine for same must in case of India-Nepal relations.

INTERNATIONAL MIGRATION IN NEPAL

History and trend: One of the big problems of research particularly in the developing countries like Nepal is the lack of availability, reliability and systematic publication of data and migration sector cannot be excluded from this situation. Hence, a detail analysis of migration phenomenon from the perspective of poverty, gender and development at various levels of spatial aggregation is difficult (KC 2003b). Even though the Government of Nepal started collecting data on migration since 1920 it was not accessible as published material. Kansakar (2003) reports that the population data published for the first time in Nepal was in the Appendix of the speech made by Prime Minister Chandra Shumsher Jung Bahadur Rana in the booklet Maharaja Chandra Shamsher Jung Bahadur Rana's Appeal to the People of Nepal for the Emancipation of Slave and Abolition of Slavery in the Country in 1925.

Another classic source of migration data was the Population Census of 1952/54. The report contains an analysis of different characteristics of the population of Nepal. Though Nepal has a census history of almost a century, more detailed account of migration data were made available only after the census 1991. The census of 2001 has a bit more detailed information, including a comprehensive account of the respective areas of destination, the purpose of migration (type of work the migrants engaged in), and gender specific data including the population structure and so on.

Nepalese labour out-migration is not a new phenomenon. Nepali migrant workers have been sending their earnings to their families for around 200 years. The first evidence of out-migration found in literature is that in early nineteenth century, the first Nepalese men migrated to Lahore (in present day's Pakistan) to join the army of Sikh ruler Ranjit Singh. Afterwards, both they and later migrants are termed as "Lahure" (cf. Thieme and Wyss 2005). Literally, the nickname lahure is given to the people who join the armed force of India, Hong Kong, Singapore, United Kingdom, and so on; but it also designates people living abroad particularly having the working class jobs. The distinction here is essential because people living abroad for study or working in the universities and 'big' organizations like UN, FAO, and ADB are not necessarily called lahures. The labourers working in the working class jobs are recently termed as 'New Lahures' (Seddon et al. 2001). This is an indication of socioeconomic position of migrant households in Nepal, who goes where and who does what.

Another metaphor used for Nepalese migrants working abroad is the Gurkhas: particularly known as the Nepalese who work in Gurkha Regiment for British or Indian forces. After a war in the Gorkha area with the British East India Company (1814/1816), an increasing number of Gurkhas (mostly, but not exclusively from present-day Nepal) also joined the British Army in India, starting a tradition that continues today (cf. Seddon 2005).

During the World War I and II, Gurkhas were sent as courtesy from Nepalese government to support allied force where they fought courageously and established an image of "Gurkhas". Even to date Gurkhas as Nepal Armies and Police are popularly recognized as good peace keeping force worldwide, some examples are their involvement in UN peace keeping force in Kosovo, Lebanon, Congo etc. In other words, Nepalese out-migration started from the history of Nepali soldiers who joined forces of other countries though it was not well accounted. With respect to the census 1942, Kansakar (2003: 107) reports, "The census seems to have not recorded the Nepali troops sent from Nepal in different fronts to assist the allied forces and might have been included only those who went abroad for livelihood".

Nepal's international border with India and China remained almost open for the movement of people from both of her neighbours. With China, it became closed one after 1950, while it has remained open with India to date with no restriction on the movement of people of both countries. Hence, because of open border, cultural similarities, and no need of documentary evidence to show migration to and from India is pre-historic and even unaccounted. Throughout the 19th century and well into the 20th, Nepalese men served in India, often accompanied by their wives and other family members. As the Gurkha settlements increased in number and size, they also attracted Nepali workers seeking civilian employment in India. The brothels developed in these new centres may well have included women from Nepal and from the surrounding areas (Seddon 2005). He further illustrates that the development of tea estates in Assam and Darjeeling in India also increased the demand for labour, which resulted in a substantial increase in the number of both men and women workers from Nepal, ultimately increased the expatriate Nepali community in those areas.

Data show that Nepal is witnessing an increasing trend of out-migration since 1942, the first year from which we have the information. In this period of six decades, the migrated population reaches from 88 thousands in 1942 to more than a million in 2008, over 12-fold growth in an increasing rate.

Not all persons represented by the figure mean the labour migration rather they are the people absent at households during census period, which also include labour migrants. Because of data problem, we have to take the whole group of out-migrants into a single category but they can be disaggregated into labour migrants, trafficked people, students, emigrants (under diversity visa [DV] program in USA, skilled manpower immigration program in UK, Canada, New Zealand, and Australia), Gurkhas, and the people working in diplomatic missions and NGOs, and so on.

The growth was not so high until 1981 but it took a bigger leap between the years 1981 and 1991. This can be related to first popular movement in 1990 that restored democracy in Nepal. This actuated labour out-migration in two ways: a) democracy provided an increased access to information and opportunity, and also to freedom and autonomy in decision-making; b) the restored democracy could not solve the problem of unemployment and people's expectation, which made them explore a better opportunity and go abroad. As a means of pull factor could be the increased labour demand from Gulf countries and other Asian countries where the economy was (and still is) booming because of their industrial development. Another leap observed in the figure is from 2001 to 2005. This corresponds with a period of political instability (the period of Maoist insurgency) and surprisingly increased development of information technology that made it easy for the people to access to information.

This trend is ever increasing. A very recent figure of DLEP shows that the size of Nepalese labour force in the year 2007/08 totalled 215,639 persons, an increase of 22.44 percent compared to the previous year (Kantipur 2008).

Patterns of migration: The Government of Nepal officially opened its door for citizens to go abroad for work in late 1980s. Before that people used to work only in India because of open border and people did not have access to other countries. After having labour agreements with a number of Gulf States the number of migrant workers has increased substantially since 1996 with the increasing demand every year.

According to the population census 2001, India remains to be the main recipient of Nepalese migrant workers with about 600,000 migrants living there. India is followed by the Gulf countries in aggregate (111,000) such as Saudi Arabia, Qatar, United Arab Emirates, Bahrain, and so on. Other countries account for about 62,000 Nepalese migrants. Europe is still not visible in terms of Nepalese migrant population size and the proportion in other developed countries is also negligible with respect to size.

A study carried out by Seddon et al. (2002) gives a good account of Nepalese workers living abroad especially in the West. They illustrate that there are few Nepalese living and working in 'the West' and they send remittances back home. Many, particularly in North America, are professionals who live with their families. These are predominantly of urban origin. According to their estimate for 1997, a total of 12,500 Nepali migrants were working in Europe and might be 2,500 in North America—making a total of around 15,000 in the West as a whole. The largest number of Nepalese in any one country is in Britain, with 3,600 (mainly Gurkhas) officially registered and 8,000 unofficial workers. Likewise, in Japan, most of the estimated 10,000-plus Nepali migrant workers are illegal.

If we take out India from the picture, Gulf becomes the prime destination of Nepalese migrant workers. According to DLEP, Malaysia (36%) remains to be the largest recipient as per the country-wise calculation till now (2008), which is followed by Qatar (29%), Kingdom of Saudi Arabia (19%), and United Arab Emirates (12%) and so on. As mentioned above European and American countries are still out of access for the Nepalese migrant workers. Clearly, one should note that the data are entirely work-related migration, which does not include students, refugees, permanent emigrants, and the expatriates.

It is also interesting to observe that probably because of open access to information and impact of globalization the out-migration towards countries other than India is being increased. Previously. people only had access to India because of a number of reasons such as transportation, information. demands from other countries, and other policies and governing rules but gradually people are moving to other countries in the world. In 1981 about 93 percent of out-migrants went to India while only 7 percent found their destination to other countries. The tendency of migrating to outside India kept on increasing and reached 23 percent in 2001 while going to India has been reduced to 77 percent in the same year.

On contrary to above calculation based on the cumulative country-wise calculation, the trend of migration to Malaysia has been reduced since 2005/06 while this trend of the Gulf countries has increased. This is because of a relatively low wage rate in Malaysia as compared to the Gulf countries. My short newspaper survey during June-July 2008 showed that the demand from Malaysia seems to be only working class labourers with the name "Production Workers" or "Production Operators" while in the Gulf countries the demand is more disaggregated. Furthermore, the demand of skilled and semi-skilled labourers like mason, mechanic, salesman/girls, security guards, and engineers is increasing from Gulf States. It is also important to note that many workers returned from Malaysia because of the work they had to engage in are found different form the work they were told they would get during the process. Another important de-motivating factor to Malaysia is the levy charged by the Government of Malaysia from workers. A foreign employment agent (broker) in Jhapa said that if levy was removed the tendency would increase again. In Malaysia, one has to pay up to 150 Ringgit per month to the government, which Nepali workers consider as a financial burden against a relatively low salary.

Gender dimension of migration: Even though, at a global level, almost half of world migrant population is female, Nepal has predominantly male out-migration, with 89 percent of the total migrant population. It is partly attributed by the patrilineal social structure where men have greater access to productive resources, public sphere activities, and a breadwinning role that men are supposed to take such steps and earn to make a living. Ideally, a general social expectation from men in Nepal is to manage resources and make available a livelihood while women are expected to maintain the family and households by allocating resources for the benefit of members. In terms of productive activities, Seddon et al. (2002) analyzed 77 percent women's involvement in agriculture whereas men involved mainly (57 percent) in outside agriculture. This suggests why male out-migration is predominantly high in Nepal.

The country-wise gender composition of out-migrants from Nepal. Hong Kong has the largest proportion of female migrants.

Hong Kong is one of the main destinations for Gurkhas, who are also accompanied by their wives and children. The Hong Kong born children of British armies received their citizenship from Hong Kong government that made them attracted to reside there and hence increased the number. Another reason could be that there has been increasing demand of domestic help which preferably women like to do.

The data show that in the western countries the proportion of women migrants is higher as compared to that of in Moslim countries like Malaysia and the Gulf countries. On contrary to the situation in Southeast Asian countries like Indonesia and the Philippines, the female out-migration from Nepal to the Gulf countries is not so motivating because of the cultural factor and the nature of jobs available. Neither it can be of target for women to apply for as a factory labourer or farm worker nor can they accompany their spouses during migration (due to possibly low wage rate to run their family there). Higher proportion of women migration in the cluster of USA, Canada and Mexico reveals the diversity visa (DV) program in the USA, increasing target of students to US education and immigration program in Canada. These are relatively gender neutral interventions as compared to the labour migration to the Gulf countries and Malaysia.

Apart from the spouses of Indian armies and other civilian workers in India, a huge proportion of women migrants are working in the Indian brothels. Since 1989, when a number of Nepali women from the red light districts of Mumbai were deported, it showed that large numbers of Nepali women are employed in the Indian commercial sex industry (Seddon et al. 2002). Maiti Nepal, a non-governmental organization working in the field of women trafficking in Nepal, estimates that about 150,000 to 300,000 girls are exploited in different brothels in India. However, a scientific investigation is needed to prove whether they are exploited and trafficked. Same situation is prevailed in Hong Kong and Middle Eastern Countries. As mentioned above, due to open border with India the actual number of migrants may surpass the government estimations.

Similarly, people trafficked (as a form of human trafficking) through illegal channels are not counted on official figures.

Remittance as a product of migration: Literally, remittance is the transfer of money by foreign workers, but literature also includes other forms of transfers such as social remittances (diffusion of various types of social practices, ideas and values), knowledge or technology remittances (knowledge, skills and technology brought back by returning migrants), and political remittances as changing identities and political awareness after return (cf. Goldring 2004). Labour migration and remittance is becoming the important mainstay of Nepalese economy. As indicated above, the official statistics does not reflect the actual situation. Seddon et al. (2002) estimate the actual remittance in Nepal is about 10 to 20 times greater than the amount shown by the official statistics, which is equivalent to almost 25 percent of national gross domestic product (GDP). This shows an importance of remittance especially to the rural households. It means rural livelihoods have never been wholly reliant on agriculture, and labour migration has long been an important feature of rural existence in Nepal.

Like pattern of migration (number of migrants) the scale of remittances differs depending upon the countries of destination but in different ways. We have observed that India is the largest recipient of Nepalese migrant workers. However, the remittances from India are not as high as the number of migrants working there. Out of total number of remittances (one remittance means the remittance sent at a time) sent back home, about 40 percent is from India and the corresponding value of remittance is about one third of total remittances entered into the country.

On contrary, a negligible number of remittances (3 percent) from outside India produce almost a quarter of the total amount of remittances. It gives a critical importance of remittances from abroad (outside India) to policy and research arena. Similarly, remittances from urban areas and rural areas of the country are also significant, though they are out of the scope of this chapter.

Remittances from abroad constituted 76 percent of the total amount of remittances received in Nepal in 2004. As migration to India is decreasing the remittance thereof is also decreasing. Using the data from Nepal Living Standard Survey 2003/04 (Lokshin et al 2007) show the largest share of international remittances came from Saudi Arabia, Qatar, and the United Arab Emirates (35 percent), followed by 30 percent from India, 17 percent from other Asian countries, and the remainder from United Kingdom, United States, and other countries.

In sum, it is revealed that the scale and pattern of migration and remittances have different consequences. One country (as the country of destination) may have relatively fewer number of migrants but would have high amount of remittances and in some cases a large number of migrants may produce a relatively smaller amount of remittances, for example, number of migrants and their remittances from India. The influence in aggregate may be different from the influence at household or individual level, so they have to be treated accordingly.

Discussion

It is revealed that international labour migration in Nepal is not a new phenomenon. It has been triggering out the process of socioeconomic transformation in the country for decades. Migration can be seen as a process as well as a product of globalization that provides people not only with easy access to information and technology but also make migrants in constant connection with their areas of origin. Probably the most positive impacts of labour migration in the local development would be the remittances produced by the migrant workers because it is the most visible product of migration.

Remittance, poverty and local development: Remittances are claimed to make an improvement in the living conditions of millions of households in migrant-sending countries. For an increasing number of developing countries, remittances form a crucial source of foreign exchange, sustaining their balance of payments. In addition, governments of sending countries have put renewed hopes on migrants as potential investors in the national economy (de Haas 2005). Countries like Turkey, the Philippines, South Korea, India, Pakistan, Bangladesh, Sri Lanka, Jamaica, Cuba, Barbados, Mexico, El Salvador, and Nicaragua have encouraged international migration as a deliberate approach to development (Nwajiuba 2005). According to Russell (2004), a prime reason for this is that labour migration can provide relatively well-paid employment, especially attractive for governments struggling to keep pace with rapid labour force increases. This can produce large inflows of valuable hard currency remittances. Consequently, governments of sending countries have put renewed hopes on migrants as potential investors in the national economy (de Haas 2005).

Hence, the increased importance of remittances for the social and economic development of rural livelihoods in migrant-sending countries is crucial. In many countries in the world, remittance is becoming a major source of investment for development. For example, the average amount received by a household can be superior to GDP per capita in many Latin American countries (Vargas-Lundius 2004). This is significant considering that only a small percentage of rural inhabitants in those countries earn incomes equivalent to per capita GDP. Likewise, in Armenia, remittances have been considered to reduce inequality as the households that receive them would otherwise be at very low levels of income. According to a survey, remittances make up 80 percent of household incomes on average in Armenia and appear to go to some of the most vulnerable households (USAID 2004).

In Tajikistan, remittances keep many struggling families at home above the poverty line and reduce the stress caused by a lack of domestic job opportunities (cf. UNDP 2005). UNDP (2005) further reports that remittances help averting rural poverty also in Somalia, "with a majority of the population living on less than a dollar per day, the injection of hard currency through remittances enables the country to purchase staple food imports and have a 'multiplier' effect on the local economy". A study of Mexico suggests that each dollar of remittance generates three dollars of spending power. In Albania, remittances have played a significant role in macroeconomic stabilization of the country, the alleviation of poverty and amelioration of the living conditions of many Albanian households. In Egypt, the returning migrants in the late 1980s set up a number of enterprises, in greater Cairo, using funds brought back from abroad (UNDP 2005).

In Nepal, one-fifth of the poverty reduction occurring between 1995 and 2004 was claimed to be due to out-migration (Lokshin et al. 2007). They further reported that 44 percent of the average household expenditure was covered by remittances in 2004. They argue, "Migration and remittances improve the welfare of households in the sending communities by stimulating local economic development.

Migrants channel remittances into productive investment at home. Even when some households spend most of the remittances on current consumption, the resulting demand for goods and services can be met by other working adults in the community, thus generating strong positive externalities". An analysis of the National Living Standard Survey data carried out by Seddon et al. (2002) also shows that 24 percent of rural households received remittances in 1996, which contributes to 27 percent on average to their total income. KC (2003b) found that the districts with higher number of population abroad have a positive correlation with development indicators that could probably be because of remittances.

The Central Bureau of Statistics (CBS) reports that in 1995-1996, the income from remittances counted for about 9 percent of total rural income for the average income rural households, which increased to 17 percent in the year 2003-2004 (CBS 2004). This income from remittances is equivalent to about 40 percent of total income contributed from agriculture in the Nepalese rural economy (THT 2005). It is also important to note that the largest proportion (57 percent) of individual remittances sent to rural households was from household members working elsewhere in 2001 (Seddon et al. 2002).

Depending upon the situation, migration can be a coping strategy for poorer households (Gill 2003), while it can also aim at improving living standards (Niehof 2004). Economically, remittance benefits migrant households by increased income in the short term. However, they may sometimes cause negative social effects, particularly through disruption in family relations and also by creating a sense of relative deprivation in non-migrant communities (Kageyama 2008).

Urbanisation: One of the prime motives of rural youths to migrate for work is to accumulate wealth through remittances, which can be used to buy land in the cities. In the context of a poor infrastructure facilities in rural areas migrants may decide to stay in city areas with modern amenities. This would require a detail investigation but an indication is the increased number of urban places and the corresponding urban population growth, which was 6.65 percent in between census 1991 and 2001 (Gurung et al. 2006). Moreover, "Expansion of infrastructures in urban areas, improvement in educational attainment, mass communication and thereby increased aspiration of rural young adults means that urban areas will continue to receive more and more people". However, urbanisation caused by rural-urban migration should be discussed under internal migration, the international migration can induce the process. Sharma (1989) has already illustrated that internal and international migrations are the largest contributors to urban growth. Whether rapid increase in urbanisation is good or bad for the country's overall development is out of scope of this chapter but labour migration can be asserted to the process of urbanisation.

Labour reorganisation and changing gender roles: This kind of predominantly male dominated out-migration results in a number of changes in gender roles and relationships. In general, women are over-worked due to additional duties and responsibilities to be carried out in the absence of their male counterparts. Kaspar (2005) conducted a study in Nepal looking at the impact of male out-migration on women's life at home. During migration, female's fields of activity hardly undergo any changes, whereas a man's lines of action change considerably with migration. A man gives up agriculture and occasional employment in the village and exchanges it for permanent employment in a foreign country. A woman in contrast, looks after the children, the household and the fields before, during and after migration (Kaspar 2005). Nandini (1999) argues women who previously worked in the labour market may find it optimal to stop working and devote all their time to home production.

In her work in China, Song (1998) concludes that male out-migration virtually causes the feminization of agriculture. It connotes that women have to bear an additional burden of household work as well as farm work in the absence of men. She further argues, "It is the women who are playing key roles in sustaining the small-scale subsistence fanning and food security at both farmers' household level and national level". Moreover, one of the important gender related impacts is the possible adverse effect on girls' education because of extra burden of workload to their mothers and support needed from daughters. In a study carried out in Sudan, Myers et al (1996: 17) noted that because of male out-migration "children, particularly girls, are missing out on schooling because they are required to help shoulder their mothers' extra work burdens in the farm and household".

Impacts on left-behind household members: When a young, able, and productive male household member leaves home, multiple adjustments need to be made among those left behind. Migration changes the relative productivity of the remaining household members; affects household preferences in terms of risk aversion and uncertainty; and provides new information—for example, on new technology, type of crops, and so on. Palmer (1985) articulates that there is 'pure gain' for migrants and their families or a 'private gain' coupled with a social loss. The pure gain supporters believe that there is a net benefit for both migrant and his family as he steadily sends remittances from his work, and the family gains by having one member less to feed. In contrast, supporters of the private gain and social loss proposition argue that the migrant gets a net benefit from his earnings whereas the community as a whole loses productive manpower. The impacts of male out-migration can be discussed under three aspects: a) increase in female headed households, b) impacts on elderly people and children, and c) changes in livelihood portfolios.

It is obvious that male labour out-migration increases the female population in the community, which also leads to the increase of female-headed households. However, in the context of Nepalese social structure the female household heads would have a de facto position with a limited decision-making power. A majority of women interviewed by Kaspar (2005) did not refer to themselves as household-heads, although they took all operational decisions. Their husbands have a major role in decision-making for strategic decisions, even if they are far away from home. However, they use this position in an ambiguous way, "Wives have a gatekeeper function, not only in deciding for which decisions they need their husbands' consultation but also in selecting and pre-interpreting information about events at home and passing information on to their husbands". This may challenge the power relation in household decision-making process.

The labour out-migration has both positive and negative consequences for their elderly parents and children. On one hand, parents can be benefited from remittances or derive pride from their child's occupational or social success in the new setting. On the other hand, departure of a young and able bodied child could reduce availability to provide routine personal care or household help (Knodel and Saengtienchai 2007). Similarly, the increased household income may increase an opportunity to invest in child education (for better schooling) but the absence of father as a discipline maker the children may slip away from the right track. My field visit also showed that though the children are sent to private schools which are functioning better than the government schools in Nepal; mothers have complains about their hardship to handle children in the absence of fathers. Children are psychologically motivated to go abroad for work while their orientation to the schools is not good. However, this needs further clarification.

The potential change in livelihood portfolios of the people left-behind. Livelihood portfolio is the bundle of activities households engage in to generate livelihood and achieve a certain level of livelihood security (Ellis 1998; Niehof 2004). Livelihood security is defined as the stability and resilience of livelihood in the long run (Kaag 2004). It is argued that labour migration is one of the livelihood diversification strategies undertaken by the households in the expectation of more secured livelihoods. However, remittances may also increase income inequalities and form new social hierarchies. There is a high possibility of younger generation people (including return migrants) to move out of agriculture and form new ways of life in the context of increasing share of off-farm income to the farming households and a discouraging incentive from agricultural sector. This would have a greater implication for the future of an agrarian community where the agriculture sector could go to the hands of less productive older parents.

Discussions: With time the perception of looking at migration has been changing because of its both negative as well as positive consequences in the areas of origin and destination. Previously, migration was seen as a product of ill-economy of the areas of origin but now it is seen more as the livelihood strategy. However, the linkages between out-migration and its local consequences have been remained to be the most overlooked dimension of migration research. Rigg (2007: 176) accentuates, "the articulation of mobility with rural livelihoods is not well understood, and nor is the complexity of the individual, household and community context within which migration occurs". Recently, scholars have pointed out a shift towards the linkages between migration and livelihoods in the areas of origin. Similarly, international organizations like IFAD, DFID, IDS and UNDP are also looking at the linkages between migration and development.

New economics of labour migration suggests that migration decisions are made jointly by the migrant and other household members who are left behind in order to minimize risks and maximize the household welfare. Hence, it is argued that migration is an integral part of people's livelihood. So it is worthwhile to understand migration within livelihood perspective to better describe the linkages between out-migration and local development, which cannot be dealt with the classical economic approach of looking at migration as a response to economic disequilibria between the areas of origin and destination.

Even though the scholars try to get away from more economistic evaluation of migration, its assertion as one of the major propelling factors does not allow. Rigg (2007) argues that it is neither easy nor desirable to separate cultural from economic analysis in migration because changing cultural preferences propel migration, and migration reinforces such changing cultures of consumption. He clearly indicates that even when cultural factors matter, economic issues are closely implicated. He gives a new perspective to look at migration more culturally: "economic factors are embedded within livelihood perspective where culture and society are not artificially separated from economy" (Rigg 2007: 169). In other words, labour migration is becoming more cultural affair than economic, as part and parcel of people's life to sustain/improve their livelihoods; more specifically to improve their wellbeing.

NEPAL: QUEST FOR ELUSIVE PEACE

Amidst the continuously expanding sphere of Maoist influence, political uncertainties and growing international interest, Nepal continues to remain one of the most volatile countries in South Asia. Recent developments have, once again, reconfirmed that while the Maoists have been successful in gradually pushing their agenda through violence and intimidation, the four-party coalition government led by Sher Bahadur Deuba is increasingly finding it difficult to evolve a coherent strategy to counter it. In fact, ever since his reinstatement on June 2, 2004, Deuba has been trying to work out a framework to deal with the eight-year old insurgency, which has claimed approximately 10,000 lives. However, the limited success of counter-insurgency operations, the government's inability to forge consensus on the peace process, the continued opposition by the Nepali Congress-led political front, the emerging differences within the government, the withdrawal/collapse of state institutions and a sustained Maoist offensive have made the government increasingly vulnerable and catapulted the Maoists into the political centrestage. In this context, Deuba's visit to India from September 8-12, 2004, was an attempt to strengthen his regime both politically and militarily.

According to the joint statement issued on September 12, 2004, both the countries viewed the Maoist insurgency as a common threat and agreed to further intensify cooperation in curbing their activities. India reassured more assistance to Nepal's security forces in addition to existing support in terms of arms, ammunition, helicopters, intelligence sharing and training. At the same time, India also reportedly pointed out that there is no military solution to the Maoist problem and the government should initiate a meaningful dialogue process. However, Deuba's success on this front will be determined, to a great extent, by his ability to retain the legitimacy of his regime and strike a balance between the key players in Nepal's politics-the King, the political parties and the Maoists. The Maoists' predominance in Nepali politics has been facilitated by the inability of successive governments in addressing the basic problems such as poverty, underdevelopment and discriminatory social order.

A fractured polity, the absence of an elected government and continuous power struggle between the King and the major political parties have provided the Maoists with an opportunity to control approximately half of the territory. Besides, the near collapse of development work and civil governance in violence-affected areas, breakdown of the rule of law, and lack of democratisation at the grassroots level sustain the Maoist activities. Consequently, the Maoists have not only set up parallel structures of governance in many parts of the country including their own visa and taxation system but have also been able to exert considerable influence in urban centres for example, the week-long blockade of the Kathmandu Valley imposed on August 18, 2004. Though the visible impact of the blockade was not significant because the Maoists 'suspended it for one month' on August 24, 2004, they were, nonetheless, able to gain significant psychological advantage particularly the capability to cut off links to the capital city at will. The deteriorating situation was further aggravated when the Maoist-affiliated All Nepal Trade Union Federation (ANTUF) enforced indefinite closure of 47 industrial establishments, hotels and transport services to press for their demands, which include among others, making public the whereabouts of its workers and leaders who have allegedly disappeared from government custody, compensation to the families of those killed by the state, removal of the terrorist tag slapped on them and increased wages and facilities to workers. Though the ANTUF agreed to withdraw its call on September 15, 2004, after the government agreed to release two of its detained leaders and make available information on the whereabouts of people 'disappeared' from custody within one month beginning September 22, 2004, it is unlikely to restore the confidence of the business community due to continued threat of extortion and the government's inability to provide protection to industries. Simultaneously, the Maoists continued with their violent campaign, attacking district headquarters, government infrastructure, security forces and civilian population. On September 10, 2004, the Maoists were reported to have exploded two bombs at the American Information Centre at Gyaneshwar in Kathmandu. No one was injured in the incident after which the US government decided to suspend all Peace Corps activities.

The absence of a comprehensive counter-insurgency doctrine has enabled the Maoists to grow from strength to strength. The main thrust of counter-insurgency operations has been the excessive use of force and towards that end the government has worked on a policy of strengthening the Royal Nepal Army (RNA) with sophisticated weapons from India, the US, the UK, Belgium and other countries. It is estimated that approximately

25 per cent of the total national budget is now allocated to security. However, despite considerable augmentation of the strength of the RNA, the situation on the ground remains alarming. Though the security forces have achieved some success in counter-insurgency operations, the task is becoming difficult due to lack of adequate state presence in the violence-affected areas. As a result, the government has not been able to supplement the success of counter-insurgency in one area with strengthening/restoration of civil governance, institutions of law enforcement and democratic process. The experience of the counter-insurgency operation has, therefore, necessitated an assessment of the broad direction of government policy and implications of continuous strengthening of the RNA. There is an apprehension that while the continuation of this approach may not be able to contain the Maoists militarily, it might catapult the RNA into an important player in Nepali politics with its own stake. It might further strengthen the King and weaken the democratic government and its ability to pursue a meaningful peace process.

The impetus to the peace process is being reinforced by the realisation that there cannot be a purely military solution to the problem. The Maoists are in a stronger position as is evident from their tough stand on talks. Reports in the first week of September 2004 said, the Maoists have ruled out the possibility of dialogue with the Deuba government favouring instead direct negotiations with King Gyanendra and have reiterated their demand for a Constituent Assembly election under the aegis of the UN. It is clear that the present Maoist demand will further strengthen the King and reinforce the perception that the government is not in a position to play a decisive role.

Consequently, the role of the monarchy becomes important. When King Gyanendra appointed Deuba in June 2004, he had spelt out three tasks before him: to take on board all major political parties on important national issues, find ways to deal with the Maoist insurgency and prepare the nation for elections. If Deuba fails to deliver on these counts, the King might be compelled to remove him from office. Given the fact that an extreme Right Wing opinion within the political spectrum wants the King to play a more active role, the success of the present government will depend largely on the King whose inflexible approach has thus far only complicated the problem.

The differences within the mainstream political formations have only added to the complications. While Deuba has been able to form a coalition government with the help of the Communist Party of Nepal-United Marxist-Leninist (CPNUML), he has failed to evolve a consensus even within the ruling coalition on issues such as ceasefire, external mediation and elections to the Constituent Assembly.

The UML reportedly favours unilateral ceasefire by the government as a prelude to the resumption of negotiations while Deuba insists that unless the Maoists show any sincere commitment towards a result oriented peace process; declaration of a unilateral ceasefire would be meaningless. On the question of the Constituent Assembly, the UML has hinted that the issue is not closed and could be addressed during the peace talks. In January 2004, the UML presented a nine-point roadmap favouring either amendments to the new Constitution or the preparation by the House of Representative. On the question of external mediation involving the UN, Deuba has rejected the idea on the ground that the issue was an internal one; the UML, on the other hand, incorporated a possible UN role in its nine-point roadmap. However, it has yet to expand on the type of role it envisages for the UN in the conflict.

Outside the government, the four-party alliance led by the Nepali Congress has refused to participate in the peace process and has announced fresh agitation against what they call 'regression'. Members of this alliance have been pressing for the restoration of parliament and a consensus government that should initiate dialogue with the rebels. They argue that the new government will command more credibility and legitimacy, and certainly strengthen the government at the time of the talks with the Maoists. Nepali Congress Chief G.P. Koirala has refused to participate or nominate a representative for the high-level peace committee formed on August 12, 2004, under the leadership of the Prime Minister. The objective of the committee is to coordinate the peace process and finalise the political agendas for negotiations. Reports suggest that he is holding a parallel dialogue with the Maoists in order to bring them to the political mainstream.

While there appears to be a broad consensus on negotiating with the Maoists, it, however, cannot be achieved until the political parties bridge their own political differences and evolve an effective negotiating strategy. In the light of this, a pertinent question emerges: does Nepal need external mediation to break the deadlock. Those who favour external mediation argue that despite two rounds of ceasefire and negotiations in 2001 and 2003, the government and the Maoists failed to reach a minimum consensus, hence an impartial body like the UN could play a vital role in facilitating the peace talks. The UN system has, on a number of occasions, expressed its desire facilitate peace talks and has sent special emissaries to explore the possibilities of securing a role. But the government has shown little inclination for any external mediation.

Does India have a role to play in breaking the deadlock? India's concerns at the stalemate between the Nepalese government and the Maoist insurgents are growing. The geo-strategic position of Nepal, open borders and a history of good relations makes Nepal important in India's strategic calculations. Internal instability in Nepal will have serious security implications for India. The exploitation of open India-Nepal borders by the Maoists, their deepening linkages with Indian leftwing extremist groups such as the Communist Party of India Marxist-Leninist (People's War), the Maoist Communist Centre of India (MCCI) and the Northeast insurgent groups and the unbridled use of India-Nepal open border for shelter, training, supplies and arms smuggling pose serious security threat to India. Further, there is apprehension that Pakistan's Inter Services Intelligence (ISI), active in border areas, could forge links with the Maoists to de-estabilise the region. Therefore, India needs to ensure that its core interests are not hurt in the confrontation between the Deuba government and the Maoists. India has been providing military assistance to Nepal based on assessments that the RNA was the only force capable of keeping the Maoists at bay. India has also taken a number of steps to contain Maoist activities on its soil and strengthen coordinated security strategies on both sides of the border.

Conceding that it may not be possible to defeat the Maoists militarily, it is in India's interest to ensure that the Maoists should not be able to exploit a divided polity. While supporting the Constitutional monarchy and multiparty democracy in Nepal, India has repeatedly emphasised that only the monarchy and Nepal's democratically elected parties can solve the Maoist problem, provided they work in unison. Towards this end, it is in India's interest to facilitate a peace process with an aim to restore and strengthen a viable and sustainable democratic government in Nepal.

2

Nepal and China in the 21st Century

A great living Chinese scholar Professor Huang Xinchuan underscored in his write up, " China is a close neighbour of Nepal. The geographical contiguity provided by great mountains and rivers has formed a background favourable to the development of long standing historical ties between Nepal and China and the forging of profound neighborly friendship between their people.

The Buddhism as well as the cultural interflow between Nepal and China had taken place as early as over two thousand years ago. Because Sakyamuni Buddha was born in Nepal, his Dharma has prevailed in China as early as in the beginning of Christian era" (from a paper presented at a seminar organized by China Study Center on Nepalese and Chinese Buddhism, Kathmandu, 2003). His account fairly depicts the nature and timing of Nepal-China relationship.

Besides, this relationship being of symbiotic nature, despite of asymmetrical size of our two countries remained complementary to each other's economy and security until most of the parts of South Asia came under the British occupation in the 17th century.

The Anglo-Nepal War (1814-16) which ended by the treaty of Sugauli was a great setback to Nepal's sovereignty. This treaty forced Nepal to cede one-third of its territory. Since then Nepal remained within the bounds of imperial Britain till 1947.

Her relationship with China got almost severed to the extent that the British even used their puppet Rana regime to attack China's Tibet.

The fall of the Rana regime in 1950 restored a new political climate. It paved the way to bring Nepal and China close once again. In 1955 during King Mahendra's direct rule, diplomatic ties were established between Nepal and China. Since then this relation is gaining momentum, though marked by occasional difficulties. In this span of fifty years of the establishment of diplomatic ties between the two countries, both have helped each other. Nevertheless, paradoxically even after 1950, Nepal continued to be within the bounds of unequal treaties imposed on it by foreign powers which had debarred it form deciding its own destiny.

However, it is gratifying that Nepal-China relationship started to move forward once again from 1955. Mr.Tanka Prasad Acharya was the first Prime Minister of Nepal to pay an official visit to China in post-Rana era of 1956. His visit was highly successful in forging economic and political relation with China. The great statesman of China Premier Zhou Enlai visited Nepal twice. He referred to Nepal-China relationship as being based on blood ties. The relationship between Nepal and China was defined as of great importance by the leaders of both countries. I do not know if history has any importance in the current trend of bilateral relationship which is entirely based on give and take; the two thousand years old relationship has much value to determine the future course of our bilateral relationship!

However, Nepal now being in a, very weak position in actual practice cannot expect to be treated by any powerful nation in equal terms. But China has proved itself as an exception. It has throughout strictly pursued its policy of Panchasheel and non- interference in the internal affairs of another country. Both Nepal and China are parts of ancient civilizations. China is a great nation since more than two thousand years ago. Nepal too has an ancient and glorious history. Till 1900 AD Nepal was the principal entry port of trans- Himalayan trade for over a millennium.^ It was the most powerful nation of South Asia. Nevertheless the imperial Britain succeeded in subduing Nepal and opening trade route from occupied Kalingpong to Nathula of Sikkim and then to the other side of the Himalayas. The British objective was to break the backbone of Nepal's economy and make this country impoverished, so that London could easily recruit "the bravest of the brave", the Nepalese in their army and use them to control their far flung colonies.

Since then to this day Nepal has not been able to restore its glorious stature which it had prior to the humiliating treaty of 1816 with imperial Britain, but even after 1816 London was apprehensive that Nepal would attack on its colonies of South Asia.

Though the British knew that China's help to Nepal would not be forthcoming, yet dozens of independent South Asian nations were impressed by the valour of Nepal and her effort to lead them against Britain even after 1816.

Nepal-China relationship will be completing fifty years of the establishment of diplomatic ties between them. Within this span of 50 years. Heads of State, Prime Ministers, important personalities and delegations of different natures of both countries have exchanged official and unofficial visits. The last visit of Chinese Prime Minister Zhu Rongji to Nepal was in 2001 at the invitation of the then Nepalese Prime Minister G. P. Koirala. This visit was highly successful. Nepal and China, besides signing half a dozen agreements, could also sign an accord to build another highway (Rasuwa-Syabrubesi) to link Nepal and China. Such an agreement could be signed after thirty nine years of the previous one, that is, the Kathmandu-Kodari highway. The first road agreement was signed between the two countries during King Mahendra's visit to China in September, 1961.

These visits helped sustain and strengthen the age-old China Nepal relations. Reviewing these visits one can barely think that the state of Nepal-China relationship still needs to go a long way in order to be strong. There are still constraints and irritants in our relationship. The presence of illegal immigrants from China's Tibet in Nepal and their separatist activities being launched from the Nepalese soil at the backing of the anti-Chinese international lobby has been a constant sore in Nepal China relations. This major irritant still continues to function covertly or overtly. It is violating our country's rule of law and also our sovereign status. Even in the dawn of the 21st century we have not been able to give priority to our national interest and guard our territorial integrity.

But things have changed so much around us. China has already emerged as a great economic powerhouse of the world. While we are still moving at snail's pace to integrate with her economically.

We Nepalese, however, still find China on our side, in support of our sovereignty, independence and territorial integrity. This is the reason why we accolade the great Chinese leaders like late Mao, Zhou, Deng and also the incumbent Chinese leadership, President Hu Jianto and others. It is to be remembered that the architect of modern China, Deng Xiaoping preferred to visit only Nepal among the South Asian nations. Such a preference of Deng emanated from his great knowledge of history and the importance of Nepal China relationship. Thus in 1978 when he was in Kathmandu, he advocated for a comprehensive Nepal-China relationship by suggesting to have people to people, government to government and party to party relations. As I came to know when the Nepalese side was requesting some industries under grant, late Deng was stressing to undertake joint economic ventures. Today every sensible Nepalese realizes that the suggestion of the architect of modern China was timely and sagacious; it was in the larger interest of Nepal. Nevertheless, Nepal then was having a policy of dichotomy and succumbing to foreign pressure to discourage benefits coming from China's miraculous economic prosperity.

There is no reason for Nepal China relations to lag behind. But, ambivalence was always persistent raising the threat of communist boggy whenever Nepal had a chance to promote ties with China. In reality Nepal-China relationship was throughout based on mutuality and within the parameters of helping each other. China has always been trustworthy, friendly and helpful. Even in its worst days it was helping Nepal economically and politically. It will not be an exaggeration to add that Nepal too has rendered a little bit of assistance to China by supporting China's One China Policy.

Nepal's success in preventing the advancing imperial British from reaching the Himalayas in 1814-16 Anglo-Nepal war, though it was costly for Kathmandu, it provided a strong security crest to China's South-Western region. This is one of the glowing illustrations of how Nepal contributed to China's security. I don't know if the Chinese historians and military strategists have ever acknowledged this part of the history. On the other hand, when China declared through its Foreign Minister Marshal Chenyi, on October 5, 1962 that, in case any foreign army makes a foolhardy attempt to attack Nepal.... China will side with the Nepalese people," the Nepalese people have treasured it in their ever lasting memory. Thus what we observe is that the great Chinese leaders from Chairman Mao, Zhou, Deng Xiaoping and from the Nepalese side from King Mahendra to Tanka Prasad Acharya, B.P. Koirala to King Birendra had consistently contributed to foster Nepal-China relationship. The patriotic people of both our countries indeed played a key role in maintaining and strengthening bilateral relationship.

Both Nepal and China have many memorable events. If evaluated properly it will give a glimpse of how they have helped each other. The annals of our bilateral relation of last fifty years unequivocally suggest that the initiative to enhance the strength of Nepal-China relationship mostly emanated from the Chinese side. This was well reflected once again when the then Chinese President Jiang Zemin told the visiting Nepalese King Gyanendra Bir Bikram Shah Dev on 2002-7-10 that, "apart from continuing the traditional practice of top leaders' visits, more exchanges should be encouraged between congresses, political parties, industrial and commercial circles, the press and non governmental organizations from both countries." He was elaborating on what late paramount leader Deng had said in the 1970's. His suggestion was a timely initiative to make Nepal-China friendship really comprehensive and everlasting. The incumbent Chinese leadership is also very friendly towards Nepal.

President Hu Jiantao in particular knows Nepal and the Nepalese intimately, as he also worked in the capacity of the Secretary of the CPC in China's Tibet for nearly two years.

Today China is a major global player and a great economic powerhouse of the world. Nepal though a medium sized nation, has huge natural resources and other potentialities. It is high time we became real economic partner as suggested by the Chinese leaders for the benefit of our countrymen. Nepal rejoices in being China's neighbor for the simple fact that her great northern neighbor China is a peace loving nation.

We have entered the 21st century. China's foreign policy has been largely guided by the twin principles of economic development and security on the basis of give and take. Such two-way relationships are not only sustainable but are also everlasting. Though in terms of market, Nepal doesn't provide as much space as other larger countries the vast untapped natural resources and the geo-political situation provide enough basis for even firmer and more meaningful relations between our two countries. So we can say without any reservation that the prospect of Nepal-China relations is bright.

CHINA'S LONG TERM GAME PLAN IN NEPAL

China's security and foreign policy objectives in Nepal are several. In fact, they could be divided into three parts. Nepal constituted one of the five fingers policy in Mao Zedong's five finger policy. Nepal and China share a long border, spanning about 1,414 kilometres. China has been playing significant role in determining the future shape of Nepali politics.

The Primary Stage

The Chinese interest in Nepal began with the Tibet factor. At a minimum, these objectives are the security of Chinese interests in Tibet as that region is dependent on the neighbouring countries for border trade. Additionally, given the regular flow of thousands of Tibetan refugees into Nepal and India every year, the Chinese objective is to nullify any negative fallout from Tibetan refugees in these countries to impact Nepal as a buffer zone. Thus, Chinese objectives in Nepal have been influencing by the Tibetan factor, including whether more than an estimated 10,000 Tibetan refugees play a destabilizing role from Nepal, to secure Nepal as a buffer zone.

In the beginning diplomatic ties between China and Nepal moved with great speed. The prime motive of China in the first phase (1955 to 1989)7 was to create infrastructure in Nepal. China also promised Nepal to protect its territory from any third country. Speaking in Kathmandu on the first anniversary of the signing of the Kathmandu-Lhasa road agreement, in October 1962, Chinese foreign minister Chen Yi lauded Nepal's history of resistance to foreign invasion and said: "I assure His Majesty, King Mahendra, His Majesty government and the Nepalese people, that in any case any foreign forces attack Nepal, we Chinese people will stand on your side" China openly exhorted Nepali assertions of independence vis-à-vis India throughout the period up to 1978.

Intense anti-Indian propaganda was directed by China into Nepal. In the mid 1980s China resumed its highway construction activities in Nepal, and in June 1984 it agreed to build a second trans-Himalayan highway, linking the city of Pokhara with the Xinjiang-Tibet highway. In 1987, Beijing decided to construct a road from Lhasa to Dazhu on the border with Nepal, further strengthening Tibet- Nepal transportation links. In 1988, a series of Chinese–Nepali moves ignored India's security interests. China no longer felt compelled to respect Indian sensibilities and began to compete openly with India for influence in Nepal. Chinese propaganda became openly critical of Indian policies toward Nepal, condemning them as manifestations of Indian expansionism. Nepal responded positively to China's overtures. The new wave brought many fundamental changes in triangle relationships. The pro Chinese approach of King Mahendra continued to provide new space for the Chinese expansion.

Second Phase

The second phase of Chinese strategy focussed on ending Nepal's overdependence on India. Till 1995 trade between China and Nepal was limited to 0.7 per cent. The rest 99.0312 per cent trade was with India. China was aware of the geographical proximity between India and Nepal. Therefore, new routes to trade in Nepal were planned. On the other hand, China encouraged Nepal to adopt the equidistance policy between India and China. In the early years, Chinese assistance was pledged in terms of projects and a number of financial involvements were initiated. From mid- 90s, the Chinese government has been pledging grant assistance to Nepal under the economic and technical cooperation programme in order to implement mutually acceptable development projects.

Nepal's Pro China Strategy

Nepal's pro China policy began with King Mahendra and was continued in successive regimes. But the Maoist government in Nepal openly invited China to balance India's excessive role in Nepal. The first country that Pushpa Kamal Dahel Prachanda visited after being sworn in as Prime Minister was China. He was 'invited' to attend the closing ceremony of the Olympic Games in 2008. Prachanda's visit lasted for five days and the special bonding between the Maoists and China became evident. There are people who argue that China is not only courting the Nepalese Maoists, but also rendering political as well material support to the Indian Maoist whose ultimate aim is to overthrow the parliamentary democracy through an armed struggle. It is very important to note that 38 official Chinese delegations visited Nepal during Prime Minister Pushpa Kamal Dahel "Prachanda's term, while the numbers of delegations from India were about one-fourth the above numbers. It is also well known that the Maoist government and China were preparing to extend the Tibet Railway to Nepal.

In a sensational maintain, Pushpa Kamal Dahel has said that the India-US axis was indulging in anti-China activities, and even a possible attack on China, from Nepali territory. "I had to quit as prime minister as my party was opposed to letting our territory used against China", Prachanda said while addressing a training programme of the Maoist cadres, according to the *Rajdhani* daily. It quoted Prachanda as having said: "The US-India plan had to face challenge from our party and that triggered the conspiracy against my government." Nepal's use of the "China card" in its dealings with India is nothing new. It may be recalled that in 2005 it was China that supplied arms and ammunition to King Gyanendra despite urgings to the contrary from the US and India. In September 2008 during a meeting between China's defence minister Liang Guanglie and his Nepali counterpart, Ram Bahadur Thapa, the Chinese announced a military aid package of USD 1.3 million to Nepal. In December 2008, senior military officials from China visited Nepal. During this visit, Lieutenant General Ma Xiaotan of the Chinese People Liberation Army pledged USD 2.6 million in non-lethal military aid to be used for the consolidation of Nepal's security forces and peace process.

DEFENCE TECHNOLOGY OF CHINA

China is accelerating reform and innovation in its defence-related science, technology and industry, promoting strategic and specialization-oriented restructuring of defence industry enterprises, enhancing the capabilities of independent innovation in the R&D of weaponry and equipment, and striving to establish a new system of defence-related science, technology and industry which caters to both military and civilian needs, and channels military potential to civilian use.

Promoting Innovation in Structures and Mechanisms

To meet the needs of weaponry and equipment development, as well as development of the socialist market economy, China is constantly reforming its management system of defence-related science, technology and industry. According to the Plan for Restructuring the State Council passed by the First Session of the Eleventh National People's Congress in 2008, the Science, Technology and Industry Commission for National Defence of the People's Republic of China has been superseded by the State Administration of Science, Technology and Industry for National Defence.

In 2007, the State Council approved Some Opinions on Deepening the Reform of the Investment System of Science, Technology and Industry for National Defence, which explicitly proposes a new investment system featuring effective government regulation and control, participation of social capital, standardized intermediary services, vigorous supervision and management, and positive military-civilian interaction.

As a result, an open development pattern for defence-related science, technology and industry is taking shape. The investment field has been further broadened, and investment structure further optimized. Ways of investment have been diversified to include not only direct investment, but also injection of capital and investment subsidies.

China is speeding up the transformation of the structures and mechanisms of the defence industry enterprises, and is in the initial stage of establishing a new system of defence-related science, technology and industry that features a small core, extensive cooperation and a large military potential reserve among civilians.

Structural contradictions in defence-related science, technology and industry have been gradually and fundamentally solved through strategic restructuring and the streamlining of the main body of the defence industry. China is steadily promoting the transformation of defence industry enterprises into joint-stock enterprises, actively exploring approaches to diversifying the structure of property rights, giving priority on helping qualified competitive enterprises to be reorganized and listed on the stock market, and encouraging specialization-oriented restructuring and the integration of the efforts of enterprises, universities and research institutes. Relevant laws and regulations have been improved to standardize and supervise the process of reorganizing the defence industry enterprises and getting them listed on the stock market.

Weaponry and Equipment Research and Production System

Establishing a sound licensing system for weaponry and equipment research and production. In accordance with the Implementation Measures for Weaponry and Equipment Research and Production Licensing promulgated in May 2005, the defence-related science, technology and industry has adopted a licensing system for weaponry and equipment research and production featuring management of categorization. While maintaining state control over weaponry and equipment research and production, the document allows the non-public sector to enter this field and compete for research and production projects. In March 2008 the State Council and the CMC issued the Regulations on the Licensing Administration of Weaponry and Equipment Research and Production, further improving the system.

Enhancing the basic capabilities of weaponry and equipment research and production. Defence-related science, technology and industry are striving to enhance the informationization of weaponry and equipment design and development, and to render product design more digitalized, modularized, standardized and reliable. It has built digital simulation and hardware-in-the-loop(HIL) simulation facilities and a number of important advanced experimentation and demonstration facilities, which has resulted in a higher design capability and R&D success rate. This sector has also increased final assembly and integration capabilities, and a number of key enterprises have realized systems integration of assembly, experimentation and testing. This has substantially raised core manufacturing capabilities by giving priority to resolving processing and technical issues in complex parts processing, precision manufacturing and special welding.

In addition, a number of large-scale basic experimentation facilities serving the entire industry have been constructed, as well as specialized testing and experimentation centres for reliability testing and burn-in screening of components and parts, and improved measures, standards and other basic support conditions for defence industries have been put in place. With the improvement of basic capabilities, a leapfrogging development in the ability to provide weaponry and equipment has been achieved.

Building a dynamic innovation system for defence-related science, technology and industry. The government has taken the lead to create a favourable environment for innovation and guide innovation activities through policies and investments. With the research institutes and enterprises of the defence industry as the backbone and with institutes for basic research and institutions of higher learning as a vital new force, China is giving full play to the advantages of integrating enterprises, universities and research institutes, and making efforts to increase its capability for independent innovation in defence-related science, technology and industry. To consolidate the foundation of human resources for the innovative development of defence-related science, technology and industry, both the national major projects of science and technology and important projects for defence scientific research and weaponry and equipment R&D have been taken as platforms to identify, cultivate, employ and attract talented people.

Enhancing Cooperation with Other Countries

Following the principles of mutual benefit and common development, China is conducting cooperation with foreign countries in defence-related science, technology and industry. It emphasizes exchanges and cooperation with developed countries in defence industry technology to draw on their experience in technological development and management.

It enhances mutually beneficial cooperation with developing countries, and engages in joint R&D and production in major cooperative projects, in accordance with the national conditions and specific requirements of the partners. On the export of military items, it adheres to the following principles: It should only serve the purpose of helping the recipient state enhance its capability for legitimate self-defence; it must not impair peace, security and stability of the relevant region or the world as a whole; and it must not be used to interfere in the recipient state's internal affairs.

China's defence-related science, technology and industry actively conduct cooperation with other countries in the field of hi-tech industries, combining military and civilian needs, and makes great efforts to develop hi-tech civilian products with high added value. Major breakthroughs have been made in developing the international market for space products.

China has exported its first satellite; and the earth resources satellite project with Brazil has played an important role in both countries' economic development. China has significantly enhanced its cooperation with other countries in aviation products and technologies, and made new headway in developing the international market for civil aircraft.

China's shipbuilding industry has exported products for civil use in series and batches, further increasing its share in the international market for such products.

3

China-Nepal ties Attain New Heights

This March 10, Nepal proved itself unwilling to allow a repeat of the mass Tibetan demonstrations that were held here from March to September 2008. Although the energy and numbers of last year's demonstrations surrounding the anniversary of the failed Tibetan uprising and Dalai Lama's flight into exile were not present this year, Nepalese riot police still took forcible measures to prevent a group of approximately 200 Tibetan demonstrators leaving the Boudha district of Kathmandu. A British activist named Daisy Karen Wood who attempted to dodge police and enter the Chinese Embassy carrying balloons and a Tibetan flag was quickly arrested. Nepal's desire to quickly suppress events that would embarrass China, its massive northern neighbour, comes as no surprise. Ties between the two countries have been increasing in recent months.

Historically, relations between Nepal and China have been relatively good. For centuries Nepal sent tribute bearing missions to China and acknowledged its superior regional force. The tension that did exist originated out of the perceived threat from India and contention over Tibet, which lies just 114 kilometres from Kathmandu. Following China's refusal to give military assistance to Nepal during the Anglo-Nepalese war of 1814-1816, Nepal invaded Tibet in 1854. China quickly intervened and the Treaty of Thapathali was signed between the two countries in 1856. Nepal recognized China's supremacy in the region and agreed to provide assistance if Tibet was ever invaded by a foreign force.

When an armed British mission arrived in Tibet from India in 1905, however, Nepal did not intervene. Having come under the influence of British India after its loss in the Anglo-Nepalese war, Nepal went as far as to tell China that it would assist the Tibetans if they ever declared independence, provided it was within British interests. When the Tibetans used the chaos of the 1911 Revolution to expel the Chinese, Nepal broke ties with China altogether.

Relations were re-established in 1955 when the Chinese began sending soldiers into Tibet. With the British gone from India, Nepal recognized Tibet as a sovereign part of Chinese territory and in 1960, a year after Tibet's failed uprising and the Dalai Lama's flight into exile, the two countries signed the Treaty of Peace and Friendship, cementing strong ties that continue today.

Now the new "Comprehensive Treaty" will bring the two countries even closer. The treaty puts into place agreements that China will not attack Nepal and will respect its sovereignty, while Nepal will solidify its acceptance of the "One China" policy. Under the policy Tibet, Taiwan, and Hong Kong are stated as indisputable parts of Chinese territory, and Nepal will not allow anti-Chinese activities on its soil. Nepal proved its willingness to fulfil such promises in the days surrounding the 50th anniversary of the March 10, 1959, Tibetan Uprising. The day after a visit by Chinese assistant foreign minister Hu Zhengyue, who arrived in Nepal last month leading a 14-member delegation, 27 Tibetans monks were arrested in Kathmandu. Eighteen were released and nine turned over to the United Nations and deported to India. The streets around the two Chinese embassies in Kathmandu were also closed off, declared "protest-free zones", and staffed with police who had orders to arrest anyone demonstrating nearby. Additional arrests of Tibetan activists were carried out and demonstrators were quickly confronted.

China welcomes these closer relations, with the additional support for its "One China" policy and assistance in controlling the more than 20,000 Tibetan refugees living in Nepal. The refugees, if they ever gave up the aging Dalai Lama's method of peaceful negotiation, could use Nepal's difficulty to control its northern border to launch attacks on Chinese forces in Tibet-something which Khampa fighters did with short-lived US Central Intelligence Agency support in the late 1960s and early 1970s. China views the establishing of closer relations with Nepal as an important step in its competition with India for regional influence. "China now seems to view Nepal as a vital bridge toward South Asia as part of strategy of encircling India," said Nepal expert Sanjay Upadya.

However, Nepal's interest in expanding relations with China is more complicated. The country has long sought to balance the interests of India and China, the two regional powers it lies between. Since the signing of the Indo-Nepalese Treaty of 1950, India has come to heavily dominate Nepalese politics. While the treaty acknowledges Nepal's sovereignty, clauses in the agreement give India a greater amount of control over Nepal than the Maoist government would prefer.

It is the overbearing influence of India that has pushed Nepal's Maoist government decisively towards China. The shift has been so strong that Premier Prachanda went as far as to break the long-standing tradition of Nepalese heads of state making their first foreign trip to India, instead visiting China, ostensibly to attend the opening ceremony of the 2008 Summer Olympic Games in Beijing. The move toward China does not necessarily mean that Nepal is breaking ties with India-the government rather seeks to decrease Indian influence. As Nepalese journalist Narendra Praṣad Upadhyaana said, "It is not that China is ideal. It is only to neutralize India. Historically, socially, and culturally Nepal is closer to India. On a political level however the Maoist government wants to avoid being controlled by India as much as possible."

This new partnership with China comes at a time of great necessity for Nepal. The country is facing growing insecurity which many experts in Kathmandu believe could escalate into a crisis within the next year. With the decade-long civil war resulting in the overthrow of the monarchy, Nepal is facing the challenges of a newly democratic nation that has innumerable political groups and organizations vying for a tiny amount of resources amid growing insecurity.

The country's police and army have become polarized, with different groups supporting the Maoists, opposition forces, and even the return of the monarchy. A number of journalists have been attacked in the past six months. Amid simmering discontent within the Maoist Army, which refuses to integrate with the regular army and continues to recruit soldiers, the expected flood of returning immigrants from jobs in the Middle East and Malaysia due to the global financial crisis makes Nepal's immediate future seem grim.

Perhaps the most dangerous threat to the country's stability, however, is the deteriorating situation in the southern Terai region. Members of the Tharu indigenous group recently declared a 14-day strike, shut down roads, and engaged in near daily clashes with police that left four people dead. The Tharus were demanding to be recognized as distinct from the Madhesis, the ethnic group that most indigenous people from the Terai are lumped into. Government negotiation ended the strike only after the situation had become so tense that police were ordered to escort petrol trucks through checkpoints and the price of fruit and vegetables in some Kathmandu markets had nearly doubled.

Though the strike has ended, the Tarai will continue to be an issue for Nepal. The indigenous groups demand that a new constitution divide the country into ethnically based autonomous states, something that could spell disaster as many of the ethnic groups in Nepal do not even acknowledge the others' right to exist. The idea of "ethnic federalism" will not be given up easily though. According to Dr Om Gurung, an indigenous rights leader in Kathmandu, the establishment of ethnically based autonomous federal states was a key promise of the Maoists during the civil war. Recently, however, the government has begun backing away from the promise, and most experts believe that such a system would set the stage for future conflict. Indigenous leaders are adamant, however, that Nepal's diverse nature requires such a system.

Dangerously, after the Maoist victory in the civil war and their subsequent international recognition, organizations in Nepal realized that agitation and violence does indeed work as a means of achieving political goals. With 70 identified armed groups operating across Nepal, most the wings of political organizations, the government and safety of the people are severely threatened. How the indigenous groups will choose to assert themselves if their demands for autonomous states are not met is still unknown.

Unless the government manages to control this growing unrest, the Maoist revolution may in fact prove to have just been the catalyst for a longer struggle for territory, resources, and representation in Nepal that the country will have to face as it struggles over the course of the next year to write a new constitution and make the difficult transition from a country at war to a country at peace.

This is a desire that can be assisted by a closer relationship with China. Over the past years China has proven itself willing to give large amounts of no-strings-attached cash and support for infrastructure building to countries that support its "One China" policy and allow it to expand its growing global influence. This is in contrast with most Western countries which demand that aid goes to specific projects and require greater oversight regarding where the funds end up. While the lack of transparency in Nepal means that much of the aid will be lost due to corruption, there is enough being offered that some effect will be felt by the population.

Along with the $16.4 million donation, after the signing of the "Comprehensive Treaty" China will add an additional 770 kilometres to the Kathmandu-Khasa highway in Tibet, effectively linking Nepal with China's massive internal railway system. Additional roads connecting Tibet and Nepal will be built and Chinese products are increasingly replacing Indian products, something that most Nepalese appreciate because of the lower cost. "China's products are sound to our pockets," said Nepalese journalist Narendra Prasad Upadhyaana.

The additional access to China is also expected to stimulate economic growth in Tibet, something that the Chinese government considers key to making the Tibetans drop their demands for autonomy. Larger groups of tourists coming from Nepal, and Tibetan salt being sold to Nepal, certainly may lessen some of the Tibetans' anger towards China, but it will not quite be the salve that the Chinese government wants it to be. As one Tibetan activist in Kathmandu said, "China does not have human rights. Nepal is following that. They are bending over for China and letting the Chinese control the police and treat the Tibetans here like animals."

The closer relationship with China is also not being viewed favorably by Delhi. Earlier this month several Nepalese opposition politicians left for India, claiming the trip was for health reasons. Their visit coincides with the presence of Nepal's disposed King Gyanendra, who has been in India since last month for a wedding. Although the Indian government allowed the Maoists to overthrow the monarchy, the new preference for China is making India reconsider its support. This is something that the Maoists must have expected. They are, however, reacting nervously to the opposition visit to India. "A new pact is being signed in New Delhi against the Maoist government," said the Janadisha newspaper, a mouthpiece for the Maoist Party. "Delhi is encircling the Maoists," said Nepalese journalist Narendra Prasad Upadhyaana. "India brought them to power and now suddenly they have gone to the Chinese. And India and China still do not have cordial relations."

NEPAL'S DETERIORATING DEFENSE AND FOREIGN POLICY

Since 1990, Nepali congress government is trying to change Nepalese foreign policy one sided, though previously it was quite balanced. More correctly after popular movement of 2005, home, defence and foreign policy of Nepal has been completely failed. Pro-Indian foreign policy is crisis on existence of Nepal. Bhutan is bordered with China. India is always against the good friendly bilateral relationship between China and Bhutan. Bhutan is protected by India. Nepal is also bordered with China. India does not wish friendly bilateral relationship between Nepal and China. Indian leaders frequently visit Nepal. But if any Chinese leader visits Nepal, it becomes matter of headache for India. Actually India wants Nepal under its control.

After the establishment of democracy in Nepal, nationalists protested against unequal treaty of 1950 (made by India) and Delhi agreement. Nepalese people protesting against Delhi Agreement were accused of communists. Communist Party was also banned with same issue. Later in 1956, King Mahendra lifted the ban over the Communist Party.

Even after the general election of 1958-59, India did not abandon exhibiting its bad intensions towards Nepal. As the existence of Nepal was endangered, King Mahendra dissolved the Parliament in 1960 and safeguarded the Nepalese nationality. If King would not have been there, the existence of Nepal would have ended up. On the initiation of King Mahendra, Indian army check posts that were kept for security after Delhi Agreement were sent back from northern Nepal. India could not speak because Nepal had very good relationships with China and other world powers. In deed, Nepalese monarch and northern neighbour China have contributed foe saving Nepal.

Initially, India was afraid of communists. Due Chinese terror, India started to use communists. Nepalese communists, being whatever revolutionary, could not get rid of India game. It is said former premier Man Mohan Adhikari was being paid on the name of freedom fighter of India. India understood that Nepali communists can be used in favour of India.

After 1990's popular movement, as Congress and UML rise to government, India found open way to interfere in Nepal. But only leader Madan Bhandari of UML protested the Indian imposition. India thought him a barrier and after his murder again India was happy. Still as India could not do as it wanted with Congress and UML, then in 2005 India convinced Maoists and now India is free for naked interference. The intensions of RAW and CIA were unified to destroy United China in the name of Free Tibet since the beginning of 2000. In between Nepal is entrapped. India always tries to maintain its supremacy either in non-aligned foreign policy or in SAARC. So, Nepal needs to resign from non-aligned policy and SAARC.

Chinese are simple and they understand the things slowly. Due to this delayed understanding by China, Nepal is in difficult situation. The strategic unification of RAW and CIA in this region is dangerous indicator for China and Nepal. Therefore China should openly come out to protest the conspiracy of imperialists against Nepal.

Chinese communist leader Mao Ze Dong, never took confidence of Nepali communists. He was in favour of Nepalese monarch because monarch always fought against imperialists. Now India is trying to capture Nepal by behaving like Ostrich with China, being broker of US and UN, and using so called Nepalese political parties. Even in 1989, India tried to capture Nepalese foreign, defence and home policies by terrorizing then King Birendra with popular movements.

Even India tried to make confused the King Gyanendra with expectation to control movement of 2005. However India was unsuccessful in doing so. Apart from surrendering to foreigners, King Gyanendra happily handed over the power to Nepalese people. India constructed 40 km long tunnel investing billions of rupees in between Jammu and Srinagar valley. But Kasmiries did not favour India. If Indian interests in Nepal are like that of to Bhutan and Sikkim, India won't be safe. It is because terrorism can be institutionalized in this situation which will be harmful to India.

Therefore we warn India to correct itself from such blunders. Indian interest is to make Nepalese defence and foreign policy in accordance to India. Since 2006, Nepal is being guided by pro-India party leaders. After the downfall of Maoist led government in May 2009, women defence minister (UML) and foreign minister (daughter of Girija), who have no diplomatic capabilities, both are pro-Indian. It seems this could be a strategy to surrender Nepalese foreign and defence policy to India. If you see list of ambassadors of Nepal to be sent to friend country, you will find smugglers, murderers and criminals who have no idea of foreign affairs. Therefore Nepalese foreign policy is shameful status in international level.

After 1990, Nepalese people never became free though were called sovereign. As the King was separated from sovereignty, in 1974 in Sikkim, under the leadership of Lendup Dorji Sikkim parliament decided to unify with India in 10 April 1975. Similarly in Nepal, using Girija Prasad (former PM), Madhav nepal (PM) and few Maoists, India is trying to capture Nepal.

The factors behind failed foreign policy of Nepal are betrayer leaders of Nepal and ever continuing interference of India. India is always involved in conspiracy to shrunken the Nepal. Nepal is situated in between large China in north and India in south. Nepal is bordered to India in east, west and south with 1880 km boarder. Besides, there is open border. Due to this, India is always engaged in attacking the Nepalese territory and also some Indian citizens commit crime in Nepal and hide in India. Indians enter Nepal with small and large scale business and ultimately demand for Nepalese citizenship.

In 2006, 4 million Indians succeed in taking Nepalese citizenship. Being landlocked country Nepal must have transportation facility in accordance to international treaties and traditions. But India violated it and wants to control over Nepal.

Late King Prithvi Narayan Shah is a creator of Nepal. Nepalese monarch was established fighting against imperialist power. In order to remain protected in between large China India, even in those times Prithvi Narayan Shah preached (1768) – 'Nepal is just like a Yam (tuber) between the two stones'. We are sandwiched between giant India and China. So, we are bound to have a balanced understanding between them.

The nation builder had preached us the same fact. "Establish good and amicable relation with China, have relation with the emperor of south understanding well that he is very clever. If the investors from foreign (India) come to Nepal, they will make our people poorer. In deed, ideology of Prithvi Narayan Shah is immortal. Therefore the monarch of Nepal and China has incredible contribution to save the country.

Such 200 years India was attacked by English imperialism in the name of East India Company. They had clear intension to demolish and left Hinduism and establish imperialism in this region. Communists do not believe in religion. JNU is popular for producing Extreme Leftists. It was Indian Congress government and policy makers like SD Muni who not only assisted but funded Nepal Maoists to wage a war against Hinduism.

However Prithvi Narayan was only one who protested it. He raised Nepalese flag, maintained originality of Himbatkhand and unified the great Nepal. From the beginning of Prithvi Narayan Shah Regime in 1868, the balanced Nepalese relationship with China and India was maintained by every Kings till 2005. Nepalese Kings never afraid of imperial powers.

Nepalese Kings never sold the country in any crisis. The balanced foreign policy and patronization of nationality is due to combined effort of King and people of Nepal. Nepal's foreign policy is focused to get rid of Indian conspiracy. If foreign policy of a country fails that means the sovereignty of the country can be finished. Therefore the nationalist Nepalese people along with the King should stand up in one side so that Indian interference could be protested.

ISSUE OF WHITE PAPER ON CHINA'S DEFENCE TECHNOLOGY

China is striving to establish a new system of defence-related science, technology and industry which caters to both military and civilian needs, according to a white paper issued. The white paper on China's National Defence in 2008, issued by the Information Office of the State Council, says China is accelerating reform and innovation in its defence-related science, technology and industry, promoting strategic and specialization-oriented restructuring of defence industry enterprises, enhancing the capabilities of independent innovation in the R&D of weaponry and equipment.

The paper says China will establish a licensing system for weaponry and equipment research and production. In accordance with the Implementation Measures for Weaponry and Equipment Research and Production Licensing promulgated in May 2005, the defence-related science, technology and industry has adopted a licensing system for weaponry and equipment research and production featuring management of categorization.

"While maintaining state control over weaponry and equipment research and production, the document allows the non-public sector to enter this field and compete for research and production projects," says the paper. In March 2008 the State Council and the CMC issued the Regulations on the Licensing Administration of Weaponry and Equipment Research and Production, further improving the system, says the paper.

The paper noted that China will enhance the basic capabilities of weaponry and equipment research and production. "Defence-related science, technology and industry are striving to enhance the informationization of weaponry and equipment design and development, and to render product design more digitalized, modularized, standardized and reliable," it says.

According to the paper, China is cooperating with foreign countries on defence-related technology following the principles of mutual benefit and common development. On the export of military items, it adheres to the following principles: It should only serve the purpose of helping the recipient state enhance its capability for legitimate self-defence; it must not impair peace, security and stability of the relevant region or the world as a whole; and it must not be used to interfere in the recipient state's internal affairs.

The paper says China's defence-related science, technology and industry conduct cooperation with other countries in the field of hi-tech industries and develop hi-tech civilian products with high added value. Major breakthroughs have been made in developing the international market for space products, it says. China has exported its first satellite; and the earth resources satellite project with Brazil has played an important role in both countries' economic development, according to the paper. The white paper, the sixth of its kind Chinese government issued since 1998, gives an overall picture of China's national defence ranging from the security environment, national defence policy, to defence expenditure and arms control.

MANNED SPACEFLIGHT PROJECT

Manned spaceflight is the centralized embodiment of the technological capabilities and comprehensive power of a state. From the "Shenzhou I" space ship blasting off in 1999 to the extravehicular activity conducted by the astronaut of the "Shenzhou VII" space ship in 2008, China's manned spaceflight has realized 7 material breakthroughs in a short period of just 9 years. At 16:41 on September 27, 2008, Zhai Zhigang, astronaut of the "Shenzhou VII", successfully made the first space walk.

HIGH-TECH WEAPONS ADD WINGS TO THE CHINESE TROOPS

Weaponry and equipment are the important material and technological foundation on which the military strength of a country is built. There's no way to import truly key technologies and if a country wants to own them, it can only depend on its own innovations. The weapons and equipment with the new-type armed helicopter, the new-type main combat tank, the big-caliber self-propelled artillery, the heavy anti-tank missile, the new-type aerial defence missile and the self-propelled anti-aircraft artillery as the mainstay have formed the armament system of the PLA Army featured with the capabilities of rapid manoeuvre and three-dimensional attack.

The PLA Navy has realized the upgrading of the ship-based and aircraft-based precision-attack weapons and the coordinated development of the armaments for submarines, surface ships and naval aviation. In the air, the PLA Air Force has the third generation of light and heavy fighters, the second generation of modified fighters, the tactical transport aircraft, new-type fighter-bomber, refueling aircraft, airborne combat equipment and new generation of near-distance, medium-distance and long-distance ground-to-air missiles. The PLA Second Artillery Force (SAF) has basically formed a ground-to-ground missile system which includes both nuclear and conventional missiles, both solid-fuelled and liquid-fuelled missiles of near, medium and long ranges with complete types of warheads. In addition, a number of new-type equipment for command and control, information acquisition, early warning and detection and information countermeasure have become the "amplifier" of the battle effectiveness of the troops.

CHINA DISPLAYS ADVANCED DEFENCE TECHNOLOGY

China displayed its military might by exhibiting a series of brand new precision assault weapons during the on-going Zhuhai airshow, which opened on Monday in South China's Guangdong Province. The weapons on show included precision-guided bombs and long-range striking systems hailed by military experts as symbols that the People's Liberation Army has entered an era of precision attack. In a rare collective appearance, the airshow also brought together a number of new air, naval and surface-to-surface missiles, reports said.

For example, the LT-2 500-kilogram laser-guided bomb and the LS-6 glide-guided bomb, developed by the China Aviation Industry Corporation I, both made debuts at the show. Both types of bombs were designed on the basis of traditional bombs, reports said. The China Aerospace Science and Technology Corporation displayed two types of precision-guided bombs FT-1 and FT-3, which enjoy a high percentage of hits and can be widely used for short-distance air raids and blockage as well as disrupting an enemy's air defence and crippling naval ships, reports said.

The China Aerospace Science and Industry Corporation (CASIC), another State-owned weapons manufacturer, exhibited around 20 types of missiles at the sixth China International Aviation and Aerospace Exhibition, Xinhua News Agency reported. The P12 strategic missile system developed by CASIC, was regarded as the most intriguing and eye-catching item on display. CASIC said the missile defence system demonstrates China's capability to defend the country's airspace and territory. Yin Xingliang, CASIC general manager, said China's missile systems had reached the technical level of developed countries in the late 1990s. Yin also said CASIC had worked for the peaceful utilization of technologies in the military industry and aerospace technologies in the civil aviation industry. After about 50 years of development, China is catching up with the worlds most advanced technology in the design of air-to-air missiles, said Jin Xianzhong, a senior missile designer, in an Internet interview with the Xinhuanet.com yesterday.

CHINA ADDS PRECISION STRIKE TO CAPABILITIES

China has been developing and purchasing weapons for precision-strike warfare. This is the hard edge of the People's Liberation Army's (PLA) doctrinal drive toward using increasingly sophisticated information technologies such as C4ISR (command, control, communications, computers, intelligence, surveillance and reconnaissance) to improve the capabilities of weapon systems (DTI March, p. 39). The PLA's near-term goals appear to be greater asymmetric capabilities to target U.S. naval assets in the western Pacific and in space as part of an anti-access strategy. Long-term, however, greater precision will be a feature of most new weapon systems.

China's growing C4ISR capabilities were demonstrated in March by its coordinated two-fleet operation to intercept two U.S. Navy ocean survey vessels. Chinese ships found and harassed the USNS Victorious, operating in the Yellow Sea, and USNS Impeccable, which was about 75 mi. south of Hainan Island. The fallout was diplomatic, as Washington and Beijing clashed over interpretations of the Law of the Sea Treaty, which Beijing contends gives it rights to deny access to military survey missions. This incident, though, was reminiscent in timing and scope to the April 2001 clash that saw China "capture" a U.S. Navy EP-3 electronic intelligence aircraft off Hainan. China's aggressive challenge of Japanese claims in the East China Sea, plus Washington's refusal to cease its survey missions could be flashpoints. In February, a provincial Communist Party newspaper contained a threat to sink U.S. survey ships. In this second of three articles on China's growing regional power, DTI examines the country's efforts to improve its ability to target and destroy threats.

Since the early 1990s, Chinese military scholars have been warning of the need for China to prepare to defend against, and if necessary, conduct military operations in space. In late 2006 reports emerged of China's use of high-power ground-based lasers to "dazzle" U.S. surveillance satellites. On Feb. 11, 2007, China launched the first successful intercept by its SC-19 direct-ascent antisatellite (ASAT) system, derived from its KT-1 solid-fuel space-launch vehicle, with an interceptor stage whose development was likely aided by China's micro-satellite programs. A target FY-2 weather satellite was probably illuminated by large phased-array radar developed for tracking Shenzhou manned space capsules. A far less-noted potential co-orbital ASAT demonstration occurred on Sept. 27, 2008, when the Shenzhou-7 manned spacecraft, which had just launched a BX-1 nanosatellite, passed within 45 km. (28 mi.) of the International Space Station. Following the U.S. Navy's shootdown of an errant satellite on Feb. 21, 2008, and a Mar. 5, 2008, announcement that Russia would resume ASAT development, it is likely that China will continue ASAT testing.

China's direct-ascent ASAT also proves that it is capable of developing a long-range antiballistic missile (ABM) system, a U.S. pursuit that China has opposed. China had an ABM program from 1963-80 that produced a short-range interceptor prototype and long-range radar. Chinese sources told DTI at the recent IDEX expo in Abu Dhabi that they have tested the new FD-2000 surface-to-air missile (SAM) in an antitactical ballistic missile (ATBM) mode. Developed with help from Russia's Almaz-Antey Co., the FD-2000 also draws from the earlier passive-guided FT-2000 SAM, which reportedly benefited from U.S. Patriot SAM technology.

These indigenous SAMs are entering PLA service, and will complement about 1,000 Almaz-Antey S-300/PMU-1/PMU-2 SAMs purchased since the early 1990s, giving the PLA air force the most formidable air-defence network in Asia. The PLA has also developed short-range SAM systems—including man-portable air-defence systems—for tracked vehicles and trucks. Among these is the TY-90 Yitian for trucks and armoured personnel carriers that was disclosed in 2005, but displayed for the first time at IDEX this year.

Increasing precision is also the hallmark of new PLA surface-to-surface missiles and air-launched weapons. New Chinese nuclear ballistic missile warheads feature smaller sharp-tip warheads, signifying higher precision. One warhead configuration for the 12,000-km.-range DF-31A ICBM places at least one warhead on a delivery bus that is apparently capable of radical maneuvering to evade ABM defences.

Medium-and short-range ballistic missiles (SRBMs) are also being upgraded for greater precision. The U.S. and Japanese navies have long been concerned with the PLA program to create an antiship ballistic missile, by placing a maneuverable terminally guided warhead on the 2,400-km.-range DF-21, and likely, on the 600-km. DF-15. Asian military sources are also concerned that a new 3,000-km. version of the DF-21 may have multiple terminally guided warheads.

An early 2009 Taiwanese estimate places the DF 15, DF-11 Mod2 and new land-attack cruise missiles (LACMs) of the second artillery missile force targeting Taiwan at more than 1,500, with newer versions having navigation satellite (navsat) guidance. In 2007 a Chinese source told DTI that the PLA will also be using two new shorter-range SRBMs, the truck-mounted 250-km. B-611M and 150-km. air-transportable P-12. Both are maneuverable, navsat-guided weapons with modular warheads. The PLA is also developing longer-range artillery rocket-based SRBMs, like the 200-km. navsat-guided WS-3. Some Chinese sources indicate that an antiradar or passive-guided 300-km. version of the WS series is possible.

Asian sources say the PLA has developed two families of strategic-range LACMs: the DH-10, which equips new units of the Second Artillery, and YJ-62/C-602, which equips PLA navy destroyers and land-based antiship missile units, and is to be developed into an air-launched version for the PLA air force. The air force is expected to equip a new version of the 1950s-era Soviet Tupolev Tu-16 Badger bomber, the Xian H-6K, with the weapon. The H-6Ks modified with more powerful engines, now have a potential 3,000-km. radius—enough to reach Guam. Rumors have long surrounded a potential long-range bomber program at Xian Aircraft Co., and a new stealthy version of Xian's JH-7A fighter bomber is also in development.

Tactical combat aircraft in the PLA air force and navy are receiving new Russian and indigenously designed air-to-air and ground-attack weapons. The air force's first Sukhoi Su-27SK fighters had the helmet-sighted Vympel R-73 missile a decade before the Raytheon AIM-9X entered U.S. service. The BVR self-guided Vympel R-77 followed the Su-30MKK into PLA service early this decade. But new Chengdu Aircraft Corp. J-10 and Shenyang Aircraft Corp. J-11B multirole fighters will carry air-to-air missiles designed by Luoyang Opto-Electric Co. (LOEC), which include the self-guided PL-12, thought to have a range approaching 100 km. in lofted delivery. Chinese sources also indicate LOEC is developing a high off-boresight air-to-air missile (AAM) similar to the South African Denel A-Darter, and a long-range ramjet-powered AAM.

Russian Su-30s in PLA service have been equipped with several guided munitions, including the Zvezda Kh-31 antiradar and antiship ramjet missile, Zvezda Kh-59 interdiction missile and optical image-correlation-guided KAB series bombs. At the

2005 Moscow air show, a Russian source disclosed that Russia had assisted China's development of electro-optical targeting pods, which have been photographed on J-10, JH-7A and some Hongdu Q-5 fighter-bombers. These will help guide two new families of laser-and navsat-guided bombs developed by LOEC and China Aerospace Science and Technology Corp. (CASC). The latter's FT family includes the 500-kg. (1,100-lb.) FT-1 navsat-guided bomb, the FT-2, which adds range-extending wings, the 250-kg. FT-3 and the 100-kg. FT-5, which is reportedly comparable with Boeing's Small Diameter Bomb. At last November's Zhuhai air show, LOEC revealed a dual-optical navsat-guided bomb. CASC's bombs can be expected to follow suit.

Precision is being packed into smaller munitions like the new 45-kg. AR-1, a laser-guided missile designed for the CH-3 unmanned combat air vehicle (UCAV), similar in capability to the U.S. Predator-1. Guizhou Aircraft Co. has likely developed a larger turbofan UCAV comparable to the MQ-9 Predator-B/Reaper. Most of China's new precision-strike systems are for sale.

Pakistan and Iran have benefited from China's ballistic and cruise missile technology, and from sales of conventional systems. Many more countries are likely to consider the $22-million Chengdu FC-1 and $41-million J-10 fighters, especially when equipped with precision-guided munitions like the PL-12 and FT-1. This form of power projection will soon be joined by the PLA's increasing power-projection capabilities, the subject of the final installment. Richard D. Fisher, Jr., is a senior fellow with the International Assessment and Strategy Centre of Arlington, Va., and author of China's Military Modernization: Building for Regional and Global Reach (Praeger, 2008).

DEFENCE TIES CONNECTING CHINA AND NEPAL

In 2005, China supplied more arms to King Gyanendra; in the same year Nepal supported the inclusion of China into SAARC irrespective of the fact that India had expressed its reservations; in September 2008,14 China invited the Nepalese defence minister Ram Bahadur Thapa as an observer to the military exercise 'Warrior 2008', and during his meeting with China's defence minister Liang Guanglie, China announced a military aid package of $1.3 million to Nepal.

In December 2008, Lieutenant General Ma Xiaotan of the PLA pledged $2.6 million in non-lethal military aid to Nepal during a visit. China is currently working on the reconstruction of the China-Nepal highway which is expected to be completed by the end of the year 2011.

Built at a cost of over $100 million, there are only two sections of the highway on the Chinese side – from Tingri to Nyalam and Nyalam to Zhangmu – that are pending completion. Once complete, the highway is expected to become a "golden gateway"15 connecting Lhasa to Kathmandu and will be China's gateway to South Asia. Along with the Qinghai-Tibet railroad, this highway has been touted as having the potential to boost Nepal's economic growth through greater trade with China. The basic aim of China is to reduce the Indian influence in Nepal. China knows that this can be achieved by creating alternative trade routes for Nepal.

Third Stage

In the third phase China has adopted an aggressive posture to weaken India's hold on Nepal. This phase continues the agenda of the first and second phase but the focus is more on encircling India. There are people who argue that China is not only courting the Nepalese Maoists, but also rendering political as well material support to the Indian Maoists whose ultimate aim is to overthrow the parliamentary democracy through an armed struggle. The sheer political capital of the Maoists, and the anti-China protests of March 2008 in various parts of Tibet including Sichuan, underscored the importance of Nepal for China, because Nepal has a sizeable Tibetan community, 20,000 according to one of the representatives of the Dalai Lama.

Kathmandu has become the latest proxy battleground between the regional powers, India and China, to demonstrate their influence. New Delhi is more and more getting worried about China's creeping influence in the still-new Himalayan republic. As Kanti Bajpai wrote in the Nepali newspaper, *Republica*: India lives in fear of its neighbours reaching out to outsiders to balance against Indian power. Unlike India, which has often borne the consequences of misjudging the political mood in Nepal and has been regularly maligned as a 'hegemon', China's Nepal policy has been largely successful. China has managed to project itself as a disinterested neighbour and a remarkably attractive alternative to 'Big Brother' India.

Even as Prachanda spoke of the need to review the Indo-Nepal Friendship Treaty of 1950, Nepal accepted the draft of a 'Peace and Friendship Treaty' submitted by China. China has invested extensively in improving the Chinese profile within Nepal. The establishment of China Study Centres is just one such move. There are at present over two dozen China Study Centres across Nepal. These provide Chinese language and culture classes and are often manned by volunteers from China. While enabling greater access to information about Chinese social and economic development, these centres also provide a convenient platform for the dissemination of Chinese policy towards South Asia and India's role therein.19 Aimed at providing training to students and teachers, the Confucius Institute at Kathmandu University which celebrated its second anniversary in June 2009, runs numerous programmes from business management to tour guide training across Nepal. Nepalese students even those in primary school now have access to Chinese language lessons and exposure to Chinese culture. Apart from these numerous local level organisations have been established including the Nepal-China Youth Friendship Association and the Nepal-China Mutual Cooperation Society to foster cooperation at all levels.

Nepal's ex- prime minister, Madhav Kumar Nepal, inaugurate the China-Nepal Boda Hospital in Kathmandu last year. This hospital which is the largest in the private sector has been hailed as "a new step to enhance Nepal-China friendship relations in the private sector." It is the second largest medical facility inaugurated by the Nepalese prime minister. The first was the Civil Servants Hospital in Kathmandu that caters to gazetted-officers, and it was also built with aid from the Chinese government.

Chinese involvement in Nepal is not limited to roads and hospitals. In August 2008 China handed over the Zhangmu-Kathmandu optical fibre cable project to Nepal. This 100 km of optical fibre cable is a new information superhighway, between China and Nepal. Moreover, Chinese contractors are now involved in the construction of the Melamchi Water Supply Project in Central Nepal to alleviate the water shortages in the capital, Kathmandu. The first phase of this three-phase project is budgeted at $317.3 million and is expected to be completed by 2013. The government of Nepal has invited Chinese support and participation in the development of Nepal's hydroelectric potential and China has already invested almost $200 million in various such projects.

It is, thus, evident that China's engagement with Nepal has been multi-dimensional and designed for the long-term. This is enabling Chinese involvement in everyday life in a manner which is seemingly benign but very much capable of shaping attitudes towards China and India in years to come. It must also be recognised that this is policy will have great repercussions for India. China's proactive policy vis-à-vis Nepal is very much part of its larger aim to erode India's influence in South Asia.

'THE CHINESE PATH': AN ARTIFICIAL CONSTRUCT

Ignoring Mao Zedong's postulate that the Chinese Revolution was a combination of the principle of Marxism-Leninism with the evolving reality of China, the Maoists talk of the Indian revolution following the Chinese path. They insist on aping the model followed in pre-Revolution China. The Maoists need to learn not just the history of pre-Revolution China but also the Indian reality. Revolution can hardly be cloned from country to country. Stalin had pointed out how theory becomes useless, devoid of practice. Mao himself called such a deviation 'seeking to catch the sparrow with the eyes closed'. There are differences between the Chinese situation and the Indian reality. Apart from the differences existing in the unfolding of the colonial heritage of the two countries, differences exist in the realm of economy, political structure, and growth. The Maoists, by invoking pre-Revolution China as India's model patently ignore history. The Maoists would do worse than paying heed to the dictum of Mao Zedong during the height of the Sino-Soviet debate in 1960.

Mao had argued, in effect, that the party which was not able to analyse the situation evolving in its own country and would rather emulate experiences of another country without analysis was a hotchpotch of revisionism and sectarianism, and would never be regarded as a party driven by the principles of Marxism-Leninism. The CPI (M) believes that it would not do to mechanically follow the revolutionary experience of other countries without a scientific analysis, something that the Maoists revel in doing. One recalls that during the 1970s, the CPC had criticised the Naxalites for raising the slogan of 'China's Chairman in our Chairman', and thoughtlessly using such terms as 'liberated zones' in the Indian context. The Maoists do not learn from history, even from the party of Mao!

Ignorance about the Element of Class Struggle in the Parliamentary System

Lenin had long ago characterised the parliamentary system as a scene of class struggle. Entangled in the web of what Lenin called 'left-wing communism', the Maoists deny India bourgeois democracy and dub as illusions institutions such as the parliament, assemblies, panchayats, and the entire electoral procedure. Their view is erroneous, lop-sided, and self-contradictory. Marxists know that the character of class domination defines a State and its political character. The CPI (M) has the programmatic understanding that the Indian State represents a class rule of the big bourgeoisie and the big landlords, led by the former who indulge in cooperation with international finance capital. In India, the bourgeois democratic revolution remains unfinished and the task is to establish real democracy. Yet, the fact can never be ignored that the parliamentary system has been a sign of progress for the masses in the sense that it has acted as a weapon for the extension of the democratic rights of the people. The democratic rights won have been the result of ceaseless struggle and do not represent gifts from above. Waves of popular struggles have overcome authorita-rianism of the 1970s, the ousting of democratic governments, the clamping down of internal emergency, and the inroads of communal forces in government.

In countering the false claim of the Maoists that the parliamentary system is a complete illusion, one needs to point out that in a capitalist society, as Lenin had pointed, the parliamentary forum affords the communists opportunities to expose the system of capitalism. In addition, it would be downright foolhardy not to take full advantage of the opportunities afforded by the parliamentary structure and to further the struggle in and out of parliament. Elections are called electoral struggle because in the process, millions of people take part and the opportunity is created to expose the role played by the State, bourgeois politics, and the bourgeois parties. An opportunity is created to pull the people out of the fold of the bourgeois parties. However, as the CPI (M) has maintained consistently, the extra-parliamentary struggle cannot be supplanted by the parliamentary struggle, but has to be supplemented by it. Why do the Maoists think, and on what objective basis, that the masses remain inert witnesses in the arena of parliamentary struggle? Why cannot the Maoists recall Lenin's saying that participation in the bourgeois democratic parliamentary system would go a long way in exposing the system before the masses and convincing them of the necessity for its removal. Will the Maoists learn from history?

Staying Away from the Daily Struggles of the People

Declaring that there remained no alternative before a revolutionary party other than conduct of long-standing and armed people's war towards an armed peasant revolution, the Maoists talk only of guerrilla warfare, liberated zones, headquarters, capturing cities and identify these tasks as the only worthwhile revolutionary tasks. They aim, through performing these tasks, to capture state power. The Maoists give great attention to military strategy and military tactics. They have, however, no time to spare for the task of enhancing the political consciousness of the people and of uniting them on the questions concerning politics, economy, and society. They ignore the importance of the trade union movement and the role the movement plays in enhancing the class-consciousness of the workers. Would they also turn their faces away from the land movement on the plea that without the completion of the democratic revolution, such movements would not lead to comprehensive land reforms? How then do they propose to make the teeming million of India conscious, *sans* movements that stand opposed to the bourgeois-landlord policies, of the need for fundamental changes? Reliance on the armed might of a minuscule part of the people is Blanquism of the worst kind.

Mao Zedong wrote that the Communists must never be isolated from the majority of the people and must take cognisance of the total situation. The Maoists would fulminate against international finance capital but would not take part in the actual struggle taking place against it across the country, a struggle in which the CPI (M), other Left parties, and the TUs have played a stellar role. The Maoists have stayed away from the struggle—to what purpose? In *People's March*, Kisan has confessed that the Maoists have not been able to build up struggle against the forces of imperialism, neither in the rural areas not in the cities and towns.

The confession reminds us of another confession by Charu Majumdar when he had lamented back in 1972 in a letter written to his wife that the involvement with the policy of annihilation, the anti-imperialist struggle had suffered. Kisan has also regretted the fact that the Maoists could not organise adequate response to the onslaught of the forces of communalism, in the struggle in which the CPI (M) and the Left parties play a commendable role.

Distorted Exposition of Guerrilla Warfare

In the worldview of the Maoists, democratic struggle and mass-political programmes have no place. They believe that the entire struggle of the new democratic revolution would be armed struggle with the guerrilla forces building up red bastions in the villages. They have devoted the bulk of the space in their document on the strategy and tactics of the Indian revolution to such guerrilla actions. It was the subsequently discredited CPC leader, Lin Biao, who had first propounded the theory that the Maoists have embraced. Lin had spoken of encircling the cities (i.e., the developed countries) by the villages (i.e., the developing world). Lin had also spoken of Mao's annihilation theory against the Japanese occupation army to mean that such action was necessary for the armed peasant revolution to succeed in the Third World. The Naxalites had lapped the theory up and were later being cautioned by the CPC about misinterpreting the annihilation theory and taking it out of context (and this was admitted by several Naxalite leaders of the 1970s in a published document).

The revolutionary path can never be one of conspiracy minus the objective and subjective conditions; there is no alchemy (as Marx noted in 1850) to bring about revolution. Making conspiracy the chief implement to bring about revolution is a sectarian and self-defeating notion. The Maoists are verily prey to this idea and in an obsessive manner. It devolves on the Party of the working class to bring within its capabilities the entire range of complexities existing in the country where the revolutionary struggle is to be launched. It must also bring together as many allies as possible. The notions of united front and coalition rise out of this consideration. Lenin points out that there is need for a revolutionary party to bring into the fold mass allies out of the fold of the bourgeoisie even if such allies are politically restless and are unfaithful, and offer only conditional support. To deny this is, according to Lenin, a form of crass failure to grasp the basic principles of scientific socialism. The Maoists are certainly victims to this folly. They are not able to understand the tiniest iota of the revolutionary path.

The Maoists appear obsessed with guerrilla warfare. We point out for their edification the conceptual framework on the same theme by Lenin. Lenin wrote that no party of the proletariat could consider guerrilla warfare the only path to adhere to.

The guerrilla warfare must subserve the other modes of struggle and it must be enriched through a drive to advance the Socialist perception and organisation. The point to note is that Lenin had underlined this thesis in the case of every form of struggle, whether through strikes, through parliamentary form, or through newspapers. Lenin explains that in a departure from the old forms of 'socialism', Marxism recognises the variegated forms of struggle, but the Maoists comprehensively reject this thesis. Their doings have inevitably created alienation from the mass of the people. The own initiative of the masses has suffered. This is the result of not attaching due importance to mass-political initiative.

Lenin is uncompromising in insisting that Marxism demands historical consideration while pondering the form of struggle. Any aberration here, Lenin pointed out, was a deviation from the fundamental principles of Marxism-Leninism. Lenin said that 'to attempt to answer yes or no to the question whether any particular means of struggle should be used, without making a detailed examination of the concrete situation of the given movement at the given stage of its development, means completely to abandon the Marxist position'. This is something the Maoists are squarely guilty of all the way. Marxism does not approve of the 'thesis' that guerrilla warfare is the only viable path during the period of revolution, and that all other paths are unimportant and irrelevant.

Mao had identified the conditions and conditionalities in China for the unleashing of armed peasant revolution and of armed revolutionary zones. These are:

- In capitalist countries, the workers build up their strength through overt and 'legal' struggles while educating themselves; they advance through utilisation of such fora as legal struggles, parliament, and political and economic strike actions. In China, there was no parliament, and no scope for utilising a legal forum.

- The peasant economy of China was 'localised'.
- With a low degree of capitalist development, China did not experience a unified, countrywide capitalist economy.
- Warlords remained isolated and engaged in warfare with other warlords.
- With the imperialist forces slicing up China for control, there was frequent inter-imperialist clashes in China.
- There was lack of central political command in China and thus there was a lack of concomitant control in the administration and the army.

Considering the reality prevailing in India, the attempt to build up 'bases' in remote villages, to set up 'liberated zones', and to encircle cities is pure fantasy. How to deal with the central political authority and the powerful army in the course of striving for a revolutionary social transformation does not concern the maoists. They do not see whether there are any circumstances which are compatible with the concept of armed struggle based on guerrilla warfare. None of the features like the capitalist development in India, the connectivity with the world economy, the experience of parliamentary democracy, socio-economic changes, the social position of the classes, the consciousness and lifestyle of the Indian people, the development of ideological instruments and media—are suited to guerrilla warfare on the basis of liberated zones.

Despite the weaknesses of mass struggles, advances have been registered in the case of both the urban and rural working classes and their organisations. Marxists regard momentum as the life force of matter. Considering the changes wrought in the Indian economy, society, politics, and politics, it would not be difficult to understand that the so-called 'guerrilla tactics' can create not permanent but transient flashes and can end up by harming the potential of greater mobilisation of forces and of greater struggles.

In his treatise *On Practice*, Mao Zedong wrote: 'We are opposed to die-hards in the revolutionary ranks whose thinking fails to advance with changing objective circumstances and has manifested itself historically as Right opportunism'. 'Their thinking is divorced from social practice, and they cannot march ahead to guide the chariot of society; they simply train behind, grumbling that it goes too fast and trying to drag it back or turn it in the opposite direction'.

The Maoist documents available with us describe the method of creating 'favourable circumstances'. They rely on the inner contradiction of the imperialist forces impacting the Indian ruling classes, creating political uncertainty and weakening administration. This will, according to the Maoists, lead to mass uprisings against the 'comprador ruling classes' and the police and the army will be affected. This, in turn, would lead to world war! If this is not day dreaming, what is?

CPI (M), in its Programme, has said: The struggle to realise the aims of the people's democratic revolution through the revolutionary unity of all patriotic and democratic forces with the workers-peasants alliance at its core, is a complicated and a protracted one. It is to be waged in varying conditions in varying phases. Different classes, different strata within the same class, are bound to take different positions in these distinct phases of the development of the revolutionary movement. Only a strong Communist Party, which develops the mass movements and utilises appropriate united front tactics to achieve the strategic objective, can make use of these shifts and draw into its ranks these sections. Only such a party bringing within its fold the most sincere and sacrificing revolutionaries would be able to lead the mass of the people through the various twists and turns that are bound to take place in the course of the revolutionary movement.

The CPI (M) believes that the flourishing and development of mass-revolutionary struggle is the primary task at this stage. To a true Marxist, simply making loud proclamations of armed struggle can never become a pre-condition for establishing one's revolutionary credentials. Since neither the working class nor the working masses would go in for violence on their own, what should be the stand of the Party of the working class? The CPI (M) Programme notes:

The Communist Party of India (Marxist) strives to achieve the establishment of people's democracy and socialist transformation through peaceful means. By developing a powerful mass revolutionary movement, by combining parliamentary and extra-parliamentary struggle, the working class and its allies will try their utmost to overcome the resistance of the forces of reaction and to bring about these transformations through peaceful means. However, it needs always to be borne in mind that the ruling classes never relinquish their power voluntarily. They seek to defy the will of the people and seek to reverse it by lawlessness and violence. It is, therefore, necessary for the revolutionary forces to be vigilant and so orient their work that they can face up to all contingencies, to any twist and turn in the political life of the country.

The Reality

The Maoists guerrillas have stated that their task comprises providing encouragement to the masses for taking part in 'political and military programmes, including sabotage and annihilation of enemies'. The results are there for everybody to see. Right from the earliest days of the Naxalite movement, the line of individual assassination has been adopted as a policy by the left sectarians. One has to pause and recall that on the eve of the arrest of Charu Majumdar, six Naxalite leaders, including Kanu Sanyal, Sourin Bose, C. Tejeswar Rao, and D. Nagabhusan Pattanayak, confessed that the CPC took great exception to the line of annihilation of the Naxalites. (This confession was later published in November 1972.) The CPC accused the Naxalites of mechanically following the people's war theory of Lin Biao, and pointed out that dipping the hand in the blood of a class enemy did not make a revolutionary Communist; on the other hand, it will ensure that the Party was no longer a Communist Party.

The left sectarians, including the PWG, the MCC and the CPI (Maoist), have indulged in mayhem over the years. Between 1991 and 2001, 2,077 people, mostly ordinary citizens, were killed in Naxalite-related violence. The method of killing is gruesome with people being burnt alive or smashed into smithereens by exploding crude or sophisticated devices. In 2002, the Maoists killed 90 people, in 2003 the figure reads 136, in 2004 it was 70, and in 2005, 122. Despite the Maoists' penchant for identifying persons as 'police informers' before killing them, 80 per cent of those killed by them represented ordinary people who are not class enemies, even by Maoists criteria. Some of those killed were in fact members or supporters of rival Naxalite groups; this was internecine struggle, pure and simple.

In Bengal, the Maoists' forays include killing 12 CPI (M) workers and 17 police personnel. They have also exploded landmines, destroyed isolated buildings in remote areas, and have tried to spread terror among the village folk. Spreading thinly across the borders of Orissa, Chhattisgarh, Madhya Pradesh, Karnataka, and Maharashtra, the Maoists have concentrated chiefly if not solely on spreading terror and causing mayhem in the name of 'revolutionary ways'. They prefer if they can to build up contiguous areas as 'zones' in the areas where they operate. Lately the rate of attrition among the left sectarian elements has been notable. In Andhra Pradesh, the rate of surrender by the PWG averaged over 550 per year. The decimation was also evident in Bihar and Jharkhand.

The Maoists utilise the increase of Maoist activities in neigh-bouring Nepal and the formation of a coordination committee of the South Asian Maoists to strengthen their terror tactics. They use the long and unguarded border between Bihar and Nepal to bring in illegal arms and to run training camps on both sides of the border. They keep in close touch with extremist outfits of Kashmir, the northeast India, and the LTTE from whom they get help with arms training. They may even have, as per reports published in the media in November 2004, links with the ISI of Pakistan.

However, the net political impact of the Maoists activities is very marginal and transient. For example, in Bihar and Jharkhand, ceiling surplus was neither taken away from the landlords nor redistributed among the landless and the rural poor. The chief source of income of the Maoists in the rural stretches is extracting levy from the landlords and the nouveaux rich of the villages. They appear far from interested in protecting the interests of the rural poor or in preserving natural resources. On the other hand, the Maoists are linked to a large and widening network of dishonest traders and businessmen. In Chhattisgarh and in Orissa, the villagers have clashed repeatedly with the Maoists who are involved in racketeering of forest resources including *tendu* leaves and *babui* fibres. Using the power of the gun to establish sway over villages and villagers, the Maoists has effectively become a source not of inspiration but of fear for the rural people. The shotgun justice of the Maoists' mass courts is well documented.

The Maoists have also increasingly become the handmaiden of the bourgeois political parties. The Naxalite poet Varavara Rao has confessed before the advocates' committee about the links that the Maoists have with the Telugu Desam Party at the local level in particular. He has also said that both the Telugu Desam and the Congress have utilised the 'services' of the Maoists in exchange for lucre.

It was recently disclosed that a minister in the BJP-run Munda government in Jharkhand put to use the Maoists to win elections in exchange for a considerable sum of money. In Bihar, the adage goes that those who represent bourgeois parties during the daylight are Maoists by the night. The confession of a former state secretary of the PWG about the outfit being in hand-in-glove with the Trinamul Congress is another case in point in this regard.

4

Nepal: New 'Strategic Partner' of China

There has been a major shift in China's foreign policy towards Nepal since the Maoist ascendance to power. China had earlier adopted a policy of 'non-intervention' in the internal matters of Nepal and largely stayed out of Nepalese internal politics. However, the demise of the monarchy and the ascendance of political parties have forced China to reshape its Nepal policy. Moreover, frequent protests by Tibetans in recent months alerted the Chinese to the possibility of the China-Tibet border being misused. Consequently, China has sought to engage Nepalese political actors at all levels, primarily to secure the border with Nepal. With the Maoists in power, China also hopes to use its ideological commonalities to suppress the Tibetan movement in Nepal.

When the Maoists emerged victorious in the April 2008 elections, China adopted a wait and watch policy because it was unsure of their intentions. After all, the Maoists were backed by India and were catapulted to the political centre stage only after a comprehensive peace agreement in which India had played a substantial behind the scenes role. However, media reports reveal that after several interactions with Maoists leaders, China has begun to feel quite comfortable with the Maoist-led government. The Maoists' ideological linkages with China and their keenness to neutralize India's influence in the region have also made them an obvious choice for engagement.

It has been reported that in interactions with Chinese the Maoist leaders gave the impression that the future of democracy in Nepal could be guided by the example of the Communist Party of China. Indeed, there are many in Nepal who argue that persistence with the Maoist tag in the party name despite joining competitive politics indicates that the party may work towards a single party system in the future, given that dictatorship of the proletariat has prime of place in the Maoist lexicon. In fact, some hardline leaders of the party have suggested a people's republic similar to that of China on a number of occasions even after Maoists joined the political mainstream. These ideas might have encouraged China to attempt to consolidate its position in Nepal by continuously engaging the Maoists at the political, economic, military and social levels, and thus secure its strategic interests in the region. In fact, twelve high-level Chinese delegations, including two military teams, visited Nepal in the course of 2008-2009. During these visits, China has repeatedly assured economic, technological and military aid to Nepal. The Maoist-led government was also asked to adopt a 'One-China' policy, not to allow Nepalese land for anti-China activities, take strong action against Tibetan refugees and grant special facilities for Chinese investments in strategic sectors. Beijing has also initiated Track-II diplomacy with Nepal and invited Nepalese scholars to undertake visits to Chinese think tanks. Some of the important visits from China to Nepal were:

- 25 February 2009: Assistant Chinese Foreign Minister Hu Zhengyue led a 14-member delegation.
- 19 February 2009: Liu Hongcai, Vice Minister of the International Department of the central committee of the CPC led a delegation to take part in the inaugural ceremony of the 8th convention of the UML in Butwal.
- 10 February 2009: A high level Peoples' Liberation Army (PLA) delegation, one of the largest delegations in two months, arrived in Nepal.
- 06 December 2008: Lieutenant General Ma Xiaotian, deputy chief of General Staff of the PLA headed a ten-

member delegation. China agreed to provide US $2.61 million worth of security assistance to Nepal.

- 01 December 2008: China's Foreign Minister Yang Jiechi visited Nepal.
- 24 July 2008: Chinese Vice-Minister for Foreign Affairs, Wu Dawei, visited Nepal. He pledged a grant assistance of 100 million yuan as economic and technical cooperation.
- 04 March 2008: Assistant Minister for Foreign Affairs of China, He Yafei, undertook a three-day visit to Nepal.

Nepal's engagements with China have also increased manifold with the visit of delegations both at State and non-state levels. Apart from visits at the official levels, private visits by political leaders, journalists and academicians are also sponsored by China as part of public diplomacy. During these visits Chinese authorities have reportedly assured all kinds of support to the Maoist government in its efforts aimed at laying the foundation for a 'New Nepal'. For the Nepalese Maoists, growing Chinese engagement is a win-win situation in line with their 'policy of equidistance', which has been deliberately adopted to counter-balance India's influence in Nepal.

The increasing level of bilateral engagement also indicates that China is wooing Nepal as a new strategic partner. This has been confirmed by the statements made by various Chinese officials.

For example, on 16 February 2009, Chinese Foreign Minister Yang Jiechi said in Beijing that China would prefer to work with Nepal on the basis of a strategic partnership. In fact, Vice Minister of International Department of the Central Committee of Communist Party of China, Liu Hongcai said in Kathmandu in February 2009 that "we oppose any move to interfere in the internal affairs of Nepal by any force." Similarly, on November 04, 2008, Liu Hong Chai, International Bureau Chief of the Chinese Communist Party, stated that "China will not tolerate any meddling from any other country in the internal affairs of Nepal- our traditional and ancient neighbour."

China has also submitted to Kathmandu a draft Sino-Nepal friendship treaty. The draft states that China will not attack Nepal and would respect Nepal's sovereignty and territorial integrity. Nepal would recognize 'One China' policy and not allow its territory to be used for "anti-China" activities. The draft treaty in fact looks more like a strategic one that is tilted highly in favour of Chinese security concerns. China needs this agreement because it does not have confidence in the democratic arrangements and future governments in Nepal, and wishes to consolidate its position while the Maoists are in power. China has penetrated the Nepalese political system by gaining the confidence of hardline communist leaders both in the CPN-UML and the CPN-Maoist. China is also known to have played a major role in facilitating the alliance between the CPN-UML and the Maoists. Prior to Jhala Nath Khanal becoming UML Chief, a four-member Chinese delegation visited Kathmandu on May 10, 2008 and met Khanal and other Maoist leaders. A senior delegation from the Communist Party of China led by vice Minister Liu Hongcai was also in Kathmandu in February 2009 to attend the inaugural ceremony of the 8th national convention of the UML. The victory of Khanal as chairman of the UML, who is close to Prime Minister Prachanda, has been crucial for the survival of the Maoist-led coalition government.

The nature of Chinese engagements in Nepal goes beyond the political domain. They might also be aimed at influencing the process of drafting of the new constitution to ensure that China's long-term interests are served, particularly in hydropower and other strategically important projects. China has also assured Nepal help in the modernization and integration of registered Maoist guerrillas into the Nepal Army.

Considering the strategic and economic interests Beijing has in Nepal, in terms of energy from hydro projects and as a transit country between China and India, China may expand its state level engagements by entering into long-term agreements at various levels. The proposed new friendship treaty marks the beginning of this process. Moreover, the treaty may enhance the bargaining power of the Maoist government vis-à-vis India to resolve some of the long standing disputes between the two countries.

MAOIST'S REVOLUTIONARY STRATEGIES

The Maoist's revolutionary strategies were very important in many insurgent movements, especially in the middle of the 20th century. However, currently their role is less important than it used to be and the changes described above significantly contributed to such a situation. In order to better understand what the role of Mao's views on insurgency has on contemporary insurgent movements it is necessary to analyse its basic assumptions and than compare them to the current situation and the insurgent movements of 1970-1990s. First of all, it should be said that Maoist revolutionary strategies and his views on the insurgent movements were very important because they turned to be quite effective in China since due to them the Chinese Communist Party "defeated its enemy, ignited fears about a possible global triumph of communism, radically altered the balance of power in Asia, and placed American, South Korean, and other UN troops in their first direct shooting war with a major communist power" (Whitson 1988:305). The Chinese Communists quickly positioned themselves as the patrons of other insurgent movements. It is not surprising, therefore, that Mao's theory of revolution, including the ideas of the mobilization of mass, people's war, the people war, and others, became a blueprint for other insurgents.

Basically, Maoist theory for revolution includes three distinct phases that, of course, "mirror the history of the Chinese Civil War" (Whitson 1988:455). This strategy has the supreme virtue of making the incredible appear credible: the revolutionaries start as a weak, vulnerable and desperate group and, by the end of the conflict, they have become an unstoppable political and military force.

In the first phase the revolutionaries are "building what Lenin called the 'organisational weapon' the political, military, logistics, intelligence and command infrastructure" (Schram

1996:347). According to Mao, the insurgents should organise where the state is weakest. In China, as in many other countries where the strategy has been attempted, such weak place of the state was rural areas. At this respect it is necessary to emphasise that this point is quite weak being applied to the late 1980-1990s because the end of the 20th century was characterised by a high degree of urbanisation even in developing countries.

Anyway, the first phase should be viewed as a preparation for the insurgency while the real action occurs in phase two when Maoist theory recommends "a strategy of avoiding direct confrontation with government forces" (Schram 1996:382). Instead, the insurgents should strike where the enemy is weak, notably remote police or army outposts, towns and villages beyond the government's reach to occupy, rail and telephone lines, anything else that is military or politically significant, but incapable of being defended adequately. In such a way, the insurgent movements need to maintain the initiative at all times by turning weakness into strength.

However, the main point of the second phase is not military. Military action is "one prong of the attack on the regime; so, too, are efforts to organize an effective counter-government in liberated areas, maintain a flood of propaganda, subvert the government through infiltration, and take all other measures that erode the regime's political foundations" (Schram 1996:422). Defeating the enemy army is not the point, destroying the confidence of the population in the government, and the confidence of the government in itself, is the ultimate goal. Military and political actions, therefore, is simply a tool to win allies in the population, or to convince an even larger audience that history is on the side of insurgents.

In such a situation, during the third phase, the insurgent movements carry out a final assault against the government, which should be destroyed and the regime completely changed.

Obviously, Maoist theory, effective it seems to be, cannot always be fully applied in the end of the 20th century and its role gradually became less and less important. Consequently, what is really important for the insurgent movements according to Maoist theory is to gain confidence of the population and attract possibly larger masses on the side of the revolutionaries, making the war against regime the People's War.

On projecting Maoist theory and strategies on the insurgent movements of 1970-1990s, it is obvious that they turn to be less and less effective and eventually they have not been used as often as before. For instance, the traces of Maoist influence are obvious in the Vietnam War, when American and South Vietnamese units defeated North Vietnamese and Vietcong forces on the battlefield time after time, but a communist regime now rules Saigon. In such a way, the military success prove irrelevant because the war was lost politically.

Furthermore, the 1980s may be characterised as a transition period, when Maoist theory was still important. For instance, peaceful revolutions in Eastern described above were successful basically due to the effectiveness of the struggle for people's 'minds', confidence of population in righteousness of ideas developed by insurgent movements in the context of total lost of confidence in the official governments. On the other hand, these movements did not use army force or attacks as suggested Maoist theory the confrontation was purely political and socio-economic but not military. However, 1990 revealed new trends in the insurgent movements, which made the Maoist theory less effective. In fact in the situation when there is only one superpower and the world undergoes the process of globalisation the insurgent movements, which basically operate in developing countries, realised the ineffectiveness of both military or peaceful revolutions if they are not supported by the US, which actually could cope with any rebelling state since this country did not face any opposition from any other country in the whole world. In such a way the military conflict, even if it has a character of the People's War, is doomed to defeat if the US take a decision to intervene.

As a result, the insurgent movements basically use the strategy of terror attacks aiming not only at the official governments but also at Americans and their allies. There are a lot of examples, revealing this trend. For instance, PLO and other Palestinian organisations are probably the most experience in such kind of insurgency for they struggle clandestinely against Israel supported by the US and their main strategy is terror attacks which aim at the weakening of the opponents and agreeing with the demands of the insurgents. The same may be said about Al-Quaeda and activity of other insurgent movements that are active even nowadays, especially in Iraq and Afghanistan, when been unable to win the military conflict and lacking resources to gain population confidence not only within a definite country but in the world because in the epoch of globalisation international public opinion is also important as well as domestic one, they had to use terrorism as the main means of struggle while the Poepl's War, the mobilization of the mass and Maoist strategies seem to be less effective and doomed to failure.

POLITICAL PARTIES AND THE PEOPLE'S WAR

After the restoration of democracy several parties began working in Nepal. Among them seven parties have representatives in parliament. The Nepal Communist Party does not hold any seats in parliament but at 7% of the vote has become a national party. There are four kinds of political forces in the country: the Liberal Rightist force, led by Nepali Congress; the Non-Liberal Rightist force, led by the former Panchayat system's successor, the Rastra Parjatantra Party; the Communal force, led mainly by the Nepal Sadvawana Party; and the Communist force, led by many parties. Expect for the Maoists, all parties participated in the 1999 election.

The Nepali Congress does not have a clear view on the Maoist People's War. Some of its leaders consider it to be a terrorist group and the problem one of law and order. That is the official line. However other members consider the Maoist problem a political issue that should be solved politically. The Rastria Parjatantra Party and Nepal Sadvawana Party do not have clear-cut views on but consider the war a political problem. All communist parties consider it a political problem, but sometimes condemn it for terrorist activities. There are slight differences in views between communist parties on the Maoist People's War. The Nepal Communist Party [UML] and Nepal Communist Party [ML] want to change society by peaceful means. The other communist parties consider armed struggle necessary for revolution, but argue that the situation is not ready to start armed struggle.

The Maoists mainly target the Nepali Congress workers. Many of them have been killed, abducted and injured. They also target Nepal Communist Party [UML] cadres, and other parties' workers. According to the Maoists they only punish those who are class enemies. They claim to not punish people because of their political ideology, but punish only exploiters, spies and enemies of people. There are always controversies as to whether victims were actually exploiters or enemies of people or just political opponents. In some events the Maoists have accepted that they have made mistakes against innocent people.

The Government and the People's War

All governments have had the same attitude regarding the Maoist People's War. All major parties have had the opportunity to form government. Governments typically consider the Maoists terrorists and the problem one of law and order. However they have different attitudes while they are in opposition. The government has never considered the Maoist problem a political problem and has never recognized the Maoists as a political force. The government has tried to solve this problem by using the police and army. Sometimes they talk about dialogue with the Maoists, but they do not take it seriously.

Governments have launched internal security and development programs in Maoist areas. They have also formed victim associations. Two commissions have recommended solutions to the government, but these have never been implemented. The government has enacted the Internal Security Law and established the Armed Police Force to control Maoist activities. These efforts have not made any progress towards solving the Maoist problem. After Sher Bahadur Deuwa became Prime Minister, both sides declared a cease-fire. For the first time the government gave recognition to the Maoists as a political party. Now both sides are trying to make an atmosphere suitable for peace talks.

The Monarchy and the People's War

Theoretically Maoists are republican. In the beginning of the people's war, the Maoists did not have a direct view on the monarch, however they considered him to represent the feudal system. Surprisingly, they had a soft attitude with regards to former King Birendra, as they considered him a nationalist. In the words of senior Maoist leader Dr Babu Ram Bhattarai: Birendra also stood his ground against expansionist Indian powers. He introduced democracy and took a keen interest in the well being of our country, for which extremist reactionaries assassinated his whole family. We should not consign him and his values to a footnote in history. Nepali history cannot afford to discard him.

However, in the 40 demands they demanded that "All the special rights and privileges of the King and his family should be ended." After the Royal Palace incident of 1 June 2001, the Maoists changed their attitude on the monarchy. In that event all of King Berendra's family was killed. So the Maoists argued for the birth of a republic out of the incident. Dr. Babu Ram Bhattrai again:

A modern day KOT PARBA took place in Narayanhiti Darbar on the night of 1 June this year. Not only did this incident destroy the entire dynasty of Birendra Bir Bikram Shah Dev, it also unexpectedly gave birth to a republic in this country. It is but natural, then, for the issues of constitutional monarchy and the birth of a republic to become an issue to be debated. He further states that Birendra's whole family was wiped out and now it is the duty of all nationalist Nepalis to help in the establishment of a republic. It is the bitter truth. If what has been said about Dipendra [Son of king Birendra] is true, it only proves that the monarchy is outdated and it is time to discard it. There is no point in carrying on with a system that has outlived its purpose. What has been proved is that it was not Dipendra who committed this act but the reactionaries, expansionists, fascists and imperialists. All this proves that anyone crowned king will only be a puppet in their hands.... From any point of view traditional, feudal monarchy is dead and the birth of the republic has already taken place.

Bhattrai has also accused the present king [brother of King Birendra] Gyainendra of organizing the massacre and has called for his overthrow.

Nepal has had a constitutional monarchy since 1990. The king has not had an active role in day to day politics. The executive/government makes all the political decisions. So the monarchy does not have any view on Maoist directly, but indirectly has concerns regarding the Maoists. As head of state the former king directed the government to solve Maoist problem. The present king states that there should not be any conditions set while holding dialogue between the government and the Maoists regarding the constitutional monarchy and the multi-party system.

NEPAL: RECENT DEVELOPMENTS

The Communist Party of Nepal - Maoist (CPN-M), the group which waged an armed struggle against the former government of Nepal, won what was a three-way power struggle with the monarchy and a collection of democratic parties with their electoral victory in the April 10, 2008 Constituent Assembly election. Over 60% of Nepali voters cast ballots in the election that had been twice delayed. What was surprising to many observers was that the Maoists won power through the democratic process. The Maoists had previously waged a 10-year insurrection between 1996 and 2006 that claimed an estimated 13,340 lives. During this period their stated aim was to establish a peasant-led revolutionary communist regime.

Now that they are in control of the democratically elected Constituent Assembly, Nepal's legislature, the Maoists are confronted by a number of pressing issues, including the drafting of a new constitution, mounting ethnic demands particularly with the Madhesis of the Terai region, and the need to revitalize Nepal's economy. Some have speculated that the Maoists won the election because many Nepalis viewed that as the best way to keep them from returning to their violent struggle for power. Addressing issues contributing to political instability and achieving a peaceful transition to stable democracy are viewed by observers as key to providing the basis for economic growth. The Maoists will likely focus on how to retain control of the next government as the Constituent Assembly (CA) determines its form. Uncertainty remains over how well Nepal will negotiate this political transition in the months ahead.

Some analysts have expressed concern that the Maoists could once again resort to widespread violence if they view their influence as curtailed too much by democratic political opposition. Although the Maoists have the most seats in parliament, they do not have an outright majority. This makes them to an extent reliant on smaller coalition partners. The fact that the Maoists were not able to place one of their own in the office of the president demonstrates that there are limits to their power in the current configuration of government. The Communist Party of Nepal Maoist (CPN-M) has been supported by the Communist Party of Nepal United Marxist-Leninist (CPN-UML) and the Madhesi Peoples Rights Forum (MPRF) in the CA. The Nepali Congress (NC) is the main opposition party. The Economist Intelligence Unit has described the CPN-M as having "established its political pre-eminence while falling short of outright dominance." The Maoist government has received criticism in Nepal for not having made progress on drafting a new constitution.

HISTORICAL CONTEXT TO THE PRESENT POLITICAL SITUATION

Nepal has been an independent kingdom since 1768. Never colonized, the country was almost totally isolated from outside influence until the early 1950s. A transition from strict rule by the king to constitutional monarchy began in 1959, when then-King Mahendra issued a new constitution and held the country's first democratic elections. In 1960, however, the king declared the parliamentary system a failure, dismissed the fledgling government, suspended the constitution, and established a partyless system of rule under the monarchy. Although officially banned, political parties continued to exist and to agitate for a return to constitutional democracy.

In February 1990, student groups and the major political parties launched the Movement for the Restoration of Democracy. The centrist Nepali Congress (NC) party joined with the leftist parties to hold peaceful demonstrations in Nepal's urban centres. In April 1990, after more than 50 people were killed when police fired on a crowd of demonstrators, then-King Birendra turned power over to an interim government. This government drafted a constitution in November 1990 establishing Nepal as a parliamentary democracy with a constitutional monarch as head of state. The king at that time retained limited powers, including the right to declare a state of emergency with the approval of a two-thirds majority of parliament.

In February 1996, the leaders of the underground CPN-M launched a "People's War" in the mid-western region of Nepal, with the aim of replacing the constitutional monarchy with a one-party Communist regime. The uprising appears to have been fuelled by widespread perceptions of government corruption and failure to improve the quality of life of citizens, including providing access to cultivable land. The Maoists ran a parallel government, established their own tax system, burned land records, and redistributed seized property and food to the poor, in 45 districts. The insurgency was waged, in part, through torture, killings, and bombings targeting police, the military, and public officials. A number of bank robberies, combined with "revolutionary tax" revenue, made the Nepali Maoists one of the wealthiest rebel groups in Asia.

The Kathmandu government faced additional turmoil in June 2001, when Crown Prince Dipendra shot and killed his parents, King Birendra and Queen Aishwarya, seven other members of the royal family, and himself reportedly after a disagreement over whom he should marry. This incident did much to undermine the legitimacy of the monarchy. King Gyanendra, the former king's brother, was crowned on June 4, 2001, and he appointed a commission to investigate the assassinations. By mid-June, the country began returning to normal following rioting and widespread refusal to believe official accounts of the massacre. In July 2001, Prime Minister Girija Prasad Koirala stepped down amid fears of continuing instability and his government's failure to deal with the growing Maoist insurgency. He was replaced by NC leader Sher Bahadur Deuba, who then became the head of Nepal's eleventh government in as many years.

Constitutional Crisis

During the summer of 2002, the government of Nepal was thrown into a constitutional crisis that interfered with its ability to effectively combat the Maoist insurgency. The crisis began in late May, when King Gyanendra, at the request of the prime minister, dissolved parliament and unilaterally declared a three-month extension of emergency rule, which had expired on May 24, 2002. The prime minister, who also scheduled early elections for November 2002, reportedly took such action after his centrist Nepali Congress party refused to support his plan to extend emergency rule. Following the prime minister's actions, 56 former members of parliament filed a lawsuit against him, claiming there was no constitutional precedent for the dissolution of parliament during emergency rule. In August 2002, the Supreme Court rejected this lawsuit. Although opponents of the prime minister agreed to accept the verdict, they emphasized the difficulty of holding free and fair elections two years ahead of schedule when much of the country was under either rebel or army control.

Although the prime minister pledged that there would be no emergency rule during the scheduled November 2002 elections, Maoist attacks and threatened strikes prompted the government to consider various measures to prevent a Maoist disruption of the polls. The government discussed imposing a partial state of emergency in areas most affected by the insurgency. However, opposition parties, which urged the government to open a dialogue with the Maoists, argued that by curbing civil liberties, emergency rule would inhibit free and fair elections. As an alternative, the government announced in September 2002 that it would hold the elections in six stages over two months, starting in mid-November, so that government troops could be transferred around the country to protect voters and candidates. After further deliberation, however, Nepal's cabinet concluded that the security situation was too risky to hold elections. On October 3, 2002, the cabinet asked King Gyanendra to postpone the national elections for one year. The next day, the king dismissed the prime minister, disbanded his cabinet, and assumed executive powers.

The King's Takeover

The security situation in Nepal deteriorated after the collapse of the ceasefire between the Maoists and the government on August 27, 2003. The Maoists favoured drafting a new constitution that would abolish the monarchy. The king opposed such a move and wanted the Maoists to relinquish their weapons. Accommodation between the king and opposition democratic elements had been thought to be key to creating the unified front necessary to defeat the Maoists. With his direct assumption of powers, and arrest of opposition democratic elements, the king decided to try to defeat the Maoists on his own. This move proved to be the beginning of the end of the power of the monarchy in Nepal.

After seizing direct power in February 2005, King Gyanendra exerted control over democratic elements, but made little progress in the struggle against the Maoists. The king reportedly thought he could take advantage of a split in the Maoist leadership and disarray amongst democrats to seize control and use the Royal Nepal Army (RNA) to defeat the Maoists. The seizure of power by the king appears to have been aimed as much, if not more so, at asserting the king's control over democratic forces. Many observers felt that a military solution to the conflict with the Maoists was not achievable and that a concerted effort by the king and the democrats was needed to establish a unified front to defeat the Maoists.

When the king assumed power he stated that he would take steps to reinstate a constitutional democracy within 100 days, which he then failed to do. Although some political prisoners were released by the king, hundreds of others remained under arrest and restrictions on civil liberties, such as public assembly and freedom of the press, remained in place. A U.N. Office of the High Commissioner of Human Rights team was established in Nepal in April 2005 to monitor the observance of human rights and international humanitarian law.

By moving against the democrats, who under different circumstances could have worked with the king against the Maoists, the king strengthened the position of the Maoists. By some estimates almost half of the RNA was occupied with palace security, civil administration, and efforts to restrict communications and civil rights. The king's legitimacy with the people was weakened due to the circumstances under which he assumed the throne, the way he seized direct rule, and due to poor popular perceptions of his son, Prince Paras Shah. The former Crown prince was unpopular with Nepalis "for his drunken antics and playboy lifestyle."

Maoist Reaction. From February 13 to 27, 2005, the Maoists reacted to the king's actions by blockading major highways linking the country's 75 districts, as well as international road links to India and China. This led to clashes between Maoists and the RNA and brought trade by road to a standstill. The army organized armed convoys which allowed limited trade to continue. The Maoists had earlier cut off land routes to Kathmandu in August 2004. During the week-long blockade in 2004, prices of some basic foods more than doubled and fuel was rationed. This increase in food prices reportedly recurred in the 2005 blockade. By blockading Kathmandu, the Maoists successfully increased pressure on the king's government and demonstrated their power.

Democratic Uprising

On April 24, 2006, mounting popular resistance in support of the political parties led King Gyanendra to hand over power to the Seven Party Alliance. This followed weeks of violent protests and demonstrations against direct royal rule in Nepal. The Seven Party Alliance that opposed the king in April included the parties as listed below. The Maoists were not part of the Seven Party Alliance, though they worked with the alliance to oppose the monarchy. This was made possible by the king's political crackdown on the democrats.

- The Nepali Congress (NC)
- Communist Party of Nepal Unified Marxist Leninist CPN (UML)
- Nepali Congress (Democratic) or NC (D)
- Nepal Sadbhavana Party (Anandi Devi) or NSP (A)
- Jana Morcha Nepal
- Samyukta Baam Morcha (United Left Front) or ULF
- Nepal Workers and Peasants Party (NWPP).

The seven parties worked together through their alliance to promote a more democratic Nepal in the face of direct rule by the king. In May 2006, six of the seven political parties formed a coalition government. On November 8, 2006, the Seven Party Alliance and the Maoists reached a peace agreement ending a decade-old insurgency that claimed over 13,000 lives. In it, the Maoists agreed to put down their arms and postpone a decision on the future disposition of the monarchy until after the election of a Constituent Assembly. Under the peace agreement, Constituent Assembly elections were to be held by the end of June 2007. The June election date slipped but Constituent Assembly elections were eventually held in April 2008.

WHY CHINA ENGAGES IN NEPAL

China does not have a development agenda *per se* that is comparable to that of Western donors, but its engagement in

Nepal and other rising countries is based on a number of core principles. These principles reflect China's own development experience and history of engagement with other states. A central principle that guides much of China's foreign policy is that of respecting the sovereignty of all states. China's position is that it will not intervene or seek to influence the domestic affairs of any country since these are the exclusive concern of the national government. This is generally referred to as China's policy of 'non-interference'. Thus, when the current Chinese Ambassador in Kathmandu took up his post, he reassured Nepal that "China will never deviate from its policy of non-interference in the internal matters of Nepal". Following from this, China's position is that the support it gives to developing countries is not conditional on political or economic reforms, improvements in governance or the protection of human rights – a position which clearly differs from that of many Western donors.

In addition to the significance it ascribes to sovereignty and non-interference, another key principle of China's engagement in developing countries is that of mutual benefit. China is not squeamish about advancing its economic self-interest at the same time as contributing to the development of other countries. It is open about the economic rationale for its engagement in the developing world. An important driver is the socalled 'Going Out' policy, which aims to sustain high levels of economic growth within China through global engagement, especially in new developing country markets such as Nepal.

In addition to these general principles that underpin China's relations with developing countries, its engagement in Nepal is informed by a variety of context-specific interests and motives. In this section of the paper we explore three main areas of China's interest in Nepal: stability, economic development and geopolitics.

Stability Policy

China's engagement with Nepal is strongly shaped by the 'One China' policy. This refers to China's own sovereignty and territorial claims, which are primarily concerned with denying official recognition to Taiwan and to claiming Tibet – officially the Tibetan Autonomous Region (TAR) – as an integral part of China. Beijing considers Tibet part of its territory, and the region is also a key source of mineral and water resources for China's development. Tibet is one of China's so-called 'core interests', which essentially means that it is not open to negotiation and China will use all means necessary to protect it. Therefore any challenge to China's sovereignty over Tibet or claims for Tibetan independence are regarded by Beijing as serious threats to China's security and territorial integrity.

China's profession of Tibet in the 1950s increased the strategic significance of Nepal since it is the main country bordering Tibet. As described above, since the profession, Nepal has been a haven for Tibetans who wished to escape Beijing's rule and it is also a transit point for Tibetan refugees seeking asylum in India and the West. China is determined that Nepal should not become a breeding ground for activists campaigning for an independent Tibet. It fears that Tibetan refugees, who enjoy considerable sympathy and support in India and the West, will use Nepal as a base to protest against the Chinese profession and to carry out 'anti-China activities'. Recent events in Xinjiang, Inner Mongolia and within the TAR add to Beijing's concerns that disturbances on its periphery could fuel unrest nearer to home.

In response to the perceived threat to China's security and territorial integrity, Beijing pursues a policy of repression against Tibetan activists. In order to implement this policy in Nepal it requires a relatively stable regime and an 'effective' security apparatus. It also requires a compliant government that will co-operate in the control of Tibetan activists. Therefore Beijing's primary objective in Nepal has been to ensure Kathmandu's recognition of the One China policy and to secure its co-operation to suppress Tibetan activists. There is a perception in Kathmandu that Beijing uses its diplomatic and economic leverage over the GoN to ensure that the authorities co-operate in achieving this objective. This was most evident in the run-up to the 2008 Beijing Olympics when for four months there were protests by Tibetans in Nepal under the slogan of 'Free Tibet' or 'Save Tibet'. The Chinese Ambassador demanded that, "the Nepali establishment take severe penal actions against those involved in anti-China activities in Nepal". There followed a crackdown by the Nepali security forces against Tibetan refugees, which resulted in over 8,000 arrests between March and July 2008. The Nepali police were accused of violations of human rights, including excessive use of force, arbitrary detention and unlawful threats to deport Tibetans to China.

The Nepali Government's policy of clamping down on Tibetan activists appears to have strengthened in recent years, as economic and other forms of support from China have increased. According to Tibetan sources, Nepal's police now help the Chinese authorities prevent Tibetans from fleeing across the border, reducing the flow of refugees into Nepal from more than 2,000 per year before 2008 to 770 last year. Nepal has also forcibly returned refugees to China, and Chinese police have reportedly entered Nepal to search for fleeing Tibetans. Meanwhile, human rights monitors have criticised Nepal for arresting Tibetans who publicly celebrated the Dalai Lama's birthday and for preventing Tibetans from voting in the 2010 elections for the leader of Tibetans in exile.

These actions by the Nepali authorities have their corollary in the regular declarations by Chinese and Nepali officials denouncing 'anti-China activities'. Successive Nepali governments have consistently stated that such activities will not be allowed on Nepali soil and have vowed to prevent Tibetan demonstrations; a message echoed by other political party leaders. One of the first public statements by the new Chinese Ambassador in June 2011 was to express his concern about growing anti-China activities in Nepal. In response the Nepali Prime Minster reaffirmed his Government's commitment to the One China policy. Likewise, Zhou Yongkang in August 2011 expressed the hope that "Nepal would continue to prevent Tibetan separatists from using Nepali soil to act against China".

This prompted Jhalanath Khanal, the outgoing Prime Minister, to pledge "that the Government will not allow any anti-China activities". The words and actions of the Nepali authorities suggest that China has successfully managed to bring pressure to bear on the GoN to ensure the suppression of Tibetan activism within Nepal. Furthermore, there appears to be increasing co-operation between Kathmandu and Beijing with regard to Tibet and increased pressure on Tibetan refugees in, or aspiring to reach, Nepal. Lobsang Sangay, the political leader of Tibetans in exile, claimed that "Nepal has become almost a satellite state of China". Western governments and human rights groups support the protection of Tibetans and their right to political freedom in Nepal, and they have condemned human rights abuses by Nepali government forces against Tibetan refugees. However, most Western governments are apparently reluctant to raise the issue directly with the GoN. Certainly Beijing's insistence on a hard-line response seems to carry more weight with the GoN than Western concerns for human rights.

There is general credit within Nepal that Kathmandu's co-operation with Beijing on the Tibet issue represents the *quid pro quo* for development assistance and other forms of support from China. In August 2011 it was reported that, "Nepal renewed its commitment... not to allow anti-Chinese activities on its soil, as a top-level Chinese delegation announced a US$50 million aid package". This juxtaposition of developments is unlikely to be coincidental. It suggests that despite China's stated policy of non-interference, it does effectively make aid to Nepal conditional on the GoN's compliance with Beijing's policy of suppressing Tibetan activism.

For Beijing then, stability in Nepal is first and foremost about containing the threat of Tibetan secession. However, Beijing's expressions of concern for stability go beyond the Tibet issue. It has been increasingly vocal in recent years in support of political stability in Nepal and has stressed the significance of completing key provisions of the peace agreement, such as the new constitution. When Zhou Yongkang visited Kathmandu in the immediate aftermath of the resignation of

Prime Minister Khanal, he conveyed Beijing's "sincere wish that Nepali political leaders can bring peace and stability back to their country as soon as possible". Likewise, there have been repeated exhortations to Nepal's politicians to resolve their differences through dialogue and to complete the peace and constitutional process. Contrary to the suspicions of some Western analysts when the Maoists came to power, China appears to have no interest in promoting an ideological agenda in Nepal. During the war, Beijing made clear that it had no connection with the Maoist insurgents despite their name; indeed in some Chinese quarters it was felt that Nepal's Maoists tarnished the reputation of Mao Zedong. In 2005 Beijing affirmed its support for King Gyanendra's attempt to stabilise Nepal through a hard-line approach towards the Maoists. This underlines that China's concern was, and is, to have an effective and reliable interlocutor in Kathmandu. Hence, in a previous era, it was perfectly content to do business with the Nepali monarchy, despite it being the ideological antithesis of the Chinese model. It is also linked to the non-interference principle of Chinese foreign policy, which holds that the policies of the host government should always be respected, no matter who it is or what it does.

In the post-CPA era China has been assiduous in trying to reach out to a range of Nepali political parties, as well as to different Nepali institutions. This is reflected in the official invitations to visit Beijing extended to the Nepali Congress and to the Madhes parties, as well as to the Maoists and the CPN-UML. In the uncertain environment of Nepali politics, China is regarded as "hedging its bets" by cultivating relations with a range of different parties and institutions. This highlights Beijing's pragmatic approach towards the politics of Nepal. It prioritises stability above ideology or political system, and is willing to do business with whoever is in power.

NEPAL'S CHINA-CARD

Why could Nepalese autocrats play a China-card effectively in the regional politics for continuing their unjust and undemocratic regime? Whenever Nepal had democratically elected governments, the Chinese autocrats lost the partners in autocratic governance giving way to the democratic countries such as India, the US, the UK and other European democratic governments to have more influence on the elected governments in Nepal than the Chinese Government. Naturally, often the Chinese Autocratic Proletarian Government got sidelined, and found ignored by elected governments in Nepal. The elected governments in Nepal tended to loosen their control over the Tibetan refugees in Nepal, and let them freely travel and engage in their activities for freedom in Tibet. Hence, the Chinese autocratic proletarian government always found democracy in Nepal as a threat to their oppressive rule in Tibet.

Whenever the Nepalese autocrats played the China-card, the first victims were the Tibetans fighting for freedom from the autocratic rule of the Chinese proletarian leaders, and another victim, of course, was the democracy in Nepal. This was true in 1960 when the former king Mahendra played the China-card to kill the infant democracy, and in 2005 when the current king Gyanendra played the China-card to throttle the flourishing democracy.

After the unification of small kingdoms and principalities into a present-day Nepal, King Prithvi Narayan Shah said, "Nepal is a yam sandwiched between two large stones." He was referring to India to the South and China to the North as two large stones, and Nepal as a yam in between them. He left his advice to his future generations to follow the policy of not aligning with only one side - either to the north or to the south in other words to achieve a good balance between them.

In balancing between the two powerful countries - one to the south and another to the north, the rulers of Nepal had sometimes played one against another when the situation favourable to do so arose. For example, in 1960s, king Mahendra played a China-card effectively for suppressing the opposition political activities on the borders with India. King Mahendra told the then-Indian Ambassador Shriman Narayan "Your

Excellency, I am obliged for the sincere steps you have taken to bring about peace on our southern border. There are still a few stray cases of trespasses and conflicts here and there. But I do realize that it is not very easy to control such incidents completely along the long Indo-Nepal border of several hundred miles. I am sure your honest efforts would continue. On my part, I and my government have now decided to request China to abandon the eastern sector of the East-West Highway and initiate a fresh survey for another road somewhere in the middle regions of Nepal." At that time, Indian authorities did not want Chinese closer to Indian borders.

Indian Ambassador, Shriman Narayan replied, "I personally visited the Indo-Nepal border quite extensively and asked the district authorities to restrain effectively the Nepalese citizens from indulging in undesirable activities against the king and his government from the Indian soil. I also met a number of workers of the Nepali Congress in Uttar Pradesh, Bihar and Bengal and plainly told them that India would no longer allow them to operate against the friendly kingdom." King Mahendra suppressed the voices of Tibetan refugees in Nepal, and stopped any political activities of them from Nepal against he Peoples' Republic of China in 1960s. Later on, King Birendra also eliminated the Khampa rebels fighting against the Chinese rule in Tibet from the northern border of Nepal in 1970s.

Before taking over the executive power on February 1, 2005, King Gyanendra shut down the offices of Representatives of Dalai Lama and of Tibetan Refugees in Nepal. Obviously, this was done to keep the Chinese Government happy. The king was sure that India and the western countries would not support his actions of usurping the power from the elected government. So, he wanted to keep at least one neighbor happy and in his favour.

Then came the February-1 putsch staged by King Gyanendra keeping the whole country in darkness for a whole week by snapping communication lines and closing the media. Describing it as an internal matter, Beijing refrained from taking any stand on the King Gyanendra's February-1 takeover. Thus,

China has taken a friendly attitude toward the king in Nepal. India, the US, the UK and the international community as a whole condemned the putsch and suspended the military supplies to the Royal Nepalese Army. The king could not convince the international community that his army would not use the arms and ammunition against the people fighting for fundamental human rights and democracy in the country. So, the embargo remained.

Pursuant to the Nepal-India Treaty of 1950, Nepal needs to consult with India to import arms and ammunition from the third party country. At that time, Nepal and India had this treaty done to cater the needs for countering the threat from the People's Republic of China that had captured Tibet by force in 1949. Pursuant to this treaty, India could halt or check any arms and ammunition passing through its territory to Nepal. India did not have any means to check the arms supply to Nepal by China if they came from China to Nepal through Tibet. Nepal could not receive weapons from Pakistan despite Pakistan's strong desire to supply weapons to Nepal after India, the US and the UK have suspended arms supply to Nepal since the February-1 move of the king because India could certainly stop any arms going to Nepal through its territory. The Nepali monarch desperately sought arms from China, and received 18 truckloads of arms and ammunition from it. According to media reports, the Chinese army escorted eighteen trucks carrying arms and ammunition to Nepal's border where plain-clothes Nepalese troops took over in November 2005.

Supplying lethal weapons to Nepal, China not only demonstrated its disregard for suppression of democracy, civil liberties and human rights but also added fuel to the further bloodshed in Nepal. It is understandable that the Chinese communists have no regards for democracy, civil liberties and human rights as the communists believe in subjection of individuals to the dictatorship of the proletariats. However, supplying lethal arms, the Chinese government added fuel to the political conflict in Nepal and had shown disregard for human blood. 'The Indian Express' wrote: the continuing Chinese arms supply to Kathmandu is more than a tactical threat to India's attempt at promoting democracy and stability in Nepal. The time is running out for the Indian Government to get its Nepal act together and compel King Gyanendra to pay the costs of the China-card he has chosen to play against India. Much like his father, Mahendra, who cozened up to Beijing in the early 1960s amidst rising Sino-Indian tensions, the present monarch thinks he can hustle India into legitimizing his power grab. Unable to engineer a split in the coalition between India and the Anglo- American powers, King Gyanendra has put all his eggs in the China basket. This was evident at the regional summit earlier this month in Dhaka, when Nepal became the most vocal supporter of immediate Chinese affiliation with SAARC.

Academic Govinda Bhatta wrote in 'Jana Bhawana' that ff media reports are any indication; foreign powers are making the Chinese military assistance to Nepal an excuse to intervene in the Nepali's internal affairs. Efforts are on to implicate Nepal in the international strategic campaign against China. Such campaigners have been saying that Nepal has tilted toward China and that there is increasing Chinese influence in Nepal. But, the fact remains that Nepal has not changed its foreign policy. We still believe in the policy of neutrality and non-alignment.

Sandhaya Jain wrote that by choosing to isolate King Gyanendra of Nepal and support discredited and thoroughly corrupt politicians and the Maoists after last February's palace coup, the Indian Government adopted a disastrous policy on Nepal. After Prime Minister Manmohan Singh and his team decided to suspend arms supplies to the Royal Nepal Army needed to combat the Maoist terrorists, King Gyanendra has been forced to look toward China.. Ironically, India broke up its long-standing policy of non-interference in the internal affairs of another sovereign state successfully lobbying the US and the EU for putting pressure on the King for restoration of democracy. On Sunday, December 11, 2005, former Nepalese Minister for

Industries and senior leader of the Communist Party of Nepal (United Marxist-Leninist), Keshab Badal told The Hindu (independent Indian newspaper) in Kolkata, "We urge the Indian Government not to lend any support to the Nepal Government that could end up with the latter turning even more repressive towards the movement for democracy in Nepal. We seek the sympathy of the Indian Government in our endeavors to replace the monarchy in Nepal with a democratic republic. The Government headed by the King is stockpiling arms and procuring weapons in preparation for the bloodiest civil war in the country."

On Sunday, December 11, 2005, leading a four-member delegation, Indian Foreign Secretary and Former Indian Ambassador to Nepal, Shyam Sharan arrived in Kathmandu for a three-day visit to Nepal.

On Tuesday afternoon, December 13, 2005 before returning to New Delhi, addressing a press conference on the Indian embassy premises at Lainchour in Kathmandu, Indian Foreign Secretary Shyam Sharan said, "there has been no change in the India's stance on the early restoration of multi-party democracy and constitutional monarchy in Nepal. Restoration of peace and stability and economic recovery in Nepal is not only in the interest of Nepal, but also in the India's interest. Unity among constitutional forces is essential to achieve the goal of peace and stability in the country. India is always ready to support all efforts aimed at bringing a peaceful resolution to the problems confronting Nepal." In his 10-minute long press conference, concerning the military assistance to Nepal, Secretary Sharan said, "At the moment we do not have Indian arms coming to Nepal but other aspects of our cooperation to Nepal including the RNA (Royal Nepalese Army) is continuing. For example, training for RNA is still continuing." On his meeting with King Gyanendra, Secretary Sharan said, "His Majesty conveyed to me that he remains committed to multi-party democracy and constitutional monarchy and that there should not be any doubt in his commitment." While answering reporters' queries, Secretary Sharan said India and China were not competing in Nepal, but both want a stable and prosperous Nepal."

On Thursday, December 15, 2005, 'Daily Times' online (a new voice for a new Pakistan) reported from New Delhi, India, quoting 'The Asian Age' newspaper that on Tuesday speaking to reporters on his return from a three-day visit to Nepal, Indian Foreign Secretary Shyam Sharan said, "We would trust that India and China are not seen as somehow competing with each other for any kind of influence in Nepal." He said, "India believes both New Delhi and Beijing share a common 'objective' of seeing the return of peace and stability to Nepal."

India has called on China to stop supplying arms and ammunition to Nepal and join international efforts to force King Gyanendra to restore democracy following his takeover in February. Indian Foreign Secretary Shyam Sharan, said on a visit to Nepal: "The international community has taken a position in order to foster the process of reconciliation among political forces here and we would hope that not only China but other countries join in that effort." "Nepal's efforts to lure a largely Tibet-focused China into showing it can play a role in south Asia may not be worth angering India. Feeling in New Delhi is already quite anti-king," a western diplomat said.

Foreign Secretary Shyam Sharan hinted that India's relations with Nepal have resumed after a deep freeze of almost ten months but it was not the business as usual yet. Secretary Sharan said his visit to Nepal was follow-on to the meeting between King Gyanendra and Prime Minister Manmohan Singh in Dhaka. At that meeting, both the king and the Prime Minister agreed to be in touch at different levels. Although Secretary Sharan refrained from making any comment on political overtones, he managed to convey the message to all persons he had met in Nepal that occasional "pin-pricks" by Nepal, such as procuring arms from China, would only complicate the relations between two countries.

On December 19, 2005, Indian Defence Minister Pranab Mukherjee said that the arms supply and military training provide by China and Pakistan to Kathmandu was a concern, and the Indian government was addressing it through its diplomatic missions in both those countries "A problem is there. We have taken it up diplomatically. Let us see how it can be resolved," said Mukherjee.

Deputy Director of the Institute for Defence Studies and Analyses, a leading security think tank in India, Commodore C. Uday Bhaskar said, "India should mount a wholehearted politico-military initiative to ensure that Nepal's military orientation remains with India. "There is a strategic dimension to India's relationship with Nepal and it has to be handled carefully," Bhaskar told IANS. An expert on South Asia at Jawaharlal Nehru University, S.D. Muni said, "I understand the matter has been taken up diplomatically. India's foreign secretary went there with a clear message but if it is more than just a one-time affair, then we have to put pressure (on Nepal)."

After a virtual embargo of arms imposed by New Delhi on the king's army, there has been furious military-diplomatic activity among Nepal, China and Pakistan. After an October-visit to Beijing where he struck a deal for the supply of certain weapon systems from China, Nepal's Army Chief of Staff General Pyar Jung Thapa returned from Islamabad on Saturday, December 17, 2005; where he was offered comprehensive training capsules for the RNA soldiers. On Sunday, December 18, 2005, in a press release, the RNA's Department of Public Relations (DPR) said that the delegation of the People's Liberation Army (PLA) of China led by Deputy Commander of Chengu Military Region Command Lieutenant General Gui Quanzhi met RNA Chief of Staff General Pyar Jung Thapa. Four other senior military officials of the PLA and the Chinese military attaché were present on the meeting at the RNA headquarters, However, no details about the meeting were given.

The cash-strapped RNA paid US$80,000 to buy 18,000 grenades and four million rounds of 7.62mm bullets from 'Poly Technologies Incorporated' in Beijing by November 15, 2005 while ignoring to pay off the older debts to India that have mounted up to over US$26 million. In a surprisingly prompt transaction, the consignments arrived in the Nepalese capital Kathmandu on November 22 a week after the payment was made. India had been selling weapons and equipment to the RNA at a 70 per cent mark-off before it suspended military supplies to Nepal in February 2005 to show concern over Nepalese King Gyanendra's power grab with the help of the army. Defence sources in Nepal said that the prompt payment to the Chinese company was made due to the commissions involved. A section of senior officers in the RNA had been unhappy with the Indian military aid, as it bypassed the commission agents.

China has increased its activities in various aspects of the Nepalese life. For example, Chinese People's Association for Friendship with Foreign Countries (CPAFFC) and Nepal-China Executives Council (NCEC) signed a Memorandum of understanding (M. O. U) on Sunday, December 25, 2005. On behalf of their respective organization, Secretary General of CPAFFC, Zhu Changbing, and General Secretary of NCEC, Rajendra Nakarmi signed on the document. According to the M. O. U, both the CPAFFC and the NCEC shall cooperate on the promotion and expansion of cooperation in the field of trade, tourism and cultural exchanges, and shall act as facilitators to promote and strengthen investment and entrepreneurial relationship between Nepal and China.

Vice-chairmen of the Council of Ministers Kirti Nidhi Bista met Chen Haosu, a visiting Chinese delegation leader and Chairman of CPAFFC. "Nepal-China relations, having a long and illustrious history of friendship, excellent relationship and exchanges, have taken a new dimension and reached a new height after the establishment of diplomatic relations on Aug. 1, 1955," said Bista at the meeting. "Nowadays, mutual understanding, respect and trust, and treating each other equally have become salient characters of China-Nepal relations," said Chen Haosu at the meeting. Leading a 12-member delegation of CPAFFC, Chen arrived in Kathmandu on Thursday, December 22, 2005 for a five-day-long visit to

Nepal. On December 26, 2005, Minister of State for Information and Communications Shrish Shumsher JB Rana inaugurated the three-day Nepal-China postage stamp exhibition held to mark the 50th anniversary of the establishment of diplomatic relations between the two countries at Nepal Art Council in Kathmandu. On the occasion, Minister of State Rana affixed the first cancellation mark on the commemorative stamp on Nepal-China diplomatic relations. (Nepalese media)

A Nepalese non-governmental friendship organization called China Study Centre (CSC) has set up its Eastern Region Chapter (ERC) in Biratnagar, about 400 km east of Kathmandu. "The founding of the CSC's Eastern Region Chapter (ERC) is of great importance because Biratnagar is a very important city in Nepal for its status of industrial area, trade centre and the second largest town of the country," said Chinese Ambassador to Nepal, Sun Heping at the inaugural function of the ERC. He said, "Therefore, there are more opportunities for China-Nepal trade cooperation and will surely bring the entrepreneurs in eastern part of Nepal closer to China. This newly founded ERC will play an important role in eastern Nepal to bridge the two countries in disseminating information on both China and Nepal."

On the occasion, Chairman of the ERC of the CSC, Jana Bandhu Karki said the founding of the ERC is a symbol of Nepal's efforts on strengthening the relationship with its "good partner and a growing economic power", China. Founded in 2000, the CSC has already set up its branches in Nepal's major cities such as Khandbari, Chitwan, Dhulikhel, Pokhara, Butwal, Lumbini and Nepalgunj.

On January 03, 2006, Xinhuanet reported that the Chinese Ambassador to Nepal said that China accorded a high priority to the construction of the proposed Koshi-Lhasa Highway linking Nepal's eastern zones with China's Tibet Autonomous Region. At an interaction program held by the Morang Trade Association, Chinese Ambassador to Nepal, Sun Heping said, "We have given this highway a high priority. Among the 10 highways that link Nepal with China, this was the most important highway. However, the Nepali Government needed to request the Chinese authorities officially for the construction of the highway." In addition, the Chinese Ambassador to Nepal said that the request to open a Consulate General's Office in Biratnagar could be considered after consultations with the government. "All of the businessmen of the eastern zones have been calling for Chinese help in the construction of the highway because it will benefit trade between China and eastern Nepal," said Kishor Pradhan, central member of Federation of Nepalese Chambers of Commerce and Industry.

King Gyanendra toyed with a plan to let China and Pakistan open consulates in the sensitive Indo-Nepal border areas; the (Indian) Government communicated its strong displeasure to Kathmandu. China is apparently ready to open a consulate at Biratnagar at the border between eastern Nepal and Bihar. Pakistan, not to be left behind, is keen to open shop at Birganj in central Nepal region that also borders Bihar. While King Gyanendra might hope that his threat to draw in China and Pakistan closer to him would force New Delhi to soften its policies, the indications are that the move could further undermine the limited support the monarchy enjoyed in New Delhi.

The (Pakistani) Foreign Office has warned the (Pakistani) Government that India and Nepal were in the process of finalizing a "secret extradition treaty" that might endanger safety of Pakistanis there as the agreement would give full power to New Delhi to get hold of any Pakistani national working or visiting Kathmandu. The (Pakistani) Foreign Office has proposed to the (Pakistani) Government that as a "counter step" Pakistan should immediately sign an agreement with Nepal to save its own citizens from being extradited to India from Kathmandu. In the light of Foreign Office and Interior Ministry's joint proposal, Foreign Office officials confirmed the cabinet has approved singing of an agreement with Nepal in one of the recent meetings presided over by Prime Minister Shaukat Aziz. In a New Year's Day message to Chinese Premier Wen Jiabao, Indian Prime minister Manmohan Singh said that the two populous Asian neighbours must make 2006 the year of India-China friendship in line with the pledge made last year.

Prime Minister Singh also said both India and China have made progress in negotiations over thorny issues such as a border dispute, which resulted in a brief but a bloody war in 1962. Indian foreign ministry officials said that Chinese Premier Wen replied to the Indian Prime Minister Singh's New Year's greeting on an equally positive note. "China is ready to work with India to continuously deepen the contents of our bilateral relations and push forward the China-India strategic and partnership in an all-round and in-depth way," said Premier Wen in his message. A formal ceasefire line has yet to be established following the war but the unsettled border has remained largely peaceful following agreements signed in 1993 and 1996. India says China occupies 38,000 square kilometers of Indian Territory in Kashmir while Beijing claims that the 90,000-square kilometers Indian state of Arunachal Pradesh belongs to China.

Ingratiating to Beijing, King Gyanendra has been using his father's policy of playing India off against China. Critics point out that this policy was made at a time when Nepal's two giant neighbours had just fought a bruising war in 1962. Today, China and India are bhai-bhai (friends) again; this strategy is hopelessly outdated. However, India's lingering memory of being 'stabbed in the back' in 1962 is so strong there is growing alarm that South Block's diplomacy toward Nepal has been 'pushing Kathmandu into the Chinese fold'. Until recently, conventional wisdom has been that rapprochement between China and India meant the two weren't competing with each other in Nepal or elsewhere. While many still adhere to this view, some aren't so sure any more. In fact, those who talk about a benign China are now often labeled in the Indian press as 'Beijing apologists' and part of a 'pro-China lobby'. King Gyanendra's strategy of obtaining military aid and buying arms and ammunition from China and Pakistan has worked brilliantly to stoke fears in New Delhi about Nepal going over to the other side. Even though the recent $1 million military grant and the 18 trucks of grenades and bullets from China last month may not have been substantial, its prominent coverage in the Indian media stoked suspicions again. However, the Sino phobia is restricted to a relatively small section of the military-intelligence establishment and the political opposition. A large number of people in the political and business sector is more worried about how India can keep pace with China's blistering economic growth and emulate its success in wooing foreign direct investment.

Indian Ambassador to Nepal, Shiv Shankar Mukherjee said India had very high stakes in Nepal and was very concerned with the latest developments in Nepal. Ambassador Mukherjee said that the constitutional monarchy should remain the symbol of unity, continuity and integrity of the nation and should not compete with the political parties for power. "The most sane, non-violent and practical way out is for the palace to reach out to parties and together bring Maoists to mainstream," said Ambassador Mukherjee. Responding to a query on the Indian embargo on arms supply to Nepal, Ambassador Mukherjee said, "We had helped Royal Nepalese Army to battle insurgency. After February 1, 2005, it was no longer the previous situation." Ambassador Mukherjee did not see it that Nepal was trying to use "China card" against India. He, however, said, "We expect all members of the international community, including China, not to add to complications."

Referring to the interview by Indian Ambassador Shiv Shanker Mukherjee to the private television in Kathmandu, Former Army Chief of Staff and Member of the Standing Committee of the Privy Council, Satchit Shumsher Rana said, "It is against diplomatic norms to give unwanted advice to the King." Mr. Rana also said, "If the King had been active in politics, he would have opened a political party and the seven parties (agitating against the king's direct rule) would have been wiped out."

In a press-meet in Beijing, Indian Foreign Secretary Shyam Sharan said that he had held talks with his Chinese counterpart li Jhaoji on the Nepalese politics and the situation evolving there. Secretary Sharan disclosed that he had conveyed India's concern over the deteriorating economy and political upheavals in Nepal, and the Chinese arms supply to Nepal in the recent days, as it would compound the political problems and prolong the ongoing Maoist insurgency, to his Chinese counterpart during the meeting. Secretary Sharan said that the Chinese made it clear to him that the China's policy toward Nepal is non-interference in the internal affairs of Nepal.

The Nepalese king deals a fake-China card. All sides except for the palace laugh off the bid to pressure India. The monarchy sought to manipulate India by threatening it with the China card. Sometimes there is a hint of arms supplies from Beijing and at other times a possibility of allowing them to open a consulate on the Indo-Nepal border. However, it is clear that there is no China card that Kathmandu can play. The Nepalese democratic political parties are dismissive of it, Western diplomats are impatient with any such suggestion and Indian diplomats certainly do not believe in its existence.

A European diplomat based in Kathmandu explained: "There is no China card. But the perception of the China card is more important than the card. It is a classical case of manipulation by the palace. If people believe that there is a China card, the king's purpose is served." The "China card" seems all about trying to force India to help legitimize the king and his actions. Even if a consignment of weapons did come from Beijing, Chinese diplomats are now backtracking. General Secretary of the Communist Party of Nepal (United Marxist Leninist), Madhav Kumar Nepal said, "I told the Chinese ambassador that if they are indeed arming the RNA, then it is not good. He told me that they have not provided any weapons." The Chinese ambassador conveyed the same message to President of the Nepali Congress, Girija Prasad Koirala. President Koirala confirmed this and added, "India should rid itself of the mental make-up arising out of the 1962 war with China. That situation cannot be repeated. It is the king who is trying to play on that fear psychosis by showing the China card. All these cards will fail. India need not get bothered with this." President Koirala said he was aware that the Indian diplomats were in constant dialogue with the Chinese and there was a lot of understanding between them. "We also appeal to the Chinese and the Pakistanis not to fish in Nepal's troubles and do anything that appears to help the autocratic king. That will not benefit Nepal and destroy the prospects for peace," said he.

As long as the Chinese occupation of Tibet will be intact, the Nepalese autocrats could play a China-card. Therefore, not only the Nepalese autocrats but also the Chinese occupation of Tibet is a threat to democracy in Nepal. The Chinese Proletarian Government would do its best to block the flourishing of democracy in Nepal, as democrats would be in favour of Tibetans fighting for the freedom from the foreign occupation of their homeland. Thus, the root cause of unstable democracy in Nepal is the loss of Tibet to the Chinese Proletarian Government making it possible for the Nepalese autocrats to play the China-card whenever the need arises.

STABILITY AND PEACE OF CHINESE VIEWPOINT

From a Chinese Viewpoint, the stability of a country is equated with the capacity of its government to control it. Where Nepal is concerned, the primary indicator of stability in Beijing's eyes is that the threat from Tibetan dissidents is extinguished, or at least contained. This entails the GoN affirming its commitment to the One China policy and Nepal's security forces co-operating in the repression of Tibetan dissidents. Beijing has successfully exerted its influence over the Government in Kathmandu to secure its co-operation in both respects, and Tibetan activism in Nepal has reduced as a consequence. In this sense then, China can be seen to have contributed to stability in Nepal.

However, this prompted the question among some interlocutors of what 'stability' means? China's understanding of the term may be at odds with that of Nepalis or Western actors. It would be misleading to suggest that there is a single agreed definition of stability shared by all Western actors, let alone by different branches of the same government. Clearly, stability may be understood differently if a Ministry's mandate is to protect national security rather than to reduce poverty overseas, and hence the term is the subject of much debate. The UK Government in its cross-departmental strategy for 'Building Stability Overseas' (BSOS) articulates a relatively inclusive definition of stability as follows:

"The stability we are seeking to support can be characterised in terms of political systems which are representative and legitimate, capable of managing argument and change peacefully, and societies in which human rights and rule of law are respected, basic needs are met, security established and opportunities for social and economic development are open *to all"*.

China's strategy towards Tibetans in Nepal, as put into effect by the Nepali Government and security forces, does not reflect the BSOS definition of stability. Freedom of political expression is clearly denied to Tibetans in Nepal and there are credible allegations of human rights violations against Tibetan activists. China's understanding of stability in Nepal is thus at odds with the UK Government's definition of the term. Likewise, China's strategy towards Tibetan refugees is not compatible with the concept of 'liberal peace', which prevails in Europe and is understood to include the rights of minorities, freedom of speech and the protection of human and political rights.

Clearly terms like 'peace' and 'stability' will be understood differently depending upon the norms and assumptions of the state concerned, and they may be interpreted to suit particular interests. But does China's strategy towards Tibetans in Nepal have a negative impact upon the argument environment? In particular, does the denial of the human and political rights of Tibetans threaten to cause violent argument in Nepal? It seems unlikely as the Tibet issue is largely unrelated to the fundamental drivers of argument in Nepal, while concern and protest about the treatment of Tibetans tends to be stronger outside the country than within. Nevertheless, from a Western Viewpoint, China's strategy towards Tibetans weakens any claims it may make to be supporting an inclusive and sustainable peace in Nepal.

Changing Balance of Limited Power

It is hard to argue with the view from Beijing that the benefits of Chinese aid, such as economic and infrastructural development, will improve standards of living among Nepalis and thus reduce tensions that might otherwise give rise to argument. At the same time, the benefits of Chinese aid may also increase inequalities and divisions, both between local Nepali communities and between Nepalis and Chinese incomers. Given the scale of Chinese investments and development in Nepal, there is considerable risk that this sizeable injection of resources will upset the balance of local power and interests, which may lead to violence. In September 2011, there was a bomb attack on a Chinese food factory in the Narsingh district of the Terai. This was reportedly carried out by the Janatantrik Tera-Madhesi Mukti Party, an armed militia battling for the independence of the Terai, which aims to expel Chinese and 'non-indigenous' populations from the region. It is the first attack against Chinese industry in the region, but it is feared there may be more to follow given the proliferation of Chinese entrepreneurs in the Terai, especially in the construction, textile and hotel industries. The risk of violence arising from the influx of Chinese companies into Nepal is likely to become a growing concern for peace and security from the Viewpoint of Beijing, as well as from Kathmandu.

CHANGING STABILITY OF INFLUENCE WITH THE WEST

China's growing role in Nepal does not just shift the balance of power and influence *vis-à-vis* India, it also affects the role and influence of Western powers, including their ability to influence the peace process. In Nepal, as in other developing countries, China's increased support for the government means that it becomes less dependent upon Western aid. This may diminish Western leverage to persuade the Nepali Government to address some of the more difficult aspects of the argument, which Western analysts believe must be addressed for peace to be sustainable. Such aspects include the human rights abuses carried out by all sides during the war. These are due to be addressed by a Truth and Reconciliation Commission, but this commission has yet to be set up. If human rights abuses are not dealt with, then impunity will become entrenched; and impunity is often an underlying driver of argument.

Western strategy makers need to be aware of this changing international context and of the implications for their own strategies for peace and development in Nepal. If the approach of Western donors is perceived to be overly prescriptive and/ or conditional – as some contend with regard to issues like integration and security sector reform – this may push the Nepali Government to seek support from other sources. The likelihood is that the Government will turn to states like China that generally provide what the Government requests – often hardware rather than 'software' – and provide it with no strings attached. This may affect the democratic quality of the systems that emerge, and it is a particular concern in areas like the security and justice sectors, where weak governance can lead to violence and insecurity.

The implication in this case is that China's growing role in Nepal is freeing the GoN from pressure to comply with Western standards of good governance and human rights. China's increased aid to the Nepali Government means that the 'donor marketplace' is expanding. By offering an alternative model of support to the traditional Western donors, China (and India) are introducing more competition into this marketplace. This weakens the bargaining position of Western donors since it means that the Nepali Government has more options regarding from whom it would like to receive development assistance and with what, if any, strings attached. It is hard to predict what will be the implications for peace and argument of an expanded donor marketplace in Nepal. It would be naïve to suggest that the agendas of Western donors are wholly benign in contrast to those of China or India. All external actors that engage in Nepal, as in other developing countries, do so based on a calculus of different interests: economic, security, developmental and geostrategic. So it does not automatically follow that a decline in the influence of Western donors will increase the prospect of argument in Nepal.

It is also important to keep in mind the basic role and agency of Nepalis themselves. The focus of this study is upon external actors, notably China, and how their engagement affects peace and argument in Nepal. The role of foreign powers in Nepal is highly significant, as this report demonstrates, especially in light of shifting balances of power and influence *vis-à-vis* the government in Kathmandu. However, ultimately it is the Nepali people who will determine whether there is a return to widespread violent argument or if sustainable peace can be secured.

What the research findings and analysis contained in this report do suggest is that strategy makers in the West, in China and in Kathmandu need to engage proactively with the changing realities; and they need to consider what it means for their policies and practice in support of peace and stability. For Western actors, the expansion of the donor marketplace means that the tools of conditionality they have used in the past to support peacebuilding will become less effective. This suggests that not just new tools, but new multi-lateral approaches, will be required if Western donors are to support peace in Nepal and in other argument-affected states. In the final section of the report we consider what such tools and approaches might include.

Altering Stability of Influence with India

Another concern expressed was that China's growing role and influence may provoke India into a response that threatens Nepal's peace. This is based on the assumption that India considers Nepal as being within its sphere of influence and so will regard China's increasing engagement as a threat. According to such views, New Delhi is apprehensive that China's expansion into Nepal is part of a wider plan to contain and encircle India.

One Indian analyst reports "a substantial amount of concern among the Indian establishment. The Chinese are making inroads across South Asia". According to this analysis, Chinese infrastructural developments in Nepal, combined with the build-up of its military capabilities in Tibet, will enable the PLA to deploy rapidly to India's borders.

Various recent events are attributed to Indian concern about China's growing role in Nepal. The petrol shortage in Nepal in early 2011 was seen by some as engineered by New Delhi in reaction to the then Government's proximity to Beijing. India also remains closely involved in Nepal's politics and reportedly it has stepped up its micromanagement of Nepali politicians to counter Chinese influence. There was a notorious controversy in late 2010 when a recording was leaked of a man with a Chinese accent offering US$6.9 million to a Maoist party leader to bribe 50 Nepali members of parliament to support a Maoist government. This affair was portrayed in India as evidence of China's meddling in Nepali politics.

However, the recording has not been verified, nor the identity of the Chinese speaker, and it is suspected in some quarters that the whole incident was an Indian propaganda exercise. Whatever the reality, these incidents indicate increased tensions between the two powers over Nepal. India's concerns about China's proximity to Kathmandu are compounded by its distrust of the Maoists – despite New Delhi's instrumental role in bringing them into the political process in 2005. The fact that the UCPN-M party still debates whether India should be considered as 'national enemy number one' illustrates that the distrust and antagonism between New Delhi and Nepal's Maoists is mutual. That said, different factions within the Maoist party are perceived to have different views about Nepal's neighbours. Thus Prachanda is regarded as being relatively pro-Beijing, while Baburam Bhattarai is considered to be more sympathetic to New Delhi. The appointment of Bhattarai as Nepal's Prime Minister in August 2011 was thus viewed in India as a reassuring development. Furthermore, the fact that Bhattarai made his first official visit to New Delhi rather than to Beijing, unlike his predecessor, may presage a swing back towards the traditional balance of power.

Another cause for concern in New Delhi has been that the Maoist regime in Nepal could lend support to Maoist rebels in India, the Naxalites. There have been rumours of Naxalites receiving military training from Nepal's Maoists, and in 2010 the Indian Ambassador lodged a protest with the GoN over "organised training" of Naxalites in Maoist camps in Nepal. However, no evidence has been provided to substantiate this allegation, and most analysts consider a connection between Nepal's Maoists and India's Naxalites to be far-fetched.

China and India are seen to have adopted different approaches to Nepal: Beijing playing a strategic 'long-game', whereas India's approach is regarded as more tactical and short-term. India's tactics include alleged attempts to obstruct and undermine key aspects of the CPA, including the constitution and integration processes. Certainly there are suggestions that Indian manoeuvring has undermined Western attempts to support the peace process. The alleged obstructionism reflects Indian concern that the integration of Maoist combatants will weaken its special relationship with the Nepalese Army.

There is a risk that such tactics – or at least the perception of them – will increase disillusionment with Nepal's peace process and may lead to its ultimate collapse. If China's growing role provokes India to intensify its involvement in Nepal's politics, this risks aggravating divisions among Nepali political leaders, destabilising the political situation and further delaying the implementation of the CPA. Indian concerns about China's expansion into its sphere of influence, allied to its distrust of the Maoists, have the potential to provoke a response that could disrupt the peace process and destabilise Nepal. However, Beijing appears well aware of India's sensitivity given the historic privileged relationship between Delhi and Kathmandu. Thus far, it has been careful not to over-play its hand; indeed it has on occasion urged the Nepali Government to work at restoring its relationship with New Delhi. Furthermore, the preceding analysis suggests that China's increased engagement in Nepal, and the shift in the relative influence of the two powers, may lead to a net gain in terms of peace and stability. If India is seen to have a destabilising influence on Nepal's peace process while China has a broadly stabilising influence, then China's increasing engagement should have a positive effect in terms of peace and stability.

Approach Implications

What are the implications for strategy makers of China's increasing engagement in Nepal, especially those concerned with issues of peacebuilding and argument prevention? While there is now broad acceptance and appreciation of the scale and significance of China's engagement in the developing world, analysts and strategy makers in the West are still getting to grips with the implications of this shift in the context. In particular, little attention has been paid thus far to the implications for argument-affected and fragile states, such as Nepal. How will China's rise affect argument drivers and dynamics? And what opportunities may it offer to consolidate peace and stability?

These a·e questions that strategy makers should ask as they considc how to respond to the threats and the opportunities resulting fr om China's rise. The final section of this report assesses the current state of play and offers some suggestions for harnessing this change positively in order to support peace and stability in Nepal. We focus primarily on the implications and options for Western governments. We pay special attention to the UK, as it is set to become the largest bilateral donor to Nepal; thus its response to China's rise will be particularly significant and may influence the approaches of other actors. The following implications are therefore relevant for all governments engaged in Nepal, insofar as they share similar interests and concerns to the UK Government. Donor representatives in Kathmandu suggested that Nepal illustrates a relatively good example of co-ordination and coherence among Western donors, and this view is corroborated by the findings of a recent European Union assessment. There are reportedly high levels of informal knowledge-sharing among donors, although formal structures and mechanisms for inter-donor co-ordination are limited. There are periodic Head of Mission-level meetings for aid co-ordination, while the United Nations convenes bi-weekly integration and rehabilitation meetings. However, there is no co-ordination structure specifically relating to argument issues, akin to the Donor Peace Support Groups that have been established in some other countries.

It appears that Chinese officials do not generally engage in the various donor coordination forums in Kathmandu; one official from a major Western embassy said he had never seen Chinese representatives in any donor forum.

It was not possible within the limited scope of this research to clarify whether Chinese representatives are invited to such forums, although apparently Indian representatives are invited to some of them. There used to be a degree of engagement between Western and Chinese diplomats in meetings of representatives of the permanent five members of the UN Security Council regarding the UN Mission in Nepal (UNMIN), but this has ceased since the exit of UNMIN in January 2011.

In part, China's absence from the various donor co-ordination forums in Kathmandu reflects the very different norms and principles that underpin Chinese aid generally, and its engagement in Nepal in particular. Beijing does not regard itself as part of the Western donors' 'club' and prefers to deal directly with the Nepali Government rather than through multi-donor structures.

However, what was notable from interviews in Kathmandu is the apparent disconnect between most of the Western donor/diplomatic community in Kathmandu and Chinese officials. This disconnect reflects in part the view expressed that it is not worth engaging with Chinese officials in Kathmandu since strategy and strategy decisions are made in Beijing. However, this seemed to be compounded by the sense of a longstanding cultural divide between Western and Chinese officials, with reference made by Western diplomats to a 'Chinese Wall', which blocks substantive exchange regarding issues of aid, development, governance or security.

Possible Entry Points

In July 2011, the UK Government launched its new strategy for BSOS. In this strategy the Government affirms its intention to "incorporate [the stability] agenda into our developing relationships with the emerging powers". Obviously the UK Government does not have a monopoly on concern with stability. Other external actors have their own stability agendas, which are likely to diverge from the UK's. This may present some challenges, but could also be an opportunity for collaboration. As described above, China has its own clear and predominant stability agenda in Nepal, based on its security concerns *vis-à-vis* Tibet, its economic expansion and its geopolitical strategy. In order to incorporate the UK's stability agenda into its developing relationship with China, the UK Government will need to deepen its understanding of China's interests in argument-affected states like Nepal. In certain respects, notably Beijing's strategy towards Tibetan activists in Nepal, China's stability agenda clearly diverges from the stability agenda of the UK and other Western governments. However, in other respects there is apparent common ground between the stability agendas of Western states and of China – for instance, the shared concern to see Nepal's peace process through to its conclusion.

Therefore as a first step it is suggested that further analysis be undertaken of points of convergence and divergence with regard to Western and Chinese stability agendas. This could serve as the basis for constructive dialogue between Western and Chinese strategy makers on issues to do with peace and stability in Nepal. Where there is a shared interest in commonly agreed aspects of stability (whatever the differing norms or motivations behind it), this could be a basis for developing common strategy objectives and even practical co-operation. Where there is a difference of Viewpoint or principle – for instance regarding the Tibetan issue – this should be identified, and attempts made on both sides to appreciate the values and interests that underpin the different strategy approaches. Clearly such an approach would require a degree of receptiveness from the Chinese side.

It would be a mistake to assume that the Chinese are oblivious to Western concerns about human rights or unaware of the different norms of foreign strategy. A senior Chinese analyst at an influential think tank affiliated to the Ministry of Foreign Affairs expressed the "hope that China and the West can work together much more closely on economic aid. But the obstacle is Western suspicion of China, and accusations that China's non-interference strategy means that China lacks any sense of morality in its foreign strategy". However, he went on to note that there is increasing public debate within China about the strategy of non-interference; and this may open space for dialogue between strategy communities in China and the West about how to promote peace and stability in argument-affected states.

The UK BSOS strategy goes on to state that the Government "will invest greater diplomatic efforts in new 'prevention partnerships' with these countries". This demonstrates awareness of the growing role that China and other rising powers play in countries at risk of argument and instability, such as Nepal. It is hoped that the findings of this research scheme may help to inform the development of a 'prevention partnership' with China based on shared objectives of peace and stability; although it is recognised that deeper and more comprehensive research will be required to establish a firm knowledge-base for such a partnership. At a minimum, this scheme should assist Western strategy makers to appreciate the challenges and limitations to their efforts to promote peace and stability in Nepal, and thereby help ensure that policies are not counterproductive.

Looking beyond the bilateral relationship between the UK and China in respect of Nepal, it is recommended that broader international dialogue about peace and stability in Nepal should seek proactively to engage Beijing as well as New Delhi. While support for Nepal's peace process appears relatively coherent and co-ordinated among Western donors, they should also be looking to connect with Chinese as well as Indian Viewpoints. This will require a more systematic attempt to build relations with Chinese officials in Kathmandu – as well as with the relevant strategy makers in Beijing – and progressively to incorporate China into an inclusive dialogue.

A further area for Western strategy makers to consider, and a possible entry point, relates to the notion of 'argument sensitivity'. This is based on the understanding that any intervention from outside – developmental, commercial or otherwise – will affect the distribution of power and resources in the local community. Interventions that do not take existing relations and dynamics into account may inadvertently provoke or sustain argument, and end up doing more harm than good. As noted above, there is a risk that the sizeable injection of Chinese resources into Nepal will upset local interests and power balances, leading to the sort of violent attack against Chinese targets witnessed in the Terai in September 2011. This indicates the value to Chinese companies of adopting a argument-sensitive approach.

The principle of argument sensitivity is not new to Nepal. It is recognised that in the past "development programmes have sometimes reinforced the social and political inequalities that are at the root of the violent, armed argument". Argument-sensitive approaches have been adopted in a number of development sectors in Nepal, notably in the forestry sector. The UK Government has promoted and supported argumentsensitive approaches both internationally and in Nepal. In its response to the multilateral aid review for instance, DFID recommends that "multilateral organisations need to improve their performance in fragile contexts... [and they] need to take a more systematic approach to developing argument-sensitive programming". While not underestimating the challenges of making Chinese engagement in Nepal more argument-sensitive, this may be an area where the West can collaborate with China. There are clear cost and security benefits to Chinese businesses of a argumentsensitive approach, while it is also in the interests of Western governments, Beijing and all others concerned with stability in Nepal. Western actors could support this by raising awareness of what it means to be argument-sensitive, and by sharing ideas and information with Chinese companies investing and operating in Nepal about ways of putting argument-sensitivity into practice.

More generally, this study suggests that the UK and other Western governments would do well to consider what the implications are when they no longer 'own' the donor marketplace. While the engagement of non-Western powers in Nepal is not a new phenomenon (especially where India is concerned), the growing role of China, and the consequent shifting boundaries of what constitutes aid, are fast changing the context in which Western donors try to support development and peacebuilding in Nepal. China is not overtly attempting to supplant the traditional donors to Nepal. However, by offering alternative options to the GoN they are weakening the bargaining position of traditional donors, with the consequence that the Western practice of linking aid to conditionalities around governance or human rights will be less effective. We should not overestimate the effectiveness of these conditionalities: some of the concern about emerging powers "overestimates the extent to which [good governance, etc.] have been furthered by direct conditionalities imposed by [Western] donors". Nevertheless, conditionalities will now be less effective than they were before, so if the UK and others wish to continue to exert a positive influence upon processes of development and peacebuilding, they will need to engage proactively and imaginatively with the new reality of a multi-polar donor context.

In close, this report suggests a number of ways in which Western strategy makers could strengthen their engagement with China on issues of peace and stability in Nepal. This is on the basis of a preliminary and light-touch research exercise. It was not possible within the limited scope of this scheme to explore fully the various forms of Chinese engagement in Nepal or how they interact with argument drivers; nor has there been a thorough analysis of all international actors. We recommend undertaking more in-depth and systematic research in some of the areas identified above, in order to generate a comprehensive evidence-base and to develop more targeted strategy recommendations. However, this report has highlighted a number of key issues to consider, and we hope it will stimulate strategy debate as well as practical action in response to the significant changes identified.

Space for Improvement

The UK Government's aid review published in March 2011 makes clear that Nepal is one of a reduced number of priority countries to qualify for UK development support. Indeed, the UK is set to become the largest bilateral donor to Nepal over the next few years.

Furthermore, the UK is one of the lead donors supporting critical aspects of peace and stability in Nepal, such as the Rule of Law. In light of the foregoing analysis of China's increasingly significant role in Nepal's development, it seems essential that there be some minimum level of dialogue between UK Government representatives and their Chinese counterparts. And this dialogue should be based on a solid understanding of each country's interests in Nepal, as well as the range and nature of its engagements.

No doubt Western donors are well aware of the changes in the global landscape and of China's rise, but it is not apparent that the consequences of this for Nepal have been fully analysed and factored into the development of aid strategies. DFID's Operational Plan for Nepal 2011–15 notes that "Nepal is of strategic significance to the UK as a fragile state in its own right and as a building block for stability in the region, positioned between China and India". However, this awareness of the regional interactions does not appear to have informed UK strategy priorities. Given the major investment by Western donors in Nepal's peace process, and the country's continuing fragility, it is particularly important to understand how China's increased engagement impacts upon the peace and argument environment in Nepal.

It is acknowledged that opportunities and entry points to influence Chinese officials in Kathmandu may be limited. Furthermore, the Chinese Embassy may indeed have limited independent agency to affect Beijing's strategy towards Nepal. However, the impression gained from interviews in Kathmandu is that there is scope for Western donors and diplomats to engage more proactively and systematically with their Chinese counterparts, be that bilaterally or through multi-donor co-ordination forums. Nor is this restricted to officials in Kathmandu; it may be that there is scope for improving information exchange and co-ordination between Western embassies in Beijing and Kathmandu, as well as with their respective foreign ministries. As China's engagement and influence in Nepal grows, this should become a priority for Western diplomats and strategy makers. The risk is that unless steps are taken soon to overcome the perceived Chinese Wall, the UK and other Western actors will find themselves responding to China's rise as a threat rather than as an opportunity. This relates to the risk that if Western donors are perceived by the Nepali Government to be too prescriptive or conditional regarding their support, then this may reinforce Nepali resentment about Western interference and ultimately push them further into the arms of China.

MAOIST INSURGENCY IN NEPAL: REGIONAL DIMENSION

A five-year old Maoist People's War in Nepal has quietly been capturing the hearts and minds of villagers and urban intellectuals, and has been growing more rapidly than anyone had ever imagined. So potent is the Maoist rhetoric of revolution that even if the insurgency fails, it may change the entire complexion of the country in just a few years. The Maoist People's War in Nepal is entering into sixth-year on February 13, 2001. In the last five-year Maoist guerrillas have captured many successful headlines, both at home and abroad. A recent article published on January 4, 2001 by Stratfor.com, an US-based intelligence consulting firm, has made an assessment on

Nepal. In an alarming note to the ruling elite as well as to the strategic thinkers of regional and global powers, the article writes: "Nepal is likely headed toward even more difficult times with the probable change of its entire political system, from multiparty democracy to communist state... China's presence in Nepal would also complicate positions of the U.S. Navy in the Indian Ocean.....India will be forced to counter Nepal's apparent slide toward Beijing through other means, perhaps increasing contacts with Bhutan, another buffer state in the region."

The so-called intelligence assessment appears to be exaggerated. For example, Maoist take-over in Kathmandu will not necessarily slide Nepal towards Beijing. It all depends on how India will react to developments in Nepal. Maoists have no governments in the world as their natural ideological friends. That being the case, the Maoists will have to define the framework of their foreign policy based on *realpolitik.* Further, the Maoist leadership is very critical of Chinese Communist Party whom they describe as "revisionists." So, Maoists have a tight rope walking and will have to follow the policy of equi-proximity with both India and China.

Regional Instability

A close study of the insurgency gives one the impression that the guerrillas have clearly entered into the strategic stalemate from the strategic defensive phase of the Maoist People's War and are only one more phase away i.e. the strategic offensive. While the insurgency has already exhausted the state and has shaken the internal stability of multi-party political system in Nepal, it also has a potential to raise the level of instability in regional balance of power.

Nepal occupies a strategic position between India and China, two nations that have unresolved border disputes and have even fought a war over it in 1962. China still occupies a section of the Himalayas claimed by India. Since the fall of the Soviet Union, China has focused more on reinforcing its southwestern border by moving troops and constructing military infrastructure. Both India and China have historically treated Nepal as a buffer state. Although Nepal is economically dependent on India, but it is relatively free of military ties to either India or China.

WHO IS BEHIND MAOISTS?

The frustrated Nepali Congress leaders as well as other anti-insurgent political groups often ask question such as "who is really behind Maoist terrorism?" The favourite past time among the Nepali ruling elite have been to see foreign hand whenever they fail to manage the country and the political situation goes out of their hand. A section of hyper nationalists, who exist inside all political parties, see India behind "Maoist terrorism", although they fail to provide convincing argument. Why would India, which itself is biting a bullet from Maoist insurgency in Bihar, Madhya Pradesh and Andhra Pradesh, would support Nepali Maoists? Their only argument is that India enjoys in political instability in Nepal and hence does not want to see strong and stable Nepal, an argument without an iota common sense.

Arguments lacking common sense abound regarding Maoist insurgency in Nepal. Former Prime Minister Krishna Prasad Bhattarai once blamed the United States for fanning insurgency when he was reported to have said that the Maoist leader Dr. Baburam Bhattarai was sheltered by the American Embassy in Kathmandu. Why would the United States, a staunchly anti-communist and a global status-quo power, whip-up Maoist insurgency in a land, which is geo-politically so far away and has little day-to-day interests? It may be noted here that the United States had withdrawn the office its military attaché a few years back indicating the declining strategic value of Nepal.

This leaves China as a potential destabilizing force. Here, too, it does not make any sense to blame China behind Maoist war because China is not a Maoist state any more. Further, it is not in the interest of China to antagonize India and Western powers under normal circumstances by politically and militarily messing in Nepal.

In this context, it does not make any sense for Americans or Indians to fan communist rebellion in Nepal even for the purpose of temporary expediency. Maoist war is thriving in Nepal thanks mainly due to the internal environment of poverty buttressed by repressive policies of incompetent and corrupt leaders. Foreigners will certainly watch the developments to protect their day-to-day interests but it is absurd to say that they are doctoring the Maoist political and military events.

Strategic Choices for Regional Actors

In the past, both India and China have sought and competed for influence in Nepal. Nepal, in the past, had tried to maintain a relationship of equi-distance (some prefer the term "equi-proximity) between the two regional heavy weights. How would these two antagonistic neighbours react to the growing instability in Nepal? What are their strategic choices? There are people in Nepal who think India would not let Maoists come to power. They argue that if Nepal government fails to disarm the guerrillas, New Delhi will not hesitate to step in with its armed forces to flush out the guerrillas. In that event what will China do? Will it stay as a spectator? Perhaps, not. What are the choices for India? Prolonged instability in Nepal is not definitely in India's interest. But sending the armed forces to quell Maoist insurgency will not be a prudent decision on the part of New Delhi either. India has already learned a painful lesson in Sri Lanka when its armed forces entered the island-nation but failed to disarm roughly 6000 Tamil guerrillas. Similarly, tens of thousands of military personnel had to be deployed in Kargil to flush out less than one thousand militants. Fighting against guerrillas in Nepal's mountainous terrain will prove highly costly, a fact already experienced by the British in 1814-16 war.

India will have to do cost-benefit analysis before deploying its force even if the beleaguered government of Nepal requests for the same. Will India's relation with Maoist Nepal be worse-off than what it is presently? Will India lose anything in Nepal in the event of a Maoist take-over? One of the 40-points of Maoists is the scrapping of the 1950 Treaty of Peace and

Friendship. This is nothing new for India as all other political parties, too, have sought a new treaty and New Delhi has agreed for a comprehensive review of the treaty. In this context, New Delhi has nothing to lose, in strategic terms, from a change of political system in Kathmandu. On the other hand, if India enters Nepal in arms, the ongoing insurgency will take the form of national liberation war in which India will get nothing but international condemnation. It will only hasten the Maoist take over. The topography is clearly in Maoists' favour and existing wide spread anti-Indian sentiment also will rally behind the Maoist guerrillas.

The growing Maoist insurgency with its link with India's People's War Group (PWG) and Maoist Coordination Centre (MCC), however, appears to have heightened India's security interests which is reflected in Uttar Pradesh, Bihar and West Bengal government's recent decision to establish additional police posts along Indo-Nepal border.

Indian Defence Minister George Fernandes recently has said that his ministry is actively considering setting up of army camps along Indo-Nepal border in Bihar to check infiltration and subversive activities against India allegedly being carried out by Pakistan's Inter Services Intelligence (ISI) from the Himalayan kingdom.

Although not openly declared but certainly one of the factors behind the decision to establish additional police posts and the contemplation for the deployment of armed forces along India-Nepal border appears to control cross border linkages between India's PWG and MCC. It is a well-known fact that the supporters of Free Tibet Movement based in India have used Nepal as a conduit to transfer men and propaganda materials into Tibet.

The government of Nepal, despite the request of Chinese government authorities not to allow anti-China activities from Nepali soil, has failed to stop Free Tibet Movement activists from sending men and propaganda materials into Tibet through the only Arniko highway (previously called Kodari highway) connecting Nepal to Tibet. The flight of Karmappa Lama into India in the winter of 2000 through the territory of Nepal has made Beijing unhappy with Kathmandu The Arniko highway (120km) was constructed in 1962-64 period with Chinese assistance despite India's objection.

The then King Mahendra had argued to silence the Indian critics by saying that, "communism does not come by taxi cab." The construction of highway was the opening of the first Chinese gateway to South Asia. The Arniko highway has remained a militarily strategic point for both India and China while Nepal has considered it as politically important in its policy of balancing the neighbours.

5

'New Front' of China on Indo-Nepal Border Policy

The Chinese clamour over Arunachal Pradesh has raised many eyebrows in India. Even as the meeting between Prime Minister Manmohan Singh and Chinese Premier Wen Jiabao in Thailand on Saturday was being looked at as an effort to cool down the tension between the neighbouring countries, the Dragon nation has opened another anti-India front. This time in Nepal. Silently but speedily China is spreading its wings in the erstwhile Hindu kingdom, mainly to unleash anti-India propaganda. Besides acquiring some major construction projects in Nepal, the Chinese are also making their presence felt by opening language centres in Nepali cities on the Indo-Nepal border. These centres are teaching Chinese language. But, what raises suspicions on Chinese intentions is the fact that these centres are open only for Nepali citizens.

The surge in Chinese activities in the neighbour country is a matter of concern for India which is already fighting terrorism being pushed into the country from Pakistan. It's a known fact that China often uses Nepal as a buffer state against India.

After the Indo-China war of 1962, the Dragon country has made constant efforts to increase its influence in Nepal. Though it did not succeed much till Nepal was under the rule of monarchy, the fall of monarchy and growing Maoist grip over Nepal has given a fillip to Chinese plans.

A clear indicator of this is the construction of Sikta barrage in Agaiya village of Banke district (Nepal). Its construction was delayed for almost three decades owing to Indian protest. But, once Maoists held sway over the Nepali government, the construction was given a go-ahead in 2006. Moreover, the contract for the project was given to Chinese firm — Sinehydro. In fact, a team of 40 Chinese engineers is engaged in the construction of the Sikta barrage in Agaiya district of Nepal. The district touches the Indian district of Shravasti. The distance from Indian border to the barrage is barely 14 kilometres. The possibility of Chinese infiltration in important zones of war on Indian border areas due to the presence of Chinese engineers cannot be ruled out.

Also, after the completion of the barrage the flow of river Rapti towards India will be diverted towards Nepal which will create acute water shortage in Indian area. Efforts have also been started to divert the flow of rivers flowing towards Indian area from Parchu lake located in Chinese area adjoining the state which may lead to floods in the borders districts of India during monsoon. Not only this, if the and Sikta barrage ever breaks down due to technical reasons it will severely impact the security arrangements made on the India border. China, thus, seems to be working on these two projects under well-planned policy to tease India. Similarly, China has established the office of 'Maitri Sangh' in Nepal adjoining Indian border territory. Meanwhile, a 10-member team comprising five Chinese and five Tibetan national recently visited Nepalganj headquarters of Banke district (Nepal). The team toured the Indo-Nepal border and secretly clicked photographs of the Rupaidiha main gate located on Indo-Nepal border. The Indian intelligence agencies, however, learnt about this when the team had already left for Kathmandu. Assistant army Nayak Devendra of Shashtra Seema Bal (SSB), when contacted, told TOI that he will report the incident to his senior officers.

Nepal's Prime Minister Mr. Madhav Kumar Nepal and Chairman of the Nepalese Congress (NC) Party Girija Prasad Koirala have assured China that Nepali soil will not be allowed to be used against China under any circumstances. Talking with the Chinese delegation led by politburo member of the Chinese Communist Party, Mr. Zhang Gaoli, separately, September 1, 2009, the two veteran politicians of Nepal, according to the high placed sources, did try to convince China towards Nepal's firm stand on 'One China Policy'. However, Beijing is not that fool to believe such parroted/repetitive assurance of Nepali politician, say Kathmandu based analyst.

"The lame duck government has not even asked official clarifications from those lawmakers from the Madhesh parties who had assured the Tibetan community in exile in India that they will raise the issue of 'Free Tibet' in Nepal's Constituent Assembly (CA) during their last meet with Dalai Lama in Dharmasala of Himanchal Pradesh, India", laments a Kathmandu based analyst who preferred anonymity. 'The recent meet of the Nepal law makers has raised suspicion in the minds of the Beijing authorities as regards the Nepalese structured stance that she remains firm on "One China Policy' of Nepal. And Beijing understands the Nepali intentions well. According to PM's political advisor Mr. Raghujee Panta, PM's upcoming visit to China, Constitution drafting process and ongoing peace process were also discussed during the meet.

DELINEATION OF NEPAL-CHINA BOUNDARY, PROBLEM AND SOLUTION OF DEMARCATION

The border areas between Nepal and China represent one of the least known areas of the world. The first regular survey of Nepal was conducted by the Survey of India in 1926-27 and that resulted in the actual demarcation of Nepal-India boundary with 10yard no man's land on either side of the land boundary. However, the demarcation of Nepal-China boundary was made through a survey from a much lower altitude. The topographical survey of 1956-58, which covered the whole of Nepal, was also conducted by the Survey of India. But this survey also could not properly delineate the boundary between Nepal and China because of the lack of proper and sophisticated instruments and equipment as well as the trained personnel to conduct survey in the high altitudes and rugged terrain. Because of the strategic importance of the Himalayas and boundary dispute between India and China as far back as 1950, when India insisted on Mc Mahon line as Sino-Indian boundary which was rejected by China. India did not provide topographical maps for a large section of the Nepal Himalayas as the aerial photographs of these regions had been damaged. When boundary talks between Nepal and China were initiated for a Boundary Agreement on March 21, 1960, its basis was the maps submitted by both countries. However, these maps were not based on proper surveys. The boundaries were drawn on sketch maps, or represented simply by a boundary line on plain paper or cloth. In order to solve the dispute resulting from such unscientific maps, the Joint Boundary Commission was constituted to survey the entire length of Nepal-China boundary as well as to resolve the territorial dispute through on-the-spot visit and assessment of the problem.

The acceptance of traditional customary boundary by both sides was the major reason for conclusion of a border agreement on as October 5, 1961. Nepal and China established diplomatic relations for the first time on August 1, 1955, that is, six years after the establishment of the People's Republic of China in 1949, and four years after the installation of democracy in Nepal in 1951. In the Agreement designed to maintain friendly relations between the People's Republic of China and the Kingdom of Nepal and in the Agreement on trade between the Tibetan Autonomous Region of China and Nepal the customary movement of people and goods along the border has been accepted..

It is to be noted that the survey for the delineation of Nepal-China boundary in 1960-61 had to be carried out with several constraints. Firstly, the survey had to be carried out from lower altitude and there was no aerial survey. Secondly, the instruments and equipment for the survey, manpower as well as proper training for high altitude survey were completely lacking. Moreover, in the absence of on-the-spot survey of high altitude areas, the drawing of the boundary line through the survey was done by recording actual location of important peaks and then drawing boundary line tentatively between the two surveyed peaks.

This mainly accounts for change in position and alignment of Nepal-China boundary between 1961 and 1982 as well as change in the total length of boundary between 1961 and 1982. A glance at the maps of 1961 and 1982 shows a major change in Humla and Mustang. The 1982 boundary maps had been prepared through ground survey on higher altitude than in 1961 and was supported by aerial survey and satellite imageries. As compared to 1961, the length of Nepal-China boundary in 1982 increased to 303 kilometres and the area has increased by 1.876 sq. km. for Nepal.

The Nepal-China border extends along the whole length of northern border of Nepal and the starting and ending point of Nepal-China boundary is the tri-junction of the boundary between Nepal, China and India.

However, because of the Sino-Indian boundary dispute as well as Nepal-India dispute over the Kalapani on the source of the Mahakali River, the demarcation started 5 kilometers ahead of the tri-junction in the west and 5 kilometres behind the tri-junction in the east. There is no man-made boundary demarcation on land as indicated in the boundary treaty maps, except for the boundary pillars.

Along the whole length of Nepal China boundary, there are 79 boundary pillars, only as against more than 1000 boundary pillars along Nepal India border with 10 yards no-man, land on either side of Nepal India boundary. Under the protocol signed and exchanged between Nepal and China on January 20,1963, the contracting parties agreed to maintain and adopt necessary measures to prevent the removal, damage or destruction of boundary pillars as far as possible, to prevent the boundary rivers from changing their course and to make a joint inspection of the entire boundary every five years. Accordingly, in 1979 a new agreement was signed between the two countries after detailed mapping and demarcation of the boundary.

THE ENTRY AND EXIT POINTS ALONG THE NEPAL CHINA BOUNDARY

The Nepal-China border is almost marked by the absence of settlement on either side. The number of settlements along the proximity of border is 10 in Nepal and 18 in China. The border settlements in Nepal are located in the districts of Humla, Rasuwa, Sindhupalchok, Dolakha and Sankhuwasabha, and the settlements on the other side of these districts also are located on Chinese side. The Gorkha district has no border settlement, but has two settlements across its border with China.

One notable feature of Nepal-China boundary is the complete absence of border check posts, except at the Kodari border. Most of the border check posts are located at a distance of more than one day's walk from the actual border on either side. The movement of the border people living within a distance of 30 kilometres on either side of the border has been regulated with the provision of multiple entry permits. However, this provision has not been able to serve the need and purpose of the border people who wish to pursue trade or visit relatives on the other side. Most of the places intended for visit for trade and social relations lie far ahead of the limit of 30 kilometres. In order to tackle this problem, the Agreement on Trade, Intercourse and Related Questions between Nepal and the Tibet Autonomous region of China was concluded on 2nd May 1966, and renewed for the third time on 2nd May 1986. In the revised Agreement, emphasis was laid on identifying areas of movement and fixing of the exact settlements rather than the 30-kilometre distance on either side. However, the survey for the identification of the specified locations of movement for the border people has not yet been initiated.

It is to be noted that on 7 November 1950, according to a letter from India ambassador to China, India's Home Minister Sardar Vallabhbhai Patel, in his letter to Prime Minister Jawaharlal Nehru, stated that Chinese Government has declined to accept the boundary treaty entered into between India and Tibet in 1914, and the McMahon line demarcated as the boundary between India and China in the North Eastern Frontier of India between Bhutan and Burma. He emphasised the need of controlling the bordering countries like Nepal, Sikkim and Bhutan as well as India's northern areas bordering China. The main purpose of India's motive behind imposing the 1950 treaty on Nepal has been guided by this concern. On the basis of this motive, during the period of Prime Minister Matrika Prasad Koirala, India sent Military mission, and the Indian army was posted at the Nepal-China border check-posts, which were removed during the period of Prime Minister Kirtinidhi Bista.

REASONS FOR KEEPING THE BORDER OPEN

The main reason to make Indo-Nepal border gradually and unknowingly open was to facilitate easy access to recruit the young and raw Nepali boys in the British Gorkha Army Regiment without any border restriction. British Army Officers did appreciate the bravery of young and sturdy Gorkha fighters during Anglo-Gorkha War, 1814-16. Second, it would be easier to sell the finished British and Indian goods and merchandise in the market of Nepal and even Tibet via Nepal with open border. At the same time, open border facilitated the import by India of Nepalese cheap raw materials for its manufacturing industries.

The third reason was to make easy and frequent visits of the Indian politicians and bureaucrats as advisors and consultants to the Nepalese Ministers and Secretaries after the democratic movement of Nepal in 1950. In the same way, wide open border also made it easy for Indian Overseers to come to Nepal as Engineers and semi-educated persons as teachers in remote-area schools of Nepal. Fourth and the most important factor for the border to remain open is social relationship at people to people level of both the nations.

There is no Treaty to make the Border Open

There is no such treaty/agreement or memorandum to keep the border open between two countries. Even Nepal-India Peace and Friendship Treaty of 31 July 1950 does not have the provision for open border system. Article-VII of the treaty says: "The government of India and Nepal agree to grant, on reciprocal basis, to the nationals of one country in the territories of the other the same privileges in the matter of residence, ownership of property, participation in trade and commerce, movement and privileges of a similar nature."

But there is no mention of the open border between two countries. It only suggests that the border management system must be reciprocated by both the countries. What it means is that if open or regulated system is enacted by one country, the same system should be implemented by the other on the basis of reciprocity.

If we examine some regulations, there is no mention of open border system. Passport Regulations-1952 says: "In case of the Nepalese residing for long or permanently settled down in any foreign country want to visit Katmandu, they will require to have the permit issued from the concerned District/City Magistrate or Passport issued by the Embassies or Consulates of Nepal in the respective country or from the Alainchikothi (as Consulate Office of Nepal) in Patna, India."

In the same way, the Sample of Rahadani/Permit-April 1862 says: "Nepalese to go out of Katmandu Valley and Nepal to Nepal via India should require to obtain Rahadani/Permit from Rahadani Goswara (Office) or Gadhi/Gaunda." There was also arrangement to provide permanent passport paying Nepali Rupees Five for one year to the general people, who come and go through Gadhi and by aero-plane from 14 April 1952.

On the other hand, if we make a study on the existing Immigration Act-1992, even the Indian nationals should produce visa to enter Nepal. Article-3 (1) of the Act says: "No foreigners are entitled to enter into the Kingdom of Nepal and reside in Nepal without having passport and visa." In this connection, the question arises: who are the foreigners?

Immigration Regulations-1992 (Second Amendment-2002), Article 2(B) defines: "Foreigner means any person, not being the citizen of Nepal at present, as it must be understood." In the regulations, no special provision has been made for Indian nationals. It indicates that the regulated border system should also be followed for the Indian nationals. If there was some memorandum or agreement to maintain open border system between two countries, the Immigration Act and Regulations would not have been issued in this manner.

Next, Article-7 of Nepal-India Joint Press Statement-23 March 2000 reads: "The two Prime Ministers agreed on the need to prevent the misuse of the open border by terrorists, criminals and other undesirable elements and directed that co-operation in this regard be enhanced. Discussions on the management of the border would continue in the Joint Working Group on Border Management between the two Home Secretaries."

This scribe had published an article in a daily newspaper on the regulation of border. In response to this article, Sanjaya Verma, Counselor of Indian Embassy, Katmandu wrote in the Letter to the Editor column of the same daily supporting this scribe that "Open border between two countries is not mentioned in any of the articles of 1950 Nepal-India Treaty.

Open border is an emblem of most intimate friendship that has existed between both countries from ancient time to this date."9 So all these facts reveal that there is no black and white document on the prevalence of open border system between Nepal and India.

How the Border is made Open

There may be a query as to how the open border system prevailed between two countries. The answer may be, it prevailed only on the basis of mutual understanding, good neighbourly relations, religious sentiment, the same topography, social similarities, and family relationship. The next factor may be political. There was a very close contact among high-ranking political leaders of both nations. While Nepalese leaders had participated actively in the independence movement of India, Indian leaders also contributed to establish democracy in Nepal.

And the open border made the movement of political leaders and bureaucrats of India and Nepal easy to shuttle back and forth without any interrogation or check in the border.

The third factor is the social one. Socially, Nepalese boys are the sons-in-law of Indian nationals and Indian girls are the daughters-in-law of the Nepalese, mostly those who reside in the frontier. As a consequence, Indian and Nepalese parents are Samdhi (parents of daughter-in-law) to each other. So the border was made open socially for frequent visits to the kith and kin on either side of the frontier. The administration did not obstruct them in practice.

Implications of Open Border System

There are positive and negative implications of open border system between Nepal and India. Negative implication outnumbers the positive one in the Nepalese context. Convenience in movement and travel, strengthening mutual ties, quick emergency response and assistance, competitive frontier market, supply of labour etc. are positive features. But there are many other negative aspects of insecure open border system.

This may be cross-border terrorism, transaction of illegal arms and ammunitions, encroachment of border and no-man's land, effect on peace and security, trans-border crime, theft and robbery, girls and women trafficking, narcotic drug trafficking, kidnapping of individuals, illegal migration, smuggling of goods and machinery, leakage in revenue collection and anti-social activities.

The terrorist and Maoist rebels have gained benefits from the open border. They have misused it for the transaction of illegal arms and ammunitions. But the common people of Nepal and India fear insecurity for their life and property. Maoists and unwanted elements create terror in Nepalese frontier time and often.

They attack mainly government offices, set fire to them and loot the bank. Some of them have been killed during fighting.

Those who manage to escape flee on the other side of the porous border with no restriction and take shelter there. In the same way those who are wounded and injured, cross the open border easily, with blood leaking from their bodies. They get treatment in the hospitals of Indian frontier. When they recover and get recharged, they go again to create terror and horror in Nepal. In such a fashion Indo-Nepal porous border has been made insecure and misused.

On the other side, not only the Indian and Nepali nationals cross the porous border without any restriction, but these days some Pakistani, Bangladeshi, Sri Lankan and even Afgan and Iranian nationals infiltrate into Nepalese territory, misusing the open border to some extent. Their similar face, attire, posture and behaviour resemble the Nepalese and Indian nationals. Some of the Pakistani, Iranian, and Myanmar infiltrators are seeking asylum in mostly western nations through United Nations High Commissioner for Refugees (UNHCR) office in Katmandu. In one sense, the porous border has helped to initiate rebellion activity in both nations to some extent. So Indo-Nepal open border management system is going to be difficult for the common people of both countries.

CHINA'S INROADS INTO NEPAL: INDIA'S CONCERNS

The political crisis that triggered off in Nepal with Prime Minster Prachanda's resignation yet again indicates not only the trials and tribulations of a fledgling democratic process but also points to the geopolitical vulnerability of the country sandwiched as it is between the two Asian giants. While India considers Nepal a part of its sphere of influence, it is increasingly being challenged by China's inroads into Nepal. In fact, the growing Nepal-China nexus should be seen in the context of India-China power competition in Asia. Essentially Nepal facilitates China's security interests in the South Asian region. This can be clearly glimpsed from Chinese ambassador, Zheng Xianglin's statement delivered at the Council of World Affairs in August 2008 that "Nepal is situated in a favourable geographical position in South Asia, and a passage linking

China and South Asia." Nepal constitutes an important element of China's South Asia policy.

One may recall Mao Zedong's five finger policy in which Nepal constituted one of the five fingers along with Ladakh, Bhutan, Sikkim and Arunachal Pradesh. The five fingers were essentially meant to serve as a 'new buffer' zone between India and China after the 'old buffer' (Tibet) came under China's sovereign control in 1951. With growing tensions in Tibet, particularly after the March 2008 uprising, China's conception of Nepal as a new buffer acquired particular significance. Its policy towards Nepal came to be driven by the need to curb the clandestine activities of some 20,000 Tibetan refugees (the second largest Tibetan refugee community in the world) in Nepal. Consequently, China has been increasingly playing a significant role in determining the future shape of Nepali politics. During each of the high-level meetings China has extracted assurances from Nepal that it adheres to the one-China principle, acknowledges Tibet as an inalienable part of China, and will ensure that no anti-China activity is allowed on its soil. Underscored in China's South Asia policy is the strategy to marginalize India's influence in Nepal. Marginalizing India would allow China not only to dominate South Asia but also provide easy access to Nepal's roughly 83,000 megawatts of hydroelectric potential.

It is interesting to note that China pronounces its foreign policy towards Nepal in a manner which presents not only a benign image of itself but which also helps assuage Nepal's fears of a domineering India. For instance, the December 2008 Yang Jiechi's assurance to protect Nepal's "sovereignty and independence" not only strengthened Beijing's diplomacy but also sought to obviate India's influence. News reports from Nepal even go further to suggest that "China intended to develop relations with Nepal in a way that would serve as a role model for bilateral ties between big and small countries." China has, in fact, laid down a four-fold policy to strengthen its bilateral relations with Nepal: "First, accommodate each other's political concern. Second, enhance the economic cooperation on the basis of mutual benefit. Third, boost people-to-people and cultural exchanges. Fourth, strengthen the coordination and cooperation in international and regional affairs."

Apart from stating a clear policy towards Nepal, China has been systematically pursuing a multi-dimensional engagement with Nepal. There has been a flurry of visits between China and Nepal in recent times. According to one news report, about 38 Chinese delegations visited Nepal in 2008 alone. China has been cultivating ties with not only the Communist Party of Nepal-Maoist (CPN-M) but also with the Communist Party of Nepal-United Marxist-Leninist (CPN-UML) and the Madhesi People's Rights Forum. Lately, China has begun taking interest in Terai politics. There are reports of a high level Chinese delegation visiting the General Convention of the Madhesi People's Rights Forum in early 2009. In April 2009, a CPN-UML delegation led by Jhala Nath Khanal visited Beijing when China had impressed upon the delegation that it wants "a new kind of relationship" with Nepal.

Besides high level visits, China's inroads into Nepal are being greatly facilitated by the systematic promotion of China Study Centres (CSCs) which are completely funded by China. The number of CSCs in Nepal has increased in recent times. According to the CSC website, there are ten local branches located in Butwal, Banepa, Sankhuwasabha, Pokhara, Biratnagar, Morang, Sunsari, Chitwan, Nepalgunj and Lumbini, besides the central organization of the CSC-Nepal in Kathmandu. According to Bhim Prasad Bhurtel, the executive director of the Nepal South Asia Centre, Kathmandu, "33 China Study Centres have been established in southern Nepal adjoining the Indian border." He also mentions that China Radio International has launched a local FM radio station in Kathmandu with the purpose of bringing China closer to Nepal. Besides CSCs, a Nepal-China Mutual Cooperation Society (NCMCS), funded by the Chinese Embassy in Nepal, was established in March 2005. The primary aim of NCMCS is to strengthen diplomatic relations between the two countries as well as to disseminate an image of a friendly China as opposed to hegemonic India. Besides, there are other associations like the Nepal-China Executives Council in Kathmandu, the Nepal-China Friendship Association in Lumbini and the Nepal-China Youth Friendship Association in Pokhara. Further, to promote bilateral cooperation and exchanges the Nepal-China bilateral consultation mechanism was constituted in 1996. Such multi-layered engagement enabled China to not only strengthen its diplomacy in the region but also project a benign and cooperative image. It may be noted that India does not have such multi-layered levels of contact and lacks innovative ways (cultural or diplomatic) of reaching out to the Nepali government and people. In fact, similar culture and traditions in Nepal create a kind of extended cultural zone for India and often therefore many of the natural linkages that exist between India and Nepal are taken for granted.

China's proactive policy in Nepal can also be discerned from the military assistance it has been providing. On December 7, 2008 during a meeting in Kathmandu between Nepal Defence Minister Ram Bahadur Thapa and the deputy commander of China's People Liberation Army, Lieutenant General Ma Xiaotian, China pledged to provide US $2.6 million as military assistance for Nepal's security sector. Earlier in September 2008, China had announced military aid worth $ 1.3 million, the first such assistance to the Maoist government in Nepal. It may be recalled that in 2006 China had provided clandestine military assistance to the Maoists in a bid to placate them. In recent times, Beijing has shown keen support for the Maoist governments' proposal to integrate some 19,000 Maoist guerrillas with the Nepal Army.

As part of economic assistance, ahead of Prachanda's now-cancelled second visit to China, China had announced a doubling of aid to Nepal amounting to $21.94 million. To attract Chinese investment in Nepal, on April 7, 2009, the Nepal-China Executives Council (NCEC) and the Chinese People's Association for Friendship with Foreign Countries (CPAFFC) signed a MoU. The trade volume between the two countries currently stands at $401 million with China selling goods worth about

$386 million, and Nepal exporting a mere $15 million. To bridge the trade deficit, China has agreed in April 2009 to provide duty free access to 497 Nepali goods in the Chinese market. There are also proposals for a second South Asian Countries Commodity Fair to be held from 6 to 10th June 2009 at Kunming where 40 Nepali enterprises are slated to participate with 30 stalls. China is the third largest country to provide FDI to Nepal, India and the US being the first and second, respectively.

Also, not to forget, China's initiative in building a road link between Lhasa and Khasa, a border town located some 80 kilometres north of Kathmandu. China has also accepted Nepal's proposal in April 2009 to open up two more custom points in addition to the existing five. China is also building a 65 km second road link, the Syafrubesi-Rasuwagadi road, which is the shortest route from Tibet to Kathmandu. As part of promoting Nepal's hydro-power projects, in 2008, China's Assistant Minister for Foreign Affairs, He Yafei, pledged to provide Nepal a loan of $125 million for Upper Trishuli 3 'A' and $62 million for Upper Trishuli 3 'B'. The plants would start operating from 2012.

There has thus evolved a multi-layered engagement between China and Nepal, causing considerable concern in the Indian establishment. Even if Prachanda's statement is to be believed that "not a single (Chinese) delegation came to Nepal on my invitation," it nonetheless does not rule out China's growing inroads into Nepal. China's growing ties with Nepal undoubtedly supports its wider South Asia policy, much to the concern of India.

More importantly, China's strategic interest has been facilitated by the rise of the Maoists in Nepal. In fact, the January 2008 speech of Prachanda which got leaked has fuelled India's concern about the possibility of Nepal inching towards a Maoist dictatorship. Indeed, ideological similarity with Communist China lends suspicion to the growing affinity between the two countries. Unlike Royal Nepal, the Maoists under Prachanda have shown in no ambiguous terms their strategic goal of reducing dependence on India and increasing ties with China. In this context, it is worth noting the draft proposal for a China-Nepal friendship treaty submitted on February 27, 2009 by the visiting Chinese delegation to Nepal led by Assistant Chinese Foreign Minister Liu Jieyi. The official reason provided was the need for a fresh treaty to meet the changing political environment in Nepal after the Maoists came to power.

For Nepal, signing a treaty with China on the lines of the 1950 India-Nepal treaty undoubtedly curtails India's special relations with Nepal. At the same time, by pledging to overhaul the 1950 treaty with India on the ground that it "does not represent the aspirations of the Nepalese people anymore" Maoist Nepal clearly seeks to reduce India's influence in Nepal. Prachanda's May 09, 2009 interview to the Times of India in which he asked, "Why should Nepal seek India's consent on its security?" seems to hint at the Maoist's search for independent foreign policy. And on the other hand are reports about China pledging support for Prachanda's decision to sack the army chief when India was trying hard to prevent it.

INDO-NEPAL OPEN BORDER: IMPLICATIONS FOR BILATERAL RELATIONS AND SECURITY

The implications of free movement of population across the international boundaries are varied and complex. Open border facilitates cultural continuity through interaction between countries having socio-religious affinity. This cultural continuity can be stretched to consolidate ethnic identity of minority groups staying across the border. In an advanced stage of political development, a well bonded ethnic entity may evolve where people and groups inside the boundary 'are likely to exhibit 'opportunism' in their alliances, interaction patterns and cultural borrowings, as they seek personal and group advantage unhampered by border restrictions of rigid loyalty.' The political risks associated with changes in the ethnic composition of the receiving country and the bilateralization of such issues can lead to complications in other areas of mutual cooperation.

Apart from socio-cultural implications the open border can prove to be a safe haven for smugglers, criminals and terrorists to carry out their activities in an uninterrupted manner.

Population movement across the international boundary have even wider ramifications. Depending on the ethnic composition of the receiving society and its geographical size, the ethnic identity of the migrants have not only the potential to threaten the identity of a nation, but fear is often expressed about their tendency to pose demographic threat by swamping the indigenous people in a small nation. An ethnically homogeneous nation is more likely to be repugnant to the immigrants who can be a threat to its ethnic identity.

Moreover, the ideological orientation of the migrants may also be incompatible with that of the establishment in the host country. In multiethnic societies, immigrants having socio-cultural similarities with an ethnic group of the host country are more likely to be welcomed by that group, but opposed by other groups, who do not share such an affinity.

Thus the dynamics of migration and its impact varies from group to group, and society to society. 'Perceived cultural affinity-or its absence-clearly plays a critical role in how various communities respond to population influx...". Conferring of citizenship rights also depends on whether the receiving country considers the migrants as potential citizens or not.

In South Asia the borders of most of the countries are penetrable. The cultural heritage of the subcontinent is converged in such a manner that ethnic groups residing in different regions in different countries exhibit an overlapping cultural bond cutting across the physical boundary of a nation state. As an observer has put it: "The identity question of India's neighbouring states; at least on the cultural plane, has thus been rendered extremely vulnerable, because India as the oldest country in the region, seems to prompt all their cultures. The vision of India's unity in ancient times was based on its cultural entity and now it is a cultural name to begin with." Population movement across the Indo-Nepal border has devoid

Nepali nationalism of its unique characteristics through cultural penetration.

According to Myron Weiner, 'what is most troubling to the governments in South Asia is the unwanted ethnic mix that migration brings into community anxiously seeking to assert their own identity.' In this context, the Indo-Nepal border reveals an interesting mixture of socio-cultural continuity and at the same time, it is considered a threat to national identity. The socio-cultural compulsions that have motivated policy makers to keep the border open can be attributed to the following historical, strategic and socio-cultural facts.

History of Socio-Cultural Continuity

The overwhelming presence of people of Indian origin in and the presence of Nepalese population in the Terai region contiguous to the Indo-Nepal border has made socio-cultural intercourse indispensable. The 1700 km long Indo-Nepal open border has not only facilitated socio-cultural exchanges that date back to centuries but have been strengthened by age old historical ties. The geographical proximity and socio-cultural affinity have determined the contour of the relationship between both the countries.

Throughout history, the movement of people between Nepal and India was unrestricted. Some archaeological remains in the Lumbini garden attest to the fact that since the third century B.C. till about the fourteenth century A.D., Lumbini was regularly visited by a large number of people from various regions of India, Tibet and Nepal (Khandadesa). In the post-Mauryan period also there existed very congenial relations among the people and that promoted their commercial activities smoothly. During the reign of Lichchhavis in the first century A.D, the region from the Ganges up to Mahabharat ranges was marked by uniformity in governance, socio-cultural activities and economic pursuits. During this period, Nepal received Gupta script, Sanskrit language, Hindu and Buddhist religious architecture from India. All these point to the fact that before its unification, Nepal was a part of Indian empires and thus within the sphere of the broader Indian cultural domain. In the medieval period, the Mallas of Kathmandu Valley traced their ancestry from the Karnatas of Simaraunagarh and the Baisi, Chaubisi and Sen Kings of the Western Himalayas and the Terai region of Nepal from Rajasthan.

In the past, both the countries belonged to the same political domain and administration which explains their cultural affinity. Till the end of eighteenth century, i.e. 1774, Terai region of Nepal was under the Sen Kings of Palpa, Makwanpur and Vijayapur. "...the territories of the Sen kingdom included the whole of Terai region of Nepal as well as some parts of northern India in Uttar Pradesh and Bihar."

In the early modern period, the Sen kings of Vijayapur and Makwanpur had accepted the suzerainty of the Sultans, the Mughals and the East India Company and annually they used to pay rents for utilising the resources of their territory. Moreover, from the 10th century to 13th century when Muslim invasion shook northern India, the Hindu kings from Mewar, Chittor, Kannuaj, Kumaon, Mithila and Videha fled to Nepal. The age old historical ties were also consolidated by matrimonial relations between the royal houses of Nepal and India. The religious ties between both the countries have reinforced the bond of relationship between the people of both the countries. In the Pasupatinath temple there is a tradition of worship by Bhatta brahmins of Karnataka in India. The Hindus of Nepal have high reverence for sacred religious places like Varanasi, Kasi etc. Though India has a preponderant Hindu population, Nepal is the only confessed Hindu Kingdom of the world. The existence of bonds between the people in both the countries have made it imperative for the policy makers to keep the border open.

The concept of a separate sovereign nation having a distinct political entity remained blurred due to the British annexation and expansion and unification of Nepal under Prithivi Narayan Shah. It was only after 1860 that the boundary between both the countries was more or less stabilised when British ceded certain part of the territory between the rivers Mahakali and

Rapti to Nepal as a mark of recognition for the help it had rendered during the Sepoy mutiny. However, Nepal was regarded as a buffer zone between India and China by the British.

Indian Migration to Nepal

The fertile land in Terai was the only source of revenue for the Nepali Kings. It financed their military conquests and provided for their luxurious life. The unwillingness of the hill folk to settle and cultivate lands in the Terai region due to malarial climate led to substantial migration from the Indian side with official patronage and encouragement. Thus Indian settlements in Terai were accomplished without taking into consideration its long-term implications.

British government's formal recognition of Nepal as a sovereign independent nation under the Treaty of 1923 led to the opening of Terai for Indian traders. Nepal neither had the capital, nor infrastructure and technology to build industries. Lack of industrialisation provided the Indian businessmen with incentive to open up new ventures in Terai. Indian businessmen took advantage of the rail transport system built by the British and established industries in the Nepal side of the border and exported the surplus commercial goods and other agricultural products to India.

In many cases, people had shops both in India and Nepal. The businessmen of both areas constantly shuttled from one place to another, and foreign goods passed more easily from one shop to another because of the open border. Moreover, any bussinessman who wanted to set up business in the Terai was given two bighas of land. The reluctance of Nepalese businessmen to settle in the Terai region can be attributed to the fact that Nepalese were agriculturists by tradition and they call themselves agriculturists even today.... A few domiciled Nepali businessmen do not rely completely on business but also do agricultural work. In the industrial sector that is dominated by the Indians, preference is given to the Indian workers as common ethnic factors enhance the predictability of their behaviour and make them trustworthy. Moreover, mobility of labourers from the hills could not be accomplished because of the problem of ecological adaptation.

Many people cross over the border to the Indian side, work as seasonal workers during the harvesting time, sometimes as vegetable sellers and hawkers. Because of the available educational opportunities many Nepalis cross over the border to attend the schools and colleges in India. The most significant among the places which attract Nepali students is Benaras, where mostly Nepali brahmins come to seek Sanskrit education. Many others prefer to migrate to India due to high wages and highly prestigious social positions accorded by the hill society to the people working in the foreign army. The voluminous presence of both Nepalese and Indians on both the sides of the border supports the system of open border, in spite of some negative implications.

There is a general perception in Nepal that Indians are taking up jobs which would otherwise have gone to the Nepalese. According to an observer on population migration, 'Indian contractors dominate in big contracts in governmental and non-governmental sectors because of their better organisation, investment and entrepreneurial capacity...A large number of immigrants working in urban areas have a strong hold on trade and commerce, even displacing Nepalese traders....Their business entrepreneurship and extensive linkages in India and abroad are not matched by their Nepalese counterparts'.

Nepalese Migration to India

The Nepalese migration to India can be attributed to the following reasons. From the beginning, Nepal disliked the idea of Gorkha recruitment in the Indian army. The clandestine method adopted by the British resulted in repressive actions by Nepali government against the Gorkhas on their return home on leave. In some cases their property was confiscated and they were given death penalty. Consequently, they were encouraged by the British to settle in Dharmashala (Bhagsu), Bakloh, Darjeeling, Dehradun and Shillong. Apart from this, many Nepalese also migrated to the districts of Darjeeling and Jalpaiguri of West Bengal to be employed in the tea gardens. Sikkim was under Nepali domination since 1775. The status quo was restored in 1812 and it became a British protectorate in 1861. This explains substantial Nepalese settlement there. Many Nepalese labourers were taken to Sikkim for working in various developmental works undertaken by the British government. After Youngshusband mission to Tibet and discovery of Chumbi valley of Sikkim, a new trade route opened between British India and China. Some of the traders and artisans, mostly the Newars and a few Sherpas, managed to move to Kalimpong and Sikkim since Nepalese were the only foreigners from South Asia permitted to carry on trading activities within Tibet. Moreover, on the Indian side of the border, many Nepalese were settled because of British policy and many of them were transfered with the territory to the British India as a result of Sugauli Treaty of 1816. The overwhelming presence of Nepalese on the Indian side of the border makes close cross border interaction inevitable.

A Case for Open Border

The historical ties between both the countries explain the necessity of the Treaty of Peace and Friendship of 1950 between India and Nepal to provide an impetus to the historical socio-cultural relations. Two clauses of the 1950 Treaty are significant and have aroused much debate and misunderstanding. Article VI of the Treaty states that 'each government undertakes, in token of good neighbourly friendship between India and Nepal, to give to the national of the other, in its territory, national treatment with regard to participation in industrial and economic development of such territory and the grant of concessions and contract relating to such development'. Article VII further states that, 'the government of India and Nepal agree to grant, on reciprocal basis, to the nationals of one country in the territories of the other the same privilege in the matters of residence, ownership of property, participation in trade and commerce, movement and other privileges of a similar nature'.

Although both the countries are bound by the 1950 Treaty of Peace and Friendship, it is pertinent to point out that though the treaty has given legality to the movement of the people across the international boundary, their socio-cultural links were deeply imbibed into the socio-cultural history of both the countries. As an analyst has put it: (India being a) "Hindu majority state where the life of its people is governed by the ethos of Hindu religion largely, in which it finds itself so close to Nepal.......Nepal's Hindu identity makes its cultural boundary contiguous with India."

The Terai region of Nepal bordering India is an extension of the Indo-Gangetic plain. The "geographical factors have been reinforced by religious, cultural and ethnic affinities between the inhabitants of Terai region and their counterparts across the border. The Terai region has, therefore, remained practically an expansion of the Indian society and economy through the centuries." The border was not regulated because as a British protectorate its southern border was secure. Moreover "the arrangement of open border was preferable to the restricted border because it saved the rulers from incurring the administrative expenditure necessary to check and regulate the border and the task involved in the control of movement of people through the border to and from India."

The concentration of Indian born population in the Terai region explains the present relations. The number of India born population in Terai according to 1991 census is 97.21 per cent of the total foreign born population residing in this region. Out of the total foreign citizens in Terai, the Indians constitute 77.6 per cent. These people cannot be prevented from maintaining familial relations by a restricted or regulated border.

Nepali Nationalism and Open Border

The issue of open border was never a problem with the ruling elites in Nepal in the early 1950s because India had played a significant role in the democracy of Nepal. But in subsequent days, the Indo-Nepal Treaty of Peace and Friendship became a contentious issue between both the countries after the introduction of Panchayat government. Most of the Nepali elites considered it as undemocratic since it was concluded by the autocratic Rana regime which did not have popular support and who took the step to consolidate their position against the growing anti-regime activities.

The Treaty has been frequently criticised by different regimes of Nepal who have, time and again, resorted to the strategy of whipping anti-Indian sentiments in a bid to prove themselves as nationalists. The settlement of Indians and the open border was exposed to bitter criticism. During the period between 1960-90, anti-Indian postures were almost synonymous with nationalism in Nepal. During this period various clauses of the 1950 Treaty were frequently violated. This can be attributed to two factors. First, the assertive monarchy and erosion of democracy after the introduction of the panchayat system. Secondly, India's overbearing role and its sympathetic attitude towards the democratic forces in Nepal led to an increase in anti-Indian feelings in certain sections of Nepali population. Moreover, reports were rife about Nepali Congress operating camps for armed training of its volunteers in India;

In this context, the King to assert his control over the throne and to legitimise his rule, encouraged Nepali nationalism with its unique ingredients of national identity and symbol, having more similarity with hill culture symbols. This could not have been possible without giving the foreign policy an anti-India tone. Legislations were passed curtailing Indians' rights and restrictions were put on further migration. A separate cultural entity was evolved by rigid implementation of national language, and measures were taken to curtail the special relations and minimise the emphasis on historical ties with India.

The reciprocal clause in the Indo-Nepal Friendship Treaty was given scant regard when laws like Industrial Enterprise Act, 1961, the New Mulki Ain of 1963, the Citizenship Act of 1964, the Land Reforms Act of 1964, the Ukhanda Land Tenure Act 1964 were enacted crippling Indians interests. To assert

Nepali national identity, Nepali language was promoted and restrictions on other languages were imposed citing the reason that other languages would hamper the development of Nepali as a national language. Hindi bulletin on radio Nepal was stopped. This was done because the close socio-economic ties of the people of Terai with India were perceived by Nepal with anxiety. As a Nepali scholar has put it, 'the Terai is the channel through which Indian influence can infiltrate into Nepal...some concerned members of Nepal's governing elite look upon the Terai as their nation's vulnerable underbelly."

Population Commission Report of 1983

As a means towards this end, in 1983, the Panchayat government decided to appoint a population commission to prepare a report on internal and international migration, which was submitted to the government in 1988. Most of its 70 recommendations for controlling internal and international migration were related to the regulation of the Indo-Nepal border. It recommended three stages for the regulation of human traffic across the border. In the first stage, people crossing the border should be made to register their name at specified border points. In the second stage, to be introduced a year after the first stage, was the entry permit system and people residing within 10 kilometers of the border would be provided with multi-entry permit system to be renewed each year and others would be issued only entry permit system. In the third stage, to be implemented at an appropriate time, regular passport system would be introduced between both the countries.

The Commission while criticising Indo-Nepal Peace and Friendship Treaty of 1950 commented that 'the treatment which Indians are successfully getting in Nepal are far from being bilateral.' Further, the report accused that due to the appointment of Indians in the skilled sector, the process of skill development among Nepali workers is retarded. To restrict the foreigners from being employed in the organised sector, the report further stressed that the work permit should be limited to the shortest possible duration. Moreover, employment of foreigners should be allowed only in proportion of foreign investment and technology in the industrial establishments, but it should not be allowed to exceed the number of the Nepalese employees. The foreign contractors employing more Nepalese in the construction works should be given concession in contract tax and other levies to discourage the trend of employing foreign workers.

In a clear violation of the 1950 Treaty, work permit was introduced by the Nepalese authority to allow Indians to work in the Kingdom. The justification for this work permit was referred to the provisions of the letter exchanged along with the treaty. According to this letter, "it is necessary for sometime to provide safeguards to the Nepali nationals from uncontrolled competition. The nature and scope of such safeguards will be determined through mutual agreement between the two governments according to need." Nepal not only took the decision unilaterally citing this letter but India's protest was dismissed. Defending the work permit system, the chief spokesman of Nepali government reportedly said that, "no grounds for objection can be advanced either at the decision to require work permits, as these are required for Nepali as well as foreign nationals for registration."

The usefulness of the treaty was also questioned by Kirtinidhi Bista, the Nepali Prime Minister in 1969. The open border has given rise to a blurred national identity and has further complicated the issue of citizenship. From time to time, Nepal has imposed various restrictions on citizenship. In the process of distinguishing migrants from genuine citizens, the people of Indian origin have suffered the most. Whereas the people of hill are accepted as citizens matter of factly, the Terai people have to go through a rigorous process to prove their citizenship. In 1988, at the peak of Indo-Nepal irritations due to the trade and transit problem, the then Minister of State for Home, Prakash Bahadur Singh stated in Kanchanpur district of Nepal that "since the pressure of external population can skew the country's economic balance, citizenship from now be available only on the basis of descent." Nepal not only started registering its citizens but stated that it would grant citizenship only to the descendants of Nepalese citizens. This was done in a move to exclude people of Indian origin. To avoid any settlers from India getting citizenship, it was decided that a genuine Nepali who possesses documents of landholding would be registered as a citizen.

People not possessing such documents would require to get recommendation from ward chairman, Pradhan Pancha, Upa Pradhan Pancha, Village Development Committee, President of Class organisation, area member of district Panchayat and district level office bearer of the class organisation in this regard. A certificate proving one's continuous service in the government or semi-government office was taken as a proof for providing citizenship certificates. Many Indian landless labourers staying in Nepal for generations were harassed through such rigid procedures. However, several citizens of Indian origin who have acquired citizenship faced the prospect of disenfranchisement. Fear regarding this surfaced when the then Home Minister, Narayan Thapa made a statement on April 9, 1989 saying that Nepal would have a fresh look at the status of the 6.48 million people of Indian origin, including even those holding citizenship certificate.

SOCIO-CULTURAL IMPLICATIONS OF THE OPEN BORDER

Socio-cultural similarities on either side of the international border, a universal phenomenon, are more pronounced in the case of Nepal-India border, because such ties have been enhanced by open border with no restrictions on the movement of people on either side. Social and cultural similarities do exist along the Nepal China boundary as well but more so in the case of Nepal India border where people have easier access and interaction. Ethnic and linguistic similarities exist along the Nepal-India border both in the south plains and hills in the east and west. The open border has naturally promoted social and cultural interaction among the nationals of both sides through matrimonial relationship as well.

The role of religious centres of pilgrimage for both Hindus and Buddhists in both countries has been responsible for strengthening the social and cultural bonds between the two countries. Nepal as the abode of Pashupatinath, and the birth place of Sita and Buddha has been the holiest place for both Hindus and Buddhists. Regular visits of pilgrims from India to the holiest places like Lumbini, Janakpur, Kathmandu Valley, Muktinath, Swargadwari, Barahakshetra, etc.have contributed to enhancing and strengthening the cultural relations between the two countries. Likewise, Nepalese pilgrims visit the holiest Hindu places of Kedarnath, Kashi, Gaya, Jagannath, Haridwar, Allahabad and holiest Buddhist places like Buddhagaya, Rajgir, Sarnath, Nalanda, Kushinagar. People's visits from both countries to places of tourist attraction as well as to important cities have contributed to strengthening friendship, mutual understanding as well as trade and cultural relations.

When health infrastructures in Nepal were not developed, a large number of people from the Tarai as well as from the hills used to go to hospitals in India across the border. During the last few decades, Nepal has been able to develop health facilities in the country, particularly in the Tarai, with the establishment of regional, zonal and district hospitals with modern medical facilities. This has resulted in the large-scale flow of patients from India into these hospitals. One noteworthy development of medical facilities in the Tarai has been the opening of the modern eye hospitals and opthalmology units in zonal and regional hospitals.

These facilities have resulted in the large scale inflow of eye patients from the bordering states of India because of quality and cheap services. A medical institution that has attracted a large number of cancer patients from India is the cancer hospital in Bharatpur with ultra modern cancer treatment facilities. The flow of Nepalese cancer patients to Mumbai is still continuing. Another important development in the medical sector is the opening of a number of medical colleges in Nepal. There are 10 medical colleges in Nepal, most of them in the private sector. Three medical colleges are located in

Kathmandu, one in Pokhara and 6 in the Tarai: Dharan, Birgunj, Bharatpur, Bhairahawa, Nepalganj and Chisapani. These medical colleges have attracted a large number of Indians including non-resident Indians seeking medical education and also patients seeking medical services in these hospitals. The flow of Nepalese students seeking medical education in India is also continuing. But gradually decreasing in number.

The legacy of ancient civilisation that existed along the entire length of Nepal-India border has been relegated to historical ruins and archaeological remains. How the ancient civilisations of Mithila, Birat, Koshala, Shakyas, etc., in the Tarai region perished has still remained an engima. It has been argued that the bad drainage system converted ancient towns and villages into malarial places and people deserted them; they were reverted to natural state as dense forest infested with wild animals and, above all, malaria. The Tharus, the Kumhals, the Dhimals, the Rajbanshis, the Dunwars, etc., are considered to be the ancient people of these civilisations. They were malaria immune ethnic groups living in the isolated patches of dense forests in the Inner Tarai in the past. The migrants from India as well as from the hills and mountain areas of Nepal squeezed them. They were gradually displaced from their traditional tribal lands, and most of them were relegated to the status of marginal and landless peasants. The existence of Kamaiya or bonded labour among the Tharus numbering some 8000 families is an instance in point. The Kamaiya system has been abolished in the country recently without any arrangement for the rehabilitation of the freed Kamaiyas.

The open border has economically benefited the nationals inhabiting both sides of the border. Those engaged in agriculture have economically benefited from the sale and purchase of agriculture and livestock products in hat bazaars taking place regularly in different places on either side. The increasing urbanisation and growth of towns in the Tarai and along the border inside Nepal has resulted in large inflow of goods from Indian side into Nepal. The open border has provided employment to the people on both sides in the transport sector as well.

Migration into Tarai prior to 1860 was constrained by restriction on the purchase of land by Indian nationals in Nepal. When the Far Western Tarai was restored to Nepal in 1860, the legal codes formulated by Prime Minister Jung Bahadur made provision for the allotment of land to Indian nationals through sale and purchase so as to appropriate income from the restored territory for himself, his families and favourites. This resulted in the large-scale migration of the Indian people from the adjoining border areas of India. Similarly Prime Minister Chandra Shumsher also initiated reclamation of the forest areas of the Tarai for agricultural purpose on the advice of J.V. Collier, an Indian Forest Officer. Collier himself became a contractor to clear the forest in Kailali district by extending railway line up to Godawari near the Siwalik foothills. Collier cleared the forest so rapidly that it alarmed the Government of Nepal which had to cancel the contract. It may also be noted that the sal forest of Nepal Tarai provided the timber for much needed railway sleepers for the expansion of Indian railways. Forests also provided the largest source of revenue to the government, even after the installation of democracy in 1951. The reclamation of the Tarai not only attracted the immigrants from India but also the hill people who were employed in government services in the Tarai. They purchased land in the Tarai and became Zamindar, the big landlords.

The installation of democracy in 1951 marked the unrestricted movement of the hill people in the Tarai as well as from India. It was further accelerated by malaria eradication programme launched in the Tarai in the late 1950s. This brought about a drastic change in the regional redistribution of population in Nepal. Malaria eradication programme was accompanied by land resettlement programmes for diverse target groups, such as landless people mostly from the hills; political sufferers; Gurkha ex-servicemen both of Nepalese, Indian and British armies; victims of natural disaster; Nepalese refugees from Burma; Tibetan refugees, and so on. The Tarai which accounted for only 35.2 percent of the total population of Nepal in 1952/54 had 46.7 percent of the total population of Nepal in 1991.

Regional Distribution of Population in Nepal

(in Percent)

Region	1952/54	1961	1971	1981	1991
Mountain	-	-	9.9	8.7	7.8
Hill	64.8	63.6	52.5	47.7	45.5
Tarai	35.2	36.4	37.6	43.6	46.7
Nepal	100.0	100.0	100.0	100.0	100.0

Source: Central Bureau of Statistics, HMG,Kathmandu, Nepal, 1991.

Population growth in the Tarai has shown the highest trend since 1961. It has been estimated that in the census of 2001 that has yet to be finalised, the Tarai only with 23.1 percent of the total land area of the country will have more than 50 percent of total population of Nepal.

The density of population in the adjoining districts of India is higher than in the adjoining areas of Nepal. However, development activities in the Tarai districts of Nepal have been responsible for migration of Indians into the Tarai. The division of Bihar state with the detachment of mineral wealth rich and industrial belt going to Jharkhand and the creation of Uttrakhand with the detachment of fertile Ganga plain in Uttar Pradesh might inevitably aggravate further the poverty of the districts of Bihar and Uttarkhand bordering Nepal and might increase immigration of Indians into Nepal. In view of the dearth of different skills among the Nepalese, the skilled manpower required for different development service activities comes from India and the process of replacing these migrant workers by Nepalese has been very slow due to strong competition from the most skilled migrant workers on the one hand and the lack of government policy and programmes to train Nepalese in these skills on the other hand. The failure of the country's education programme to produce manpower with different technical skills has resulted in the production of educated mass with limited demand base in the country's economy. The large number of unemployed educated youth in the country is creating serious social, economic and political problems for the family, society and the nation. There is no denying of the fact that the emerging Maoist problem of the country is related to this reality.

The socio-cultural aspect of migration involving migration of family members, kith and kin, relatives, local communities, is notable in the case of Indian migrants into Nepal Tarai from across the adjoining districts of India. One of the important socio-cultural aspects of migration on either side of the Nepal-India border is marriage migration. Usually age and sex selectivity of migration is characterised by predominance of able-bodied males. But in the case of migration on either side of the Nepal-India border, it is characterised by predominance of females over males. The 1991 census of Nepal revealed 378, 692 Indian born population in the Tarai, of which only 93,345 persons or 24.7 percent were males and 285, 347 persons or 75.3 percent were females. The available figure of Nepal born population in the four States of Bihar, Sikkim, U.P. and West Bengal, according to the 1981 census of India, recorded higher proportion of females in Bihar (39.0 %), Sikkim (52.7 %) and U.P. (56.5 %), while West Bengal had only 41.1 percent. In India as a whole the proportion of Nepal born females constituted 52.3 percent of the total, while in Nepal the India born females constituted 71.9 percent of the total. The India born population in Nepal accounted for 2.4 percent of the total population of Nepal, while the Nepal born population in India constituted 0.07 percent only. In the Tarai districts, the India born population represented 4.4 percent of the total population of Tarai. In the States of Bihar, West Bengal and U.P., Nepal born population accounted for 0.21, 0.001 and 0.09 percent respectively, while it was 6.84 percent of the total population in Sikkim. This clearly indicates the impact of India born population in Nepal compared to that of Nepal born population in India.

Communal disturbances in India have a direct bearing upon the increase in the magnitude of Indian immigrants into the Tarai. The sudden spurt in the increase of Muslim population in Nepal between 1981 and 1991 is a clear-cut instance. The Muslim population increased from 399,197 persons in 1981 to 653,218 persons in 1991, which means an increase of 38.9 percent over a decade. 96.7 percent of the Muslim population confined to the Tarai constitute 7.32 percent of the total population of the Tarai. The sudden increase in Muslim population may be attributed to the growth of garment industry in Nepal to a greater extent and to other activities to a certain extent, because the Muslim community possesses diverse occupational skills which other communities usually lack. Similarly, since 1984 the number of Sikh immigrants into Nepal has considerably increased. At present, there are six Gurudwaras in Nepal, namely, in Kathmandu, Lalitpur, Birganj, Nepalganj, Butwal and Dhangadhi of which the latter four are in the Tarai.

Quite obviously, development of agriculture, industry, commerce, transportation and other related activities in the Nepal Tarai has been attracting Indian immigrants from across the border. The very high growth of population in the Tarai has resulted in a growing demand for employment within the Tarai region itself.

The population living on either side of the Nepal-India border is overwhelmingly dependent on agriculture, and seasonal employment was open to them in the past in the agricultural sector in Punjab. With increased disturbances in Punjab, migration of population to this region virtually stopped. The ever-increasing immigrants from across the border into the Tarai have displaced the local population from their employment opportunities and they are migrating to the urban areas from the hills, particularly the Kathmandu Valley, and also to the urban areas of the Tarai. It is a universal phenomenon that migrants are hard working people and they can devote more time to their work because they are free from the day to day obligations of their families and society. This has indeed resulted in hatred among the local people towards the immigrants as they find it difficult to compete with the outsiders. The eagerness of the immigrants to secure citizenship certificate by hook or by crook has rather delayed the process of distribution of citizenship certificates to the bonafide population under constitutional provisions.

Large-scale migration of the outsiders in Northeastern India, Kashmir and Punjab has actually displaced migrants who have settled in these areas for generations, giving rise to the movement for 'sons of the soil'. There is every danger of this situation cropping up in Nepal as well, if efforts are not made to regulate migration. Indians of Nepalese origin being driven away from Northeastern states of India is a glaring instance. Nepal-India migration in the real sense represents the mutual exchange of poverty rather than prosperity.

The most serious and adverse impact of open and uncontrolled Nepal-India border has been in the form of growing and anti-social and lawless activities. The ever increasing crimes along the border has been a major concern for both governments since early nineteenth century, and the Treaty of 1855 was aimed at controlling these problems. However, the policy of open border has rather enhanced such activities. The unrestricted movement across the border has indeed been responsible for all sorts of criminal, anti-social and illegal activities such as robbery, theft, murder, smuggling of goods to evade custom duties, narcotic drugs trafficking, trafficking of girls, arms smuggling, smuggling of archaeological arts and artifacts and manuscripts, kidnapping for rnsoms, etc.

Since 1980s, Nepal-India border has developed into a thorough passage for the cross border movement of terrorists. In view of growing terrorism in Uttar Pradesh-Tarai border in Nepal, members of the Lok Sabha demanded the sealing of the Nepal India border. When Nepali political leaders and intellectuals raised their voice for controlling and regulating the movement of people across the border, their counterparts in India termed the Nepalese concern as an anti-Indian stand.

The use of muscle men for booth capturing and for electoral manipulations on either side of the border during elections is also not uncommon. Complete sealing of the major entry points to control such practices a day or two before elections has not been so effective as there are no provisions for patrolling along the border. It has been alleged that criminal elements have been harboured and provided protection by the political leaders and influential persons on either side of the border. This sort of activities also exists along the Nepal-China border. It is alleged that some of the influential political leaders on the Nepalese side in collaboration with the border customs officials are involved in smuggling of the Tibetans to the monasteries in Kathmandu, for which they are paid handsome amounts. The Tibetans who illegally cross the Nepal-China border are handed over by the Home Ministry to the UNHCR representative in Kathmandu, who in turn hands over them to the office of the Dalai Lama in India.

It is said that Tibetans in the rural areas who intended to raise their children as monks and nuns on account of their cultural tradition or for monetary gain are smuggled into Nepal as refugees. Nepalese professing Tibetan Buddhism and living along the Nepal-China border also get their children admitted to the monasteries in Kathmandu or in the monasteries run by the Dalai Lama. Most of the religious institutions in which there is manpower shortage to run temples, monasteries, churches, mosques, etc. are facing difficulty because men and women from the urban and developed rural areas have access to education, social awareness and modern amenities and way of life. So these religious institutions are attracting people from the backward and poor rural areas. The monk and nuns in numerous Tibetan Buddhist monasteries in the Kathmandu Valley and in other parts of the country can be cited as an instance in point. Similar situation exists in Sanskrit Pathshalas and Vedic Pathashalas and also in the religious Islamic Madrashas in the country.

In recent years, there has been sudden spurt in crimes such as theft, robbery, kidnapping and murder on both sides of the border as well as increase in terrorist activities on the Indian side. Open border has provided safe passage to criminals and terrorists. The incursion of Indian police inside Nepal without permission in search of criminals who fled into Nepal has hurt the sentiments of the Nepalese and is reported to have generated hatred against India. There has been a number of intrusions/ hot pursuits by Indian police-Manebhanjyang in December 1987, Delhi police raid in March 1994 and several other incidents near Nepalganj, Bhairahawa and Birganj, 90 per cent of these cases are of Indian origin (Mehata, 2001:21). The incursion of Indian police without permission of the Nepalese authorities in connection with manhunt in Baneswaor, Kathmandu is still fresh in the mind of the Nepalese. Such unauthorised incursions by the Indian police with blatant violation of international law and code of conduct need to be avoided.

Apart from tampering with the Nepal India border by the local people in the Indian side, the Indian government itself has been involved in the violating the norms of international boundary treaty. The construction of dams on the rivers flowing from Nepal just across the Nepal India boundary on Indian side has resulted in flooding and submergence of large tracts of Nepalese terri ries. It started with the Bagmati river. Recently, the construct n of dm over the Mirchiya river in India has submerged a large tract of Nepalese territory and threatened the submergence of the international heritage site of Lumbini, the birth place of Lord Buddha.

The recent deployment of the Nepalese army in the border customs checkposts needs serious reconsideration because of its sensitive nature and role in the national defence It has demoralised the customs personnel, and police already working in these checkposts are indirectly branded as corrupt. There is no guarantee that army personnel also might not follow the suit of corrupt customs personnel and police deployed in the border check-posts. The deployment of army in the border customs check-posts might cause unforeseen and unwarranted incidents. The recent sad incident along the disputed India-Bangladesh border is a glaring example of how hostility may arise between the two friendly countries. Considering the unresolved boundary demarcation along Nepal-India border, such army deployment needs serious consideration. Recently, clash between the local Indian and the Nepalese people regarding the Nepal-India border occurred in Kakarbhitta in the Mechi River.

There is a general feeling in Nepal that the Indian leaders and diplomatic personnel have a tendency to look upon Nepal with suspicion and distrust, particularly regarding Nepal's relations with China and Pakistan. This attitude reminds one of the British colonial legacy. During the exile of King Rana Bahadur Shah to Benares, the British East India Company became successful in exploiting the situation by entering into a treaty with the Nepalese King in 1801. One of the clauses of the treaty states, "The principals and officers of both Governments will cordially consider the friends and enemies of either State to be the friends and enemies of the other; and this consideration must ever remain permanent and in force, from generation to generation". (Aitchison, 1863:196). Though the treaty was abrogated by the treaty of 1804, most of the Indian leaders and diplomatic personnel as well as news media have not given up this colonial legacy from their mind.

Regarding the purchase of arms and ammunitions by Nepal from other countries, Nepal was required to have permission to import them via Indian territories from the Government of India. This preconditions envisaged by the British (Husain, 1970:170-9) was followed by the independent Government of India as it was incorporated in the letter of exchange of 1950 treaty. According to the 1965 Nepal-India Agreement on Arms Assistance, Nepal's response was rather lukewarm, because it was having arms assistance and purchase from other countries. In view of Nepal's confrontation against the rebel Khampas among the Tibetan refugees in Nepal who made forays in Chinese territories from across the Nepal-China border and the need for training the Nepalese army in modern weaponry and warfare so as to make them competent enough to work in the UN Peacekeeping Force, importation of arms, ammunition and vehicles by Nepal in 1989 became a pretext for India to impose economic blockade on Nepal which, however, hurt the Indian traders and businessmen rather than the Nepalese majority of whom live in the rural areas. During the 1950-51 revolution against the Rana regime, the Nepali Congress had to purchase arms from Burma because of India's unwillingness. After the installation of democracy, during the period of Prime Minister Matrika Prasad Koirala, those arms and ammunition in the hand of the Mukti Sena (who were posted in Nepal as para-military force) were destroyed in Khumaltar, Lalitpur under the supervision and presence of the Chief of the Indian Military Mission in Nepal. During this period Indian military check-posts were established along the important border posts along the Nepal-China border.

The attitude of Indian politicians and news media to view with suspicion any assistance Nepal gets from China and the debate in both Houses of Indian Parliament on Kathmandu-Kodari Highway linking Kathmandu with Lhasa and terming them as "military road capable of moving tanks" bear ample testimony to this fact. However, Prime Minister Indira Gandhi had to say, "China is a neighbour of Nepal and naturally they would like to remain friendly with China also. When the Chinese constructed a ring road around Kathmandu and Lalitpur, some Indian papers carried the news that the road is wide enough to land jet fighters. Frequent strains in relations between Nepal and India at the government level are not due to political, geographical, economic or cultural reasons, but due to the amateurish handling of some of the issues by Indian politicians (Sharma, 1970:2).

Recently the statement of Mr. K. R. Malkani of the Bharatiya Janata Party questioning the sovereignty and independence of Nepal and the statement of Mr. Thakerey. President of Shiva Sena in favour of Indian military intervention following the Royal Palace massacre are instances in point to hurt the sentiments of Nepalese and the friendly relations between Nepal and India. Indian news media are also responsible for spreading false news. The exaggerated and false news telecast through Indian televisions relating to the incidents and disturbances in Kathmandu in the aftermath of the Royal Palace massacre have been largely responsible for the drastic decline in the tourist flow from India and other countries.

Jawaharlal Nehru, the first Prime Minister of India who aspireed for and established cordial relations between Nepal and India, while addressing a press conference in New Delhi on 18 January 1961, had said, "Broadly speaking, our relations depend not really on any person's goodwill, on Nepal's goodwill, on that government or this government..............They depend on geography and history, which cannot be easily done away with" (Bhasin, 1970:55). The concept of territory and boundary is imbedded in the animal kingdom and mankind cannot be an exception. Many wars and battles have been fought over territorial and boundary dispute and are still continuing in the absence of mutual rapprochement over the demarcation of boundary between the two States. One must not forget the Nehru-Zhou-en Lai concept of Hindi_Chini Bhai Bhai turning into Sino-Indian war of 1962 over the border dispute..So Nepal and India must not overlook the issue of undefined border between the two countries. It is quite disheartening to note that both countries have not been able to resolve the boundary issue even during time span of two decades since the formation of a Joint Boundary Commission in 1981. The recent understanding reached between the two governments during the meeting between Prime Minister Atal Behari Vajpayee and Prime Minister Girija Prasad Koirala to complete the boundary demarcation within three years is praiseworthy. However, seriousness and an action plan required for its completion are still lacking.

There is a need of revision of the border treaty maps regularly at least every 5 year, because Nepal India boundary run through the inhabited area as well as along the rivers. Man made features are naturally appearing on both sides of the border with possibility of tampering the boundary and the no man's land as well as changes in the natural course of the rivers. This will certainly avoid misunderstanding and dispute that might arise, if the status of border is no monitored. An uncontrolled and open border, as stated earlier, constitutes the breeding ground for anti-social, criminal and illegal activities.

Regulation of the Nepal-India border had become urgent. In both Nepal and India, voter's identify card has become compulsory for the voters, and this will facilitate, to some extent, the task of regulating the movement of population on either side of the Nepal-India border. The need for both Nepal and India to provide employment to their citizens in their respective territories has become urgent in view of the growing xenophobia against immigrant workers. There is no denying the fact that Maoist insurgency in Nepal is basically related to the problem of growing unemployment. The unrestricted flow of migrant workers might further aggravate this problem. Similarly, India must have faced the same problem to a certain extent due to the migrant workers from Nepal. Both Nepal and India must realise the urgency of exploring an effective and pragmatic mechanism for the benefit of both countries and people. Therefore, keeping in view the welfare and development of people of the two countries, there is an urgent need to check and regulate the free as well as illegal movement of people and goods across the unpatrolled open border through intensive research, joint reviews and fruitful dialogues on diverse aspects of Nepal-India open border so that Nepal-India friendship can be further strengthened.

INSECURE BORDER MANAGEMENT OF NEPAL

Nepal is situated between two emerging Asian giants, China and India. The frontier of Nepal is surrounded on its south, east and west by India and on the north by China. China has expanded its economic market almost all over the world against the background of its emerging political scenario. And India is attaining economic prosperity in South Asia by enhancing its global political image. Historically, Nepal was elongated 1,415 km east to west from Tista to Kangra with an area of 267,575 sq. km. But it was shrunk to Mechi and Mahakali, after the Treaty of Sugauli on 4 March 1816 and subsequent Boundary

Treaties of 11 December 1816 and 1 November 1860 with British East India Company. As a result, present Nepal's territory has been limited to an area of 147,181 sq. km having 885 km east-west length.

Nepal has a regulated border management system with China, whereas there is an open border between Nepal and India. This paper analyses how Nepal's open border with India is faced with external threats due to cross border terrorism. It further analyses the implications of open border system in order to maintain law and order, peace and security not only in both the nations but also in other countries of South Asia. Besides, it describes what border management strategies are available between the two countries and how they are working in practice. It also emphasizes that the existing border management system needs some change to prevent cross border terrorism.

Historical outlook

Nepal-China border management : There is a regulated/ controlled border system between Nepal and China from historic time. It has a demilitarized zone of 20 km on either side of the borderline. However, there is a frequent infiltration of Tibetan refugees in a disguised manner to move to Dharmashala of India where the Dalai Lama resides. It is notable that compulsory ID Card system has been recently introduced for the inhabitants of Nepal-Tibet (China) frontier from 1 January 2006 to cross the border point. But earlier, authentic ID was not required for the inhabitants of 30 km of both the frontiers.

Nepal-India border management : If we look back at the history of border management of Nepal with India, it was a closed border system in ancient period. There was restriction on entry into Nepal, especially for third country nationals. In course of time, controlled border system was informally initiated after the Treaty of Sugauli of 1816 with the East India Company. Eventually, western people would require special permission from the Prime Minister. The open border system started unknowingly after the Boundary Treaty of 1860. However, passport or travel document was necessary to cross the border till 1957. The border between Nepal and India became more open after India's independence in 1947. It was wide open after the establishment of democracy in Nepal in 1950. The border became further wide open after the construction of Tribhuvan Highway in 1957 linking Katmandu, capital city of Nepal, to an Indian frontier town, Raxaul.

As a result, anyone could cross the international border and shuttle back and forth, many times a day, without any interrogation. As a consequence, Passport/permit system gradually and unknowingly disappeared after the connection of roadway. On the other hand, there was a kind of closed border system during economic blockade by India from 23 March 1989 to 30 June 1990 as India unilaterally closed its entire 22 border crossing points and 15 transit points for Nepal. Meanwhile, India has also adopted a kind of discretionary system from time to time. It unilaterally implemented the temporarily closed border system in some of the sensitive border crossing points.

For example, the Falelung border point of Taplejung district of Nepal is a case in point. This point was closed for the Nepalese nationals to go to India during 2004. But before this, India was allowing Nepalese nationals to enter India from this point, after depositing ID or Citizenship Certificate.

As another example, India has laid down unilaterally that the Nepalese nationals, who enter India from third country, must produce visa.

Tanka Lal Shrestha (Nepalese working in German Embassy, Kathmandu), while travelling by Indian Airline flight on 26 January 2005 from Lahore to New Delhi was obstructed by Immigration Officer asking him to produce visa. Earlier, ID card was sufficient for the Nepalese nationals.

In due course of time, open border system changed into regulated system for the air-route passengers travelling from Nepal to India and vice versa. ID Card system was introduced for air passengers of both the countries from 1 October 2000.

It was done after Indian Airline Aircraft with flight number IC-814 which took off for New Delhi from Katmandu had been hijacked on 24 December 1999. The plane ultimately landed at Kandahar, Afganistan.

Very recently, open border was transformed into regulated system in one of the land-routes at Nepalganj-Rupaidiya border crossing point from 1 November 2005. Both the governments have introduced regulated border management system to this point, as ID Card system has been made compulsory.

This is, more or less, a short account of the historical background of Nepal-India border management system. All these points show that Indo-Nepal border management is complex, as history tells.

Border Talks End in Stalemate, Again

China's growing presence in South Asia is accompanied by a hardening of its stance on the territorial dispute. This became evident at the last round of border talks held in Beijing between September 26-27, 2005. Defence analysts attribute the Chinese intransigence in resolving the border dispute to the rapidly shifting military balance of power in Beijing's favour on the Tibetan plateau. Since 1999, there has been a constant probing of the line of actual control, via frequent border crossings by Chinese border patrols in a manner designed to test Indian resolve, psychology, vulnerabilities and border intelligence.

With the near completion of the 1,118 kilometer (695 miles) Qinghai-Tibetan railway and other military infrastructure projects in Tibet, China "may be tempted to resort to force or coercion more quickly to press diplomatic advantage, advance security interests or resolve disputes," according to an unnamed senior Indian military officer.

The Chinese have also rebuffed India's pleas for a quick boundary settlement within a fixed timeframe. Even on Sikkim, the Chinese have deliberately decided to "go slow" on the implementation of their verbal promise after obtaining a written commitment on Tibet from India in June 2003 during Prime

Minister Atal Bihari Vajpayee's visit to China. From the Chinese standpoint, the concept of give and take vis-a-vis India could also damage China's image in South Asia as the predominant power.

China Opposes India's Bid for U.N.S.C. Seat

Another sign of pro-active containment of India is Beijing's opposition to any move to expand the veto-holding permanent membership of the U.N. Security Council. With the exception of China, the remaining four permanent members have voiced their support for expansion of U.N.S.C. permanent membership, with the United States supporting Japan while Russia, France and Britain are supporting India's bid. The Chinese Foreign Ministry spokesperson has now made it clear that while Beijing is willing to see India occupy a seat in the semi-permanent or non-permanent category, it remains opposed to having its Asian rivals — India or Japan — sitting in the U.N.S.C. permanent membership category. The fact that China has now emerged as the major obstacle to U.N.S.C. reforms can be attributed to divergent world views held by Beijing and other world capitals. Similar to how the U.S. seeks to prevent the emergence of a peer competitor at the global level, China wants to prevent the rise of a peer competitor at the regional level. This stance leads Washington to support a multipolar Asia (with a strong Japan and powerful India to balance China) but a unipolar world (with the United States as the sole hyper-power without any peers). In contrast, Beijing prefers a unipolar Asia-Pacific (with China as the sole superpower without any peers) and a multipolar world (with the U.S., E.U., Russia and China as four major power poles). In contrast with both Washington and Beijing, New Delhi champions multipolarity at both regional and global levels. Beijing's attitude to the expansion of the U.N. Security Council is a clear indication that it will not countenance the emergence of an Asian peer competitor.

The East Asia Summit

In early 2005, Beijing dispatched its diplomats to Laos (then "country convener for India" within the A.S.E.A.N. regional grouping) and other Southeast Asian capitals to dissuade them from lobbying for India's membership (albeit, unsuccessfully) in the East Asia Summit (E.A.S.) scheduled for its first inaugural meeting in Kuala Lumpur in December 2005. However, with the exception of Malaysia, Beijing did not find any takers for its anti-India stance primarily because nearly all Southeast Asian countries supported India's participation in the E.A.S. seeing it as a useful counterweight to China's growing power. Having failed to keep India (and Australia and New Zealand) out of the new regional grouping, the Chinese Foreign Ministry attempted to dominate the emerging East Asian Community (E.A.C.) by dividing it into two blocs: the core or primary states with China as the leading, dominant player inside the A.S.E.A.N.+3 (China, South Korea, Japan) and the peripheral or secondary states of India, Australia and New Zealand (or, "outsiders" as the People's Daily editorial of December 7, 2005 described them).

Beijing remains leery of India's great power pretensions and attempts to extend its influence in China's backyard. Seeing New Delhi's "Look East" policy as part of a wider "congage China" strategy unveiled by the Washington-Tokyo-New Delhi grouping, the thrust of Chinese diplomacy is to confine India to the periphery of a future East Asia Community and to foil India's efforts to break out of the South Asian straitjacket. The People's Daily commentator reacted sharply to the Indian prime minister's proposal for an Asian Economic Community (A.E.C.): "India's proposal is not warmly responded [to] as each country has its own considerations."

Apparently, China's "own considerations" are primarily geostrategic in nature. Beijing fears that India's participation in the core group would shift the balance of power and make the E.A.C. less susceptible to domination by China. Therefore, in the run-up to the East Asia Summit in Malaysia and days after obtaining observer status in S.A.A.R.C., China's message to India was crystal clear. Finding India relegated to the outer circle, an Indian diplomat expressed his disappointment over the decision to entrench the A.S.E.A.N.+3 framework within the E.A.S.: "To state that A.S.E.A.N. is in the driver's seat, the passengers have a right to know where they are going."

Energy Fuels Feud

Both face growing demand for energy and are locked in fierce competition for stakes in overseas oil and gas fields in Asia, Africa, Latin America, and the Middle East. In the energy competition stakes, however, China currently has an overwhelming lead because China has linked energy to its national security policy for longer than India has. Moreover, China has been more successful in diversifying its energy resources, developing a varied network of oil suppliers from Africa to Latin America.

China's superior financial muscle and diplomatic clout also enables it to win friends and contracts for natural resources. As 2005 progressed, Chinese oil firms went out of their way (excessively overpaying for assets) to thwart India's attempts to secure international energy assets in Kazakhstan, Ecuador, Angola, Nigeria, and Myanmar. Clearly, India's efforts to secure supplies cannot succeed unless and until New Delhi creates incentives (arms, aid and diplomatic support) or economic dependencies (via trade) for the supplying country to sell oil and gas to India. Ironically, the day India's oil minister, Mani Shankar Aiyar, left for Beijing to discuss energy-cooperation joint ventures, Myanmar announced that its gas would be flowing east to China instead of north and west to India. Despite the conclusion of energy cooperation agreements, China is likely to go solo in its quest for energy security; energy competition, rather than energy cooperation, will be the norm.

As finding new sources of oil becomes more difficult, there are bound to be areas of friction between Asia's two fastest growing economies. While China views the Andaman Sea off Myanmar's coast as an important source of oil to fuel the economic expansion of China's western provinces, India sees China's presence in the Bay of Bengal an unwelcome development. The Chinese Navy has asserted its legitimate right to operate in the Indian Ocean to ensure security of its oil and trade transiting through the region. China already has better relations with the two largest energy suppliers — Saudi Arabia and Iran — than does India. With Pakistan as its long-term military ally, China also has closer relations with four important Islamic countries (Saudi Arabia, Iran, Pakistan and Bangladesh) than India, the United States and Japan.

As a major trading country and a future world power, China is now laying the groundwork for a naval presence along maritime chokepoints in the South China Sea, the Malacca Straits, the Indian Ocean and the Strait of Hormuz in the Persian Gulf through acquisition of naval bases in Cambodia, Myanmar, Bangladesh and Pakistan to protect its long-term economic security interests.

Sooner rather than later, China's military alliances and forward deployment of its naval assets in the Pakistani, Bangladeshi and Burmese ports would prompt India to respond in kind by seeking access to the Vietnamese (Cam Ranh Bay), Taiwanese (Kao-hsiung) and Japanese (Okinawa) ports for the forward deployment of Indian naval assets to protect India's shipping and trade routes and access to energy resources from the Russian Sakhalin province.

NEPALI PRESS AND THE PUBLIC

The restoration of multiparty democracy in 1990 ushered in a new era of liberalism, freedom and pluralism in the public sphere. Following the promulgation of the new constitution, sweeping legislative and legal reforms have been introduced, ensuring freedom and dignity of the fourth estate.

In general, the Nepali press upholds the Anglo-American ideals of the press (Pokhrel, 1998). The press often claims itself to be the "Fourth Estate," and given its pivotal role in waging a campaign against the autocratic Panchayat Regime (1970-1990) and subsequently contributing greatly in the restoration of democracy in 1990, the Nepali mainstream press holds significance in the political development in Nepal. American media scholar James Carey's observed that journalism and politics cannot be thought as two separate independent domains of activity; rather, they are related actively, symbiotically; and they can only be known via their mutual and active adaptations which are cooperative and antagonistic by turns; one can only be known in the light of the other (Carey, 1999). Carey's observation holds true in case of Nepal.

But few realize Carey's remark that without journalism there cannot be democracy, and without democracy there cannot be journalism either (Carey, 1999). Kathmandu's press— after all more than half of the 800 plus dailies, weeklies and other periodicals in the country are published in this city— is preoccupied more with Lippmannian ideal of centralization (national standards, national politics, national economy, and national culture) than with Deweyian ideals of decentralization (local standards, local politics, local economy and local culture). With the exception of a few newspapers, almost all dailies, even two-page tabloids of seemingly local nature, prefer to attach in their mastheads the "prestige" phrase "the national newspaper." So much so that *Sandhyakalin,* the largest selling and the popular local tabloid, claims to be "the national daily" although a cursory glance would suffice to determine its very local taste.

Kathmandu's nine broadsheet national dailies— actually national in scope—do spare one page each for local issues and this space is regularly devoted to straightforward factual reporting. While private owned media tend to be creative and innovative in some respects, the government owned publications, which include two national dailies, a weekly, and four magazines, devote their entire resources for government propaganda and national politics. The official media are numerically small but very influential and resourceful. In contrast, the private press is numerically superior, free and assertive but deficient in resources. They have to compete among themselves for a limited readership and subsist largely on market sales. One of the reasons for low readership is that Nepal is still predominantly an oral culture, and with literacy rate less than forty per cent and private sector media just over a decade young, Lerner and Schramm's observation that Nepal's communication system is in the initial stage of development may still hold true. The situation is somewhat different, at least in Kathmandu. The City's 70.62 per cent (*NHDR, 1998,* p. xxiii) literacy rate is the indication, if not of availability then of a good potential of newspaper readership. The city's per capita income of $400, which is double the national average, is an indication of greater purchasing power of the public as compared to people from the rural areas. But, unfortunately, newspaper sales are extremely low. Even the largest selling dailies do not exceed a circulation of 100,000 copies. The combined copies of all dailies may not even reach 400,000 copies a day, which means less than a quarter of the population of the city rely on newspapers for their daily diet of news and current affairs. This only points to the need to attract more readerships, and one way to do this as they are doing in America is to apply public journalism techniques. Public journalism, touted for its deliberative values, may be used to explore the reasons behind public resignation from the press as well as public affairs.

6

Nepal-Relations with China

The first recorded official relations with China and Tibet occurred near the middle of the seventh century. By the eighteenth century, Nepalese adventurism in Tibet led to Chinese intervention in favour of Tibet. The resultant Sino-Nepalese Treaty of 1792 provided for tribute-bearing missions from Nepal to China every five years as a symbol of Chinese political and cultural supremacy in the region. In the Anglo-Nepalese War of 1814-16, China refused Nepal's requests for military assistance and, by default, surrendered its dominant position in Nepal to the growing British influence. However, it appeared to be expedient for Nepal to retain the fiction of a tributary relationship with China in order to balance China against Britain.

Nepal invaded Tibet in 1854. Hostilities were quickly terminated when China intervened, and the Treaty of Thapathali was concluded in March 1856. The treaty recognized the special status of China, and Nepal agreed to assist Tibet in the event of foreign aggression. Relations between Nepal and China and Tibet continued without critical incident until 1904, when British India sent an armed expedition to Tibet and Nepal rejected Tibet's request for aid to avoid risking its good relations with Britain. Beginning in 1908, Nepal stopped paying tribute to China.

By 1910, apprehensive of British activity in Tibet, China had reasserted its claim to sovereign rights in Tibet and feudatory missions from Nepal. In 1912 Nepal warned the

Chinese representative at Lhasa that Nepal would help Tibet attain independent status as long as it was consistent with British interests. Nepal broke relations with China when the Tibetans, taking advantage of the Chinese revolution of 1911, drove the Chinese out.

When the Chinese communists invaded Tibet in 1950, Nepal's relations with China began to undergo drastic changes. Although annual Tibetan tribute missions appeared regularly in Nepal as late as 1953, Beijing had started to ignore the provisions of the 1856 treaty by curtailing the privileges and rights it accorded to Nepalese traders, by imposing restrictions on Nepalese pilgrims, and by stopping the Tibetan tributary missions. The break between Kathmandu and Beijing continued until 1955, when relations were reestablished with China. The two countries established resident ambassadors in their respective capitals in July 1960.

In 1956 the Treaty of Thapathali was replaced by a new treaty under which Nepal recognized China's sovereignty over Tibet and agreed to surrender all privileges and rights granted by the old treaty. In 1962 Nepal withdrew its ambassador from Tibet and substituted a consul general. An agreement on locating and demarcating the Nepal-Tibet boundary was signed in March 1960. Within a month, another Treaty of Peace and Friendship was signed in Kathmandu. The Sino-Nepal Boundary Treaty was signed in Beijing in October 1961. The treaty provided for a Sino-Nepal Joint Commission to agree on questions regarding alignment, location, and maintenance of the seventy-nine demarcation markers. The commission's findings were attached to the original treaty in a protocol signed in January 1963.

During the Sino-Indian conflict of 1962, Nepal reasserted its neutrality and warned that it would not submit to aggression from any state. Although the warning was directed at China, Nepal continued to support China's application for membership in the United Nations. A potential source of irritation in Sino-Nepalese relations was relieved in January 1964 when China agreed to release the frozen funds of Nepalese traders from Tibetan banks.

An agreement to construct an all-weather highway linking Kathmandu with Tibet was signed in October 1961—a time when neither Kathmandu nor Beijing had cordial relations with New Delhi. The Kathmandu-Kodari road opened in May 1967 but did not yield any commercial or trade benefits for Nepal. Because of the severe restrictions imposed by Beijing even before the road was opened, Kathmandu had closed its trade agencies in Tibet by January 1966. Although the highway had no economic or commercial value and was not viable as an alternate transit route, it was of strategic military importance to China. The highway established direct links between two major Chinese army bases within 100 kilometers of Kathmandu to forward bases at Gyirong in Tibet. Throughout the latter half of the 1960s, Nepal's relations with China remained fairly steady. One exception was the belligerent activities of the Chinese officials in Nepal who eulogized and extolled the successes of the Cultural Revolution (1966-76) during the summer of 1967.

The emergence of a strident and confident India in the early 1970s introduced some new dimensions in Nepal's China policy. King Birendra did not abandon the policy of equal friendship between China and India but wanted to woo China to counter India's growing influence in the region. China had implicitly recognized India's predominance in the region, however, and was willing to oblige Nepal only to the extent of pledging support in safeguarding its national independence and preventing foreign interference.

In an open challenge to India's primacy in Nepal, Nepal negotiated a deal for the purchase of Chinese weapons in mid-1988. According to India, this deal contravened an earlier agreement that obliged Nepal to secure all defence supplies from India. Nepal's overtures to China also had economic implications. Ever since an economic aid agreement between China and Nepal had been concluded in 1956, China's steadily increasing economic and technical assistance was being used to build up Nepal's industrial infrastructure and implement economic planning. According to a 1990 report, an estimated

750 Chinese workers were in Nepal, most of them working on road-building crews and small-scale development projects. The foreign trade balance also was in Nepal's favour. China reportedly has ceded some territory to Nepal to facilitate boundary demarcation and has endorsed Nepal as a zone of peace.

THE DYNAMISM OF CHINESE FOREIGN POLICY

The essence of Nepal's long term China policy should be anchored in an assessment of the rapid politico-social transformations underway in this country and more importantly in how these transformations can be consistent with augmenting Nepal's own economic development and more generally Nepal's national interests. This old Chinese aphorism literally alludes to the ever changing nature of things-"Thirty years the East River, thirty years the West River" (the river is the same but its course changes). Its application runs in the realm of philosophy but equally in Chinese politics and foreign policy. Analyses of Chinese politics and international relations generated in the western media commonly make the mistake of straight-jacketing China in a "time bubble" situated in the past and not in the present and therefore focus too closely on a static interpretation of Communist ideology, on Tibet and Xianziang and human rights, on nationalism, Tianamen, on Chinese military modernization, and so on and so forth. But as a noted Chinese scholar points out, "China has been changing in a constantly changing world...Chinese society is being de-politicized. China is now enjoying sustained economic growth, its society is diversifying and the influence of ideology is reduced".

Countries like Nepal in the process of consolidating bilateral relations with China should appreciate the nature of this change and craft their policies accordingly. The essence of Nepal's long term China policy should be anchored in an assessment of the rapid politico-social transformations underway in this country and more importantly in how these transformations can be consistent with augmenting Nepal's own economic development and more generally Nepal's national interests. Whether by coincidence or otherwise, China has appeared to witness profound changes during the course of every thirty years.

From the May Forth Movement in 1919 to the founding of the New People's Republic of China in 1949, China was engaged in a struggle against imperialism and feudalism; from 1949 to 1978 which broadly marks the year of Opening Up and Reform, China expended considerable efforts towards modernization and the laying down of a groundwork for its future rise; and for 30 years from 1978 to the hosting of the Olympic Games in 2008, China actively participated in the international division of labour and worked hard for its resurgence.

Moreover, the number 9 which is considered auspicious in China has been used to present an extraordinary formulation that conveys the dynamism and flexibility of the Chinese state, namely that it was in 1949 when Socialism saved China; that in 1979, Capitalism which saved China; that in 1989 it was China which saved Socialism; and finally, that in 2009, it is China which is saving Capitalism! The point is that China has been changing rapidly and her foreign policy has also reflected this, yet routinely China is presented in much more static terms with repercussions in the policy sector. Nepal should make every effort therefore to understand the broad spectrum of the Chinese state and situate its policy accordingly so as to the lay the foundations of a bilateral relationship that has the potential to be one of the most pivotal in Asia in the years ahead.

As Yang Jiemian of The Shanghai Institute of International Studies and younger brother of the current Chinese Foreign Minister Mr. Yang Jiechi has pointed out, "in the past three decades China has abandoned the erroneous ideology-centric approach to developing relations with foreign countries according to their social systems and replaced it with a more balanced approach to energetically developing relations with countries with differing social systems, cultural values and heritages and at different development levels". Indeed, this is the reason why the number of countries with which China enjoys diplomatic relations has increased from 120 in 1979 to 171 by 2008, and furthermore why China and particularly the Chinese Communist Party as the ruling party has over time disregarded ideological differences in party to party contacts.

Marking a shift in the Communist Party of China's rather narrow focus on developing international relations solely with Communist parties in other countries, even as early as the mid-1950s, in a meeting with a delegation of the British Labour Party, Chairman Mao Zedong commented that "We believe that different social systems can coexist peacefully". Subsequently in a meeting in October 1954 with Indian Prime Minister Nehru, Chairman Mao stated that "two countries, or two parties; can cooperate in spite of different ideologies and social systems". It is therefore somewhat surprising when many analysts in Nepal and even abroad seem to naively assume that the People's Republic of China and the Maoist Party of Nepal enjoy special (exclusive) rapport, whereas in fact this would be a gross underestimation of the great flexibility and nuance that inheres in the Chinese system. What should be pointed out here is the broader framework which animates Chinese foreign policy itself, which is that "China has laid out well-structured and mutually reinforcing plans in its diplomatic strategy under the guideline of regarding relations with major powers as the linchpin, with neighbouring countries as of primary importance, with developing countries as the foundation and multilateral diplomacy as an important arena in its diplomatic activities". These three sets of relationships with major powers, neighbouring countries and the developing world which are perceived to be at the core of China's foreign relations are further perceived to be "mutually reinforcing, mutually supportive and mutually-impacting....,[with] multilateral institutions [serving] to link the three together, lumping bilateral, regional and global issues as part and parcel of an integral whole".

What does this mean in the context of Nepal-China relations? What it means is that if Nepal truly wishes to promote this bilateral relationship to a strategically important level,

Nepal can no longer afford to bask in the 2000 year history between the two countries and dwell on the architects and princesses of yesteryear. Substantial efforts are required to first understand the significance of Nepal to China (and vice versa) at the bilateral level, then regional level and finally at the global level, and then set out to create a policy framework that cuts across ideological and party divisions.

The friendship at the people to people level has been enduring and solid between our two countries but at the level of policy many gaps and weakness are clearly visible; these must be eliminated gradually in order to elevate Nepal-China relations to a broader plane, to deliver tangible benefits to people on the ground, and finally to demonstrate that Panchasheel or the Five Principles of Peaceful Coexistence are very much relevant in the effective conduct of contemporary diplomacy.

The Deng Xiao-ping era in China witnessed the traditional concepts of struggle, war and rivalry being eclipsed by new concepts of international cooperation centred on reconciliation, peace and harmony in China's foreign policy, which explains why from a position of more or less "self-enclosure" in the 1960s and 1970s wherein China's contacts with the outside world were largely limited and wherein China stood on the edge of the international arena, China is now unequivocally at the centre of the world stage and an insider to the mainstream international system. China is now party to nearly 300 international treaties and more than 130 international organizations, and participates actively in almost all regional mechanisms in its periphery such as the Asia Pacific Economic Cooperation Organization, 10+1, 10+3, the Shanghai Cooperation Organization, besides playing a pivotal role in working towards the creation of a stable security regime in East Asia based on the Six-Party Talks on the North Korean nuclear issue.

In other words, China's foreign policy has undergone a process of modernization in the past 30 years which shows that it is becoming more scientific, professional, democratic and institutionalized. This is nowhere more apparent than in the fact that after 30 years of reform, "foreign policy decision-making in China has been transformed from a unitary approach to an integrated, multi-echelon one" whose most salient feature perhaps is reinforced inter agency coordination. In other words, "an integrated structure of diplomatic work is taking shape: diplomatic activities in China have been broadened to involve all institutions including government agencies, political parties, and civil society groups in all fields-political, economic, academic, cultural, scientific, technological and military."

NEPAL: FOREIGN EMPLOYMENT AND NEED FOR A REFINED FOREIGN POLICY

Most of the people use to go to different countries in order to look for foreign employment, higher education, migration etc. In the globalization age, the mobility of the people from one country to another country has become the potential destination for the foreign employment or migration in the recent years.

In 1768, since the unification of the country- Nepal, the Nepalese people have gradually started to settle their livelihood across the national border. In the history of foreign employment of Nepal, the Nepalese people had formally taken initiative for having employment in the foreign countries in the early 19th century. It is noticed that migration had taken place since 1814 through Gorkha Soldiers recruited under the British Army.

The Nepalese people have started to move in the Gulf countries since 1985 for foreign employment. Such trend for foreign employment has been increasingly continued in the recent years. It is also recorded that 107 countries are open for foreign employment as decided by the Nepal Government. Different data in relation to the employment in the foreign countries are available. The inconsistency of available data may confuse the people (Readers). However, it is also estimated that more than 1.4 million Nepalese citizens are working in various sectors in various countries.

It is noted that Malaysia is the top destination country where around 73,000 Nepalese people are estimated to be working in the countries like Qatar, Saudi Arabia, UAE, Kuwait, Bahrain, Israel etc. It shows that people are taking keen interest in foreign employment. This has greatly helped reduce unemployment problem on the one hand and generate much income and volume of remittances on the other. It can be claimed that the remittances have helped support for the social transformation and increase of business relation with the foreign countries.

The contribution of remittance to GDP was increasingly significant over the years. It is also reported that the remittances are also informally channeled, and that of remittance from the formal channel is recorded to have been as approximately US $ 1 billion every year in the country. Looking at the contribution in the national economy the remittance has played a vital role during a decade- long armed conflict and reducing poverty to some extent. This is a good indication for the interest the country. But it has to be maintained the country's position outside the world. In fact the remittance is the invisible source of national income. It is also expected that it may increase in the following days if its source or mechanism is developed in a transparent manner, and if its channel is through banks. Besides them remittance policy, system, process, cooperation, coordination, documentation, programs, promotions etc. must be required to be improved.

As mentioned earlier, the Nepalese workers are taking keen interest for the foreign employment in order to find out better opportunities. However, there exists challenge as well as opportunities. It is also reported that most of the Nepalese workers have been exploited not getting the amount of remuneration as mentioned in their agreement papers. They have not been informed the nature of their job. As a result, they have to face accident, physical abuse, injuries, grief and even unexpected deaths etc. due to the unknown nature of their jobs. In some of cases, their jobs have not been secured because of not meeting employer's needs. In such circumstances, new jobs have to be looked for. They will have to approach to the broker for seeking new jobs for them who may cheat them in terms of taking much commission from job seekers. This type of exploitation is happening time to time. These are the bitter experiences and obstacles the Nepalese workers have been facing. Such incident takes place due to lack of awareness, orientation, training, inadequate information, alien culture and language barriers, fraudulent activities etc. It is therefore, necessary that all the concerned persons have to be very serious in order to avoid cheating and illegal activities.

To avoid such unpleasant incident the Nepalese workers who are going abroad, they should be properly oriented or trained about the labour legal provision of the labour law of the said countries, discipline, manner, technology and technical and other related awareness. Likewise, it is essential to monitor channels, terms and conditions before the implementation of actions.

The management of foreign employment and remittance are facing complexities. To minimize them, there should be an agreement through the diplomatic channel between both the countries of demand and supply of job. It is also required to sincerely handle the issues created. Recently, it is also mentioned that the Government of Nepal has signed labour agreements with the Republic of Korea, State of Qatar and the United Arab Emirates (UAE). Since the signatory countries are committed to be responsible and accountable for settling issues amicably, it is expected to protect the Nepalese workers going abroad in order to make this sector much secure, utilization of the remittance in investment sector or in productive sector promoting foreign employment.

The policy should be strengthened and appropriate policies should be adopted for looking after long term point of view. The administrative sector handled by the bureaucratic level has to make them very effective and efficient for strengthening regulatory activities and to resolve the problems. The recruiting agencies have to take responsibility and accountability for making their dealing transparent. The Nepalese workers, who want to go to the interested country have to be very serious. They should have necessary information and details of jobs are to be collected whether the agency is reliable or not. The new Foreign Employment Act and the Labour Migration policy have to be implemented to protect the labour rights of the concerned persons.

The present diplomacy agendas – economic, social, culture, tourism, hydro-power, trade and commerce etc. under the Nepal's foreign policy are to be seriously considered in a positive way. In the new context, foreign employment is also one of the burning or crucial agendas of diplomacy among them the present diplomacy must facilitate to promote many economic sectors including poverty reduction.

As mentioned earlier, the remittances have generated national economic growth. This is the high time to put emphasis on the top priority. Certainly, foreign employment has caused many implications on carrying out the foreign policy in a pragmatic way. However, the diplomatic missions have to take timely initiations and to play active role to control and protect foreign employment and to maintain bilateral relation and responsibilities in relation to the Nepalese workers in the foreign labour market. It can be suggested that the labour desk should be installed if it is required in the particular identified missions as per heavy size of the labour market. The government/ diplomatic mission has to take into account for establishing welfare fund and make contributions from its own resource and collecting a certain amount of contribution from the Nepalese workers going aboard and working in the foreign countries where they are working.

It is also essential to reorient on foreign policy in the days ahead. There should be mutual coordination and cooperation between the delivering and receiving countries. To raise voice, on behalf of the Nepalese workers the frequent exchange visits at high level, diplomatic level, bureaucratic levels and track II levels are required for making good relationship between both the countries. In addition, there should be a close coordination among the ministries of labour, finance, foreign, and departments under their respective ministries to establish good networking between the concerned countries for effective solution to avail opportunities from the foreign employment to boost up Nepalese economy

NEPAL-CHINA RELATIONS 2007

China and Nepal are close neighbours on the two sides of the Himalayan Mountains and have a long history of friendly ties. It is said that more than two thousand years ago, Manjushri came all the way from the Wutai Mountains in China to Nepal. He cut open the mountain with his sword and drained the water from the lake, thus creating the Kathmandu Valley. This beautiful legend gives vivid expression to the ardent desire of our two peoples for friendship. Historical records show that the friendly exchanges of China and Nepal date back to as early as the mid-7th century. At that time, China and Nepal already started exchanging emissaries. Fahien, a Chinese eminent monk in the Jin Dynasty and Huen Tsang, another Chinese eminent monk in the Tang Dynastry, came to Lumbini, birthplace of Lord Buddha, on pilgrimages. Songtsen Gompo, King of the Tubo Kingdom in the Tang Dynasty married a Nepalese princess Bhrikuti. The Nepalese artisan Arniko built a Buddhist pagoda in Lhasa in the Yuan Dynasty. The White Pagoda in Beijing's Miao Ying Temple was also built under his supervision. All these stories and historical facts show that China-Nepal traditional friendship is solidly based.

Since the establishment of diplomatic relations in 1955, the friendship and cooperation between China and Nepal. This owes much to the commitment and dedication of several generations of Chinese and Nepalese leaders. Such friendship is a great asset of our two peoples. The leaders of, both past and present, have brought about the flowering of China-Nepal friendship with their wisdom, vision and unremitting efforts. Thanks to their untiring efforts made over half a century, exchanges and cooperation between China and Nepal in political, diplomatic, economic and trade, cultural, educational and other fields have borne rich fruit. Indeed, China-Nepal relations have become a model of friendly cooperation for countries of different social systems and neighbouring countries to live in friendship and harmony.

To look back the friendly history of China-Nepal relations, three obvious characteristics can be easily concluded, which have enabled China-Nepal friendship to maintain its strong momentum of growth over the years. The first is trust. The two countries never threat each other, harm each other or doubt each other; but always respect each other, believe each other and help each other. The Chinese Government and people firmly pursue the principle of non-interference in the internal affairs of other countries, have never interfered with the internal affairs of Nepal and highly respect the road of development chosen by the Nepalese people. We believe that the Nepalese Government and people have the political wisdom and capabilities to solve their own problems. On our part, we appreciate the understanding, solidarity and support that the Government and people of Nepal have given to China in its endeavour for peaceful development.

The second is equality. The Chinese Government and people firmly pursue the principle that a country is equal with others no matter how big or small it is. Following that, China has all along developed relations on the base of equality with Nepal. We consistently support Nepal in its effort to safeguard sovereignty, independence and territorial integrity. In the past 50 years, abiding by the Five Principles of Peaceful Coexistence, through equal dialogue, communication and coordination, China and Nepal have made excellent cooperation and achieved great accomplishments in bilateral political relations, regional affairs and international forums.

The third is sincerity. China treats Nepal as its closest neighbour and best friend. Although China isn't a rich country, it has provided assistance and cooperation to Nepal in all the fields within its own capacity. Over the past 50 years, with China's financial and technical assistance, more than 30 projects have been completed in Nepal. As recognized by people of all circles in Nepal, these projects have played a constructive role in the social and economic development of Nepal. The Arniko Highway, the Ring Road, stadium and the Birendra International Convention Centre, assisted by China, are among the best examples. In return, the Nepalese Government and people has shown friendly sentiments to China and delivered its valuable support to Chinese people. We highly appreciate the strong support Nepal has given to us over the years on the questions of Taiwan and Tibet and other major issues related to China's sovereign rights and interests.

In recent years, the relations between China and Nepal have developed more rapidly. The top leaders exchanged visits frequently and the two countries carried out cooperation smoothly. In the political field, frequently high-level visits have greatly enhanced the mutual understanding and trust between our two countries. In the year of 2006 only, in which great changes took place in Nepal, H.E. Mr. Tang Jiaxuan, the State Councilor of China, H.E. Mr. Wu Dawei, Vice Foreign Minister, visited Nepal, expressing our strong and continuous support to Nepal despite of the changes in Nepal's politics. Likewise, Hon. Mr. K.P. Sharma Oli, Deputy Prime Minister and Minister for Foreign Affairs of Nepal, visited China, reiterating that the new Government of Nepal would insistently support China on the issue of Taiwan, Tibet and other issues of China's core interests. In January, 2007, H.E. Mr. Li Tieying, Deputy Speaker of National People's Congress of the People's Republic of China, paid a visit to Nepal, which has strengthened the exchanges and cooperation between the parliaments of the two countries.

The bilateral economic and trade relations have kept a healthy developmental momentum. According to the Chinese Customs, the total trade volume in 2006 reached US$ 268 million, with 36.5% increase over previous year. During the bilateral visits in 2006, the Chinese Government has announced to provide grant assistance of RMB120 million and concessional loan of US$ 200 million to Nepal.

We are also glad to see that the people-to-people contacts between our two countries have unfolded rapidly and smoothly over the past years. In 2001, the two countries signed the

Memorandum of Understanding on Tourism Cooperation, including Nepal into the list of the tourism destination for outbound Chinese travelers. Later on, the two countries signed "Air Service Agreement", according to which, Air China opened a direct air link between China and Nepal in 2004, by route of Chengdu-Lasha-Kathmandu. In addition, the China Southern Airline has also started operating air service between Guangzhou and Kathmandu since February, 2007. Likewise, the Nepal Airline is operating air service between Kathmandu and Shanghai, Kathmandu and Hongkong.

China and Nepal have also maintained sound coordination and cooperation in regional and international affairs such as peace, development, human rights and UN reform. We share the common views on many issues related to our mutual concern. The relations between the two armies are an important component of the overall relations between China and Nepal. In the past years, the military relations and cooperation between China and Nepal have experienced continuous development. Nearly all the former Army Chiefs and Defence Secretaries of Nepal have visited China. The Defence Minister and the General Chief of Staff of China have also visited Nepal. China has rendered help and assistance to Nepal within its own capacity. The two armies have conducted good cooperation in personnel training as well. Since 1998, the Nepal Army has sent officers and soldiers to study in Chinese military universities. In the academic year of 2006/2007 in particular, 21 officers and soldiers of the Nepal Army went to China for training. China has also sent military officers to participate in the adventure trainings organized by the Nepal Army since 2002.

As looking across the globe, it is easy to come to the conclusion that peace, stability, cooperation and development are the calling of the times and the common aspiration of the mankind. Both China and Nepal face a historical opportunity to develop. By seizing this opportunity, the two neighbouring countries should build on past achievements and push ahead to bring China-Nepal good-neighborliness, friendship and cooperation to a new height. No matter what changes take place in Nepal, China's friendly policy towards Nepal will remain unchanged.

In recent years, Nepal has been affected by conflicts and instability. As an immediate neighbour and close friend of Nepal, China has shown great concern. We have also tried our best to play a constructive role in urging all sides in Nepal to solve problems through dialogues and talks. To our great joy, under the endeavors of diligent, sapiential and brave Nepalese people, Nepal is now heading to a road of peace, stability, economic development and social prosperity. The Chinese Government and people respect political system and road of development chosen by Nepalese people, and sincerely hope that all constitutional forces in Nepal will set store by the fundamental interest of the country and people, and seek to appropriately settle the current difficulties and problems through dialogues, based on the maintenance of Nepal's independence, sovereignty and national integrity. The Chinese Government welcomes the progress made in the peace process. We believe that all the concerned parties in Nepal would continue to push forward the peace process, benefit the Nepalese people and make contributions to the peace, stability and development of this region.

The Chinese Government will continue to pursue a policy of friendship towards Nepal and attach great importance to developing the comprehensive and friendly relations with Nepal. We are committed to developing friendship and partnership with our neighbours, and strive to become a good neighbour, partner and friend of them. This is a solemn and long-term pledge of the Chinese Government. China will never change its friendly policy towards Nepal irrespective of changes both internationally and in our two countries.

The Chinese Government is committed to pursuing cooperation with Nepal in all areas. As developing countries, China and Nepal are both faced with the arduous tasks of economic and national development. Strengthening cooperation of mutual benefit and promoting common development are our shared aspirations and serve our mutual interests. China is ready to increase friendly exchanges with the Nepalese Government, political parties and people of all walks of life, and expand bilateral exchanges and cooperation in politics, economy, trade, culture and tourism. China will continue to support economic and social development in Nepal to the best of its capacity.

POLITICS OF NEPAL

The politics of Nepal function within a framework of a republic with a multi-party system. Currently, the positions of President (head of state) and Prime Minister (head of government) are occupied by Ram Baran Yadav and Madhav Kumar Nepal, respectively. Executive power is exercised by the Prime Minister and his cabinet, while legislative power is vested in the Constituent Assembly. Until May 28, 2008, Nepal was a constitutional monarchy. On that date, the constitution was altered by the Constituent Assembly to make the country a republic.

POLITICAL CONDITIONS

1990–1996: Parliamentary Monarchy

Until 1990, Nepal was an absolute monarchy running under the executive control of the king. Faced with a people's movement against the absolute monarchy, King Birendra, in 1990, agreed to large-scale political reforms by creating a parliamentary monarchy with the king as the head of state and a prime minister as the head of the government. Nepal's legislature was bicameral consisting of a House of Representatives and a National Council. The House of Representatives consisted of 205 members directly elected by the people. The National Council had 60 members, 10 nominated by the king, 35 elected by the House of Representatives and the remaining 15 elected by an electoral college made up of chairs of villages and towns. The legislature had a five-year term, but was dissolved by the king before its term could end. All Nepalese citizens 18 years and older became eligible to vote.

The executive comprised the King and the Council of Ministers (the Cabinet). The leader of the coalition or party securing the maximum seats in an election was appointed as the Prime Minister. The Cabinet was appointed by the king on the recommendation of the Prime Minister. Governments in Nepal have tended to be highly unstable; no government has survived for more than two years since 1991, either through internal collapse or parliamentary dissolution by the monarch.

In the first free and fair elections in Nepal in 1991, the Nepali Congress was victorious. The 1994 election defeat of the Nepali Congress Party by the Communist Party of Nepal (Unified Marxist-Leninist) (CPN(UML)) made Nepal the first communist-led monarchy in Asia, with Man Mohan Adhikary prime minister.

In mid-1994, parliament was dissolved due to dissension within the Nepali Congress Party. The subsequent general election, held 15 November 1994, gave no party a majority and led to several years of unstable coalition governments. As of the May 1999 general elections, the Nepali Congress Party once again headed a majority government. There have been three Nepali Congress Party Prime Ministers since the 1999 elections: K.P. Bhattarai (31 May 1999–17 March 2000); Girija Prasad Koirala (20 March 2000–19 July 2001); and Sher Bahadur Deuba (23 July 2001–2003). The final distribution of seats in Parliament gave the Nepali Congress 113; the CPN(UML) 69; the RPP 11; the RJM 5; the NSP 5; the Workers and Peasants Party 1; and the United People's Front 1. Nepali Congress Party has divided to Nepali Congress Party led by G. P. Koirala and Nepali Congress (Democratic) led by Sher Bahadur Deuba. Amongst the elected MPs, 39 MPs belong to Nepali Congress (Democratic). Former Prime Minister and Influential Leader Krishna Prasad Bhattarai has expressed his support for Nepali Congress (Democratic). Both Congress parties regard Krishna Prasad Bhattarai as their main leader.

King Gyanendra discharged Sher Bahadur Deuba and on 4 June 2003 appointed Surya Bahadur Thapa as Prime Minister.

1996: Maoist Insurgency

In February 1996, the Communist Party of Nepal (Maoist) began a violent insurgency in more than 50 of the country's 75 districts. About 11,000 police, civilians, and insurgents have been killed in the conflict since 1996. In July 2001 Prime Minister Deuba announced a cease-fire, which the Maoists pledged to observe, as part of a government effort to seek a negotiated solution to the conflict. Although Maoist-instigated intimidation and extortion continue, the killings have largely subsided since the cease-fire was announced. The government and Maoists held talks in August and September 2001.

Political parties agreed in 1991 that the monarchy would remain to enhance political stability and provide an important symbol of national identity for the culturally diverse Nepali people. The King exercises limited powers, including the right to declare a state of emergency in the event of war or armed revolt, with the advice and consent of the Council of Ministers and the Prime Minister. According to the constitution, the King's declaration of a state of emergency must be approved by a two-thirds majority of the lower house of the Parliament.

2001: Royal Massacre

On June [illegible] 2001, Crown Prince Dipendra was officially reported to have shot and killed his father, King Birendra; his mother, Queen Aishwarya; his brother; his sister, his father's younger brother, Prince Dhirendra; and several aunts, before turning the gun on himself. Although he never regained consciousness before dying, Crown Prince Dipendra was nonetheless the king under the law of Nepalese royal succession. After his death two days later, the late King's surviving brother Gyanendra was proclaimed king.

2005–2007: Suspension of Parliament and Loktantra Andolan

On 1 February 2005 King Gyanendra suspended the Parliament, appointed a government led by himself, and enforced martial law. The King argued that civil politicians were unfit to handle the Maoist insurgency. Telephone lines were cut and several high-profile political leaders were detained. Other opposition leaders fled to India and regrouped there. A broad coalition called the Seven Party Alliance (SPA) was formed in opposition to the royal takeover, encompassing the seven parliamentary parties who held about 90% of the seats in the old, dissolved parliament. The UN-OHCHR, in response to events in Nepal, set up a monitoring program in 2005 to assess and observe the human rights situation there.

On 22 November 2005, the Seven Party Alliance (SPA) of parliamentary parties and the Communist Party of Nepal (Maoist) agreed on a historic and unprecedented 12-point memorandum of understanding (MOU) for peace and democracy. Nepalese from various walks of life and the international community regarded the MOU as an appropriate political response to the crisis that was developing in Nepal.

Against the backdrop of the historical sufferings of the Nepalese people and the enormous human cost of the last ten years of violent conflict, the MOU, which proposes a peaceful transition through an elected constituent assembly, created an acceptable formula for a united movement for democracy. As per the 12-point MOU, the SPA called for a protest movement, and the Communist Party of Nepal (Maoist) supported it. This led to a countrywide uprising that started in April 2006. All political forces including civil society and professional organizations actively galvanized the people. This resulted in massive and spontaneous demonstrations and rallies held across Nepal against King Gyanendra's autocratic rule.

The people's participation was so broad, momentous and pervasive that the king feared being overthrown. On 21 April 2006, King Gyanendra declared that "power would be returned to the people". This had little effect on the people, who continued to occupy the streets of Kathmandu and other towns, openly defying the daytime curfew. Finally King Gyanendra announced the reinstatement the House of Representatives, thereby conceding one of the major demands of the SPA, at midnight on 24 April 2006. Following this action the coalition of political forces decided to call off the protests.

Twenty-one people died and thousands were injured during the 19 days of protests. On 19 May 2006, the parliament assumed total legislative power and gave executive power to the Government of Nepal (previously known as His Majesty's Government). Names of many institutions (including the army) were stripped of the "royal" adjective and the Raj Parishad (a council of the King's advisers) was abolished, with his duties assigned to the Parliament itself. The activities of the King became subject to parliamentary scrutiny and the King's properties were subjected to taxation. Moreover, Nepal was declared a secular state abrogating the previous status of a Hindu Kingdom. However, most of the changes have, as yet, not been implemented. On 19 July 2006, the prime minister, G. P. Koirala, sent a letter to the United Nations announcing the intention of the Nepalese government to hold elections to a constituent assembly by April 2007.

December 2007 to May 2008: Abolition of the Monarchy

On 23 December 2007, an agreement was made for the monarchy to be abolished and the country to become a federal republic with the Prime Minister becoming head of state. Defying political pundits, who had predicted it to be trounced in the April 2008 elections, the Communist Party of Nepal (Maoist) became the largest party amidst a general atmosphere of fear and intimidation from all sides. A federal republic was established in May 2008, with only four members of the 601-seat Constituent Assembly voting against the change, which ended 240 years of royal rule in Nepal. The government announced a public holiday for three days, (May 28—May 30), to celebrate the country becoming a federal republic.

Current (2008 onwards)

Major parties such as the Unified Communist Party of Nepal (Maoist), Communist Party of Nepal (Unified Marxist-Leninist) and the Nepali Congress agreed to write a constitution that replaces the interim one within the time limit of 2 years. However, incooperative and "selfish" behaviour of the political parties has been cited as the major cause behind the derailing of the peace process. The Maoists, as the largest party of the country, took power right after the elections were held and named Pushpa Kamal Dahal or Prachanda as the Prime Minister of the country. CPN UML also joined this government but the Nepali Congress took part of the main opposition. People soon saw that the country's situation deteriorated and political turmoils were in store. Prachanda soon fell into a dispute with the then army chief Rookmangud Katwal and decided to sack him. But the President Ram Baran Yadav as the supreme head of military power in the country revoked this decision and gave the army chief additional time in office. An angry Prachanda and his party quit the government, majorly citing this reason and decided to be the main opposition to the government headed by CPN UML and co-partner Nepali Congress afterwards.

Madhav Kumar Nepal was named the Prime Minister. The Maoists have been to this date demanding superiority of civilian supremacy to army supremacy. This created turmoils in the country and showed vividly that development was a dream far away and the political leaders were just wrangling for power. The Maoists have been forcing closures or commonly known as *bandhs* in the country and have also declared autonomous states for almost all the ethnic groups in the country, seen as a part of revenge against the action that foiled their decision to sack the army chief. Political leaders are discussing plans to end this turmoil, but none of the talks have been successful. Rising inflation, economic downturn, poverty, insecurity and uncertainty are the major problems. Many analysts opine that this freedom has brought anarchy to the country. Many don't even believe the political parties will be successful on writing a constitution.

NEPAL'S FOREIGN AID POLICY, 2008

A new dimension of foreign aid's contribution is visualized in Nepal in helping restore and stabilize peace and democratic governance through peace-funding and other supporting activities in the aftermath of the decade-long (1996-2006) conflict as the country currently faces a challenge of successfully heading towards transformation from the prevalent state of transition. The efforts and initiatives begun in that direction with the Millennium Summit (2000) that set out the Millennium Development Goals (MDGs), Monterrey Conference on Financing Development (2002), the Rome high-Level Forum on Harmonization (2003), and the Marrakesh Roundtable on Managing for Results (2004), culminated into the Paris Declaration on Aid Effectiveness (2005). This mainly consists of five areas: Country Partners' Ownership of the development agenda; Alignment of assistance to the Country Partners' systems, priorities and procedures; Harmonization of donors' activities so as to avoid duplication; Focus on Results or 'outcomes' rather than mere 'outputs'; and Mutual Accountability and Transparency of donors and the government in fulfilling this commitment. Nepal has been a firm supporter of this Declaration and attaches great significance to its implementation (MOF, 2008).

Foreign aid needs to be directed towards achieving the overarching national goal of inclusive growth and poverty reduction. With a view to attaining these specific goals, Government of Nepal should strive for mobilizing concessional loans, grant aid, budget support and expedite efforts for promoting aid effectiveness, technical assistance, revenue mobilization, and building capacity and partnership, developing framework for international non-governmental organizations (INGOs), ensuring leadership and ownership of GON, enhancing private sector, promoting role of civil society, soliciting an increased level of cooperation from donors, and maintaining financial discipline and transparency in fund transfers through INGOs/NGOs. To attain the objectives major strategies should be to:

1. Formulating economy-wide and sectoral perspective plans
2. Ensuring transparency and accountability
3. Enhancing the quality of aid

4. Strengthening aid coordination
5. Project/Program identification, selection, design and securing sustainability
6. Promoting aid effectiveness through implementation reforms
7. Creating a foreign aid management information system
8. Promoting institutional effectiveness
9. Streamlining public financial management (MOF, 2008).

Graham Hancock in his publication "Lords of Poverty" (1997) said that "aid is not help"; Jaffery Sachs, who wrote "The End of Poverty" (2005) argued for making the investments needed to end poverty and questioned: "Can the rich afford to help the poor?"

Eric D. Beinhocker in his publication "The Origin of Wealth" (2005) campaigned for radical remaking of economics through creating wealth. The foreign aid must create wealth in developing countries and, therefore, Nepal needs more foreign aid to create wealth in Nepal. In "Global Economic Prospects 2008" the World Bank laid emphasis on technology diffusion in the developing world (WB, 2007). Nepal also needs foreign aid for diffusion of technology especially in the field of climate change to preserve biodiversity, and to match the wind of economic development in the region.

At the backdrop of theoretical underpinnings foreign aid is essential not only for sustaining development activities and poverty reduction, but also for improving efficiency to enhance competitiveness of both government and the private sector, which would be instrumental in maximizing benefits from globalization and liberalization. Foreign aid has played a crucial role in the process economic development and poverty reduction in Nepal for more than five decades since the inception of the First Five Year Plan in 1956. The donor communities have been generous to provide external assistance to Nepal uninterruptedly during and after the political change in 1990. However, recent experiences with the performance of foreign aid have been frustrating attributable to both internal as well as external factors.

Nepal's prime challenge is how to integrate the national economy with regional as well as global economies and maximize the benefits from globalization, liberalization and privatization by enhancing competitiveness in the area of comparative advantages, and reduce absolute poverty to zero by 2025 through mobilizing domestic capital, technology, raw materials, and entrepreneurship in collaboration with bilateral and multilateral cooperation. Since Nepal is passing through a critical juncture of poverty and stagnation, Nepal needs greater quantum of foreign aid from neighbouring countries especially India and China and other industrialized economies not only to sustain inclusive growth and accelerate process of poverty reduction, but also for achieving endurable peace and stability in the country through implementation of reconstruction, rehabilitation and reintegration programs. As envisaged in the Three-Year Interim Development Plan, 2007-2010 Nepal's priority is on developing hydropower, infrastructure - especially road, tourism and trade and investment sectors. Therefore, foreign aid in Nepal should be directed towards addressing these priorities in cooperation with private sector.

Nepal should be ready to bear with suppressed growth during transition but ensuring peace and stability, which will help promote overall tranquility in the region. Under the changing context, Nepal's economic prospects are conditioned to the quantum of bilateral, regional and multilateral cooperation provided by neighbouring countries especially India and China, the donor communities representing industrialized nations, and international financing institutions to initiate mega-projects on priority areas.

It is, therefore, necessary to explore the possibility of moving Nepal and India towards Free Trade Area (FTA). This would help abridge Nepal's alarmingly growing trade deficit with India, and create an atmosphere to generate win-win economic effects to both countries. This would also help appreciate the value of Nepalese currency at par with Indian currency. In my opinion, the open border between Nepal and India, manifestation of our unique relationship, strongly demands for FTA. This would be an appropriate supplement to foreign aid.

Nepal as a close neighbor must strive to catch up spillover economic effects of rapidly galloping China's economy (11.6% growth rate) destined to surpass GNI of US economy at the end of 2050. The quantum of foreign aid flow from advanced economies to Nepal is relatively small and, therefore, there is need to gear up the size of external assistance to a maximum level by improving the status of democracy, human rights, governance with scaling back of corruption. The government must claim for its flagship with the programs sponsored by international non-governmental organization. The foreign a policy paradigm demands a shift from donor driven to demand driven. It is also necessary to revitalize the economic strength of Nepalese economy to galvanize multilateral loans on a greater scale to expedite mega-projects ensuring inclusive, sustainable high growth.

CHANGING SINO-INDIA RELATION AND NEPAL

As the famous traditional proverb goes, "Nepal is a yam between two boulders", the boulders seem to have come much closer — further sandwiching the yam. Of late, our neighbours have put Nepal in their top watch-list. Recent marathon visits of senior leaders from our two neighbours underscore Nepal's strategic importance for them. However, neighbours can remain good friends until their concern doesn't hurt your sovereignty. The latest concern expressed covertly and overtly by our neighbours has crossed all limits in mutilating our sense of sovereignty.

The two Asian giants are in an intense race to become the super power in global perspectives. The competition has got new dimension after nuclear deal was signed between India and US. Thus, difficulties observed in Sino-India relationship is ought to leave multidimensional effect in Nepal. Therefore, it is high time for Nepal to adopt appropriate foreign policy in changed scenario.

King Pritivinarayan Shah in his 'Dibya Upedesh (Devine Instruction)' had called southern neighbour as 'cunning' and had instructed his successors to remain close with northern neighbour for national benefit. This is the first clear statement given by Nepalese rulers to theorise foreign policy. But after the rise of Janga Bahadur Rana, Nepal developed intimacy with East India Company. From such intimacy, Nepal got back its lost territories in Banke, Bardiya, Kailali and Kanchanpur from the East India Company. But in the form of its compensation, neo-independent India made Mohan Samsher, the last Rana Prime Minister to sign the most infamous 1950 Nepal-India Treaty. Through the treaty, India ensured its political and economic dominance over the sovereign Himalayan nation.

After King Mahendra sacked democratic government and imposed party-less Panchayat system, Nepal maintained closer relation with China. During the active regime of King Birendra, Nepal had successfully suppressed 'Khampa Rebel', an armed plot designed by CIA to foster 'Free Tibet Movement'. China's feeling of gratitude towards Nepal for its effort to strengthen internal security of China is showing its influence till now. But during each democratic regime, Nepal's relation with China and India remained inconsistent. However, due to excessive influence of India in Nepalese politics, the presence of China in Nepali politics remained dimmer and weaker in democratic Nepal.

After the formation of government under the leadership of Unified Communist Party of Nepal (Maoist), immature foreign policy adopted by Nepal to remain close with both China and India has made Nepal's foreign policy weaker. Hesitation to maintain political and economic ties with China and lack of effort to set bottom-line in the issue of Madhesh and Sharing of Water Resources has exposed Maoists' ability in foreign diplomacy. In the near future, threat of clash between China and India is growing. Therefore, to cope with difficult changing regional scenario, Nepal needs to perform excessive homework to formulate appropriate foreign policy.

Competition for limited energy supply, border dispute, diverse view over utility of water and immense desire of both Asian giants to snatch regional power is adding fuel in the eroding China-India relationship. After US got formal entry in the politics of South Asia through India-US nuclear deal, China had pointed towards the necessity of making the deal inclusive. American and Indian analyst argue that the term 'inclusiveness' used by China is directed towards developing Pakistan as a nuclear rich country along with India to maintain regional balance. If we agree with this view it will be easier for us to conclude that Sino-Indian relationship has worsened after Indo-US nuclear deal. Several other incidents are further deteriorating China's relation with India. It has brought more complication in regional politics.

China's border dispute with India got shape after China invaded India on 1962. Since last few years, border tensions between the two courtiers are on the rise. India accuses China of illegally occupying more than 14,000 square miles of its territory on its northern border in Kashmir. But China is claiming over more than 34,000 square miles land in India's northeastern State of Arunachal Pradesh.

China is even insisting the Tawang district, a pilgrimage site for Tibetans in Arunachal Pradesh, to be ceded to China. But India has made it clear that any areas with settled populations would be excluded from territorial exchanges. To pressure India on the issue, China is strengthening its military infrastructure along the border and establishing a network of road, rail, and air links in the region. India's strategist believe that through such suspicious activities, China is intending to revive 1962's war. To strengthen defence system, China has adopted policy of making massive investment in the development of transportation network. It is proved from the huge amount recently poured by China in Tibet and Xinjiang province for strengthening transportation system.

To fuel the conflicting situation, India too has announced different development activities in disputed land. In Siliguri corridor, a most vulnerable place of India, which is also a meeting point of India, China, Nepal, Bangladesh, Bhutan and Burma; and in the disputed land of Jammu and Kashmir, India has recently strengthened its defence system. This has manifested the tension growing between the Asian giant.

Despite accepting Tibet as a part of China by Indian government, the declaration is widely criticised at public level in India. Rivers like Ganga, Sutlej, Brahmaputra, Sindhu, etc., which are regarded as the lifeline of South Asia, originate from Tibet. Thus, to ensure safety corner in water conflict which is supposed to happen in near future, India, with help of other western nation, is assisting 'Free Tibet Movement'. India had already criticised China's idea of diverting rivers which originate from the Tibetan plateau for the purpose of building world largest channel.

Within Asia, both China and India takes each other as their major opponent. In political circle of South Asian Region, India's influence is pervasive. However, in the public level, China is more popular. These power thirsty Asian giants are eager to exploit resources of their neighbour countries for their economic and strategic prosperity. China and India, both have exhibited their eagerness to utilise 30-80 trillion cubic feet natural gas embedded in Bangladesh and 51 trillion cubic feet embedded in Burma. Such aggression of China and India is another potential cause which may invite conflict between them.

Both China and India are the largest consumer of energy. Study made by International Energy Agency (IEA) and several other institutions has concluded that energy demand of these countries will increase in tremendous ratio in the near future. Currently, China and India are respectively fulfilling 50 and 70 percent of total energy consumption from import.

Both countries are importing significant portion of energy from Saudi Arabia, Iran, Kazakhstan, Azerbaijan, Tajikistan and other countries located in the surrounding of the Caspian Sea. Similarly, African countries like Nigeria and Sudan are also addressing energy demand of China and India. In all above energy supplying countries, political instability is rampant.

Therefore, to control over the limited supply of energy, conflict is ought to rise between China and India. Strategically, Nepal is of immense importance for both China and India vis-à-vis preserving their interests in the region. After the Beijing Olympics, overwhelming interest exhibited by the Chinese authorities towards Nepal, exhibits Nepal's strategic significance.

At the same time, India is intending to show that Nepal has become a center of criminal activities in the international arena. After recent Mumbai blast, Indian media had alleged Nepal for providing safety to Pakistan based terrorist group.

Subhahuddin Ahamad, a 'think tank' of Lashkar-e-Taiba, the Indian media claimed, was in Kathmandu, he was plotting the Mumbai attack being based in Kathmandu. Indian media strongly carried this issue. And at the same time, the Indian authorities gave extreme pressure to Nepal to sign the extradition treaty. It also has manifested the growing interest of India towards Nepal.

After Deputy PM and Defence Minister of Nepal pointed towards the necessity of triangular consensus between Nepal, China and India to resolve Kalapani issue, horrified Indian establishment immediately sent its foreign minister to Nepal to manage the situation. Immediately after the visit of Indian FM, Nepal publicly agreed to exclude China from Kalapani issue. Such horrifying state of India is loaded with several serious meaning. Similarly, Power Ministry of India has passed a policy to facilitate each household with electricity in coming five years. At the same time India is heading to fulfill increasing demand of drinking and irrigation water. Building intercontinental waterways and larger channel is major agenda of India to foster its economy. In all these events, it is easy to find the role of Nepal and its resources.

From all above fact, it is clear that regional significance of Nepal is increasing in the changed scenario. Therefore it is very high time for Nepalese authority for required preparation to formulate appropriate foreign policy.

CHINA WANTS PRACHANDA TO STAY IN NEPAL

In a televised address to the nation on May 4, the Maoist Prime Minister of Nepal, Pushpa Kamal Dahal, popularly known as Prachanda, dramatically announced his resignation. The move comes in the wake of opposition to his decision the previous day to sack the 61-year-old Army Chief Gen Rukmangad Katawal following the General's opposition to the demand of Prachanda for the integration of members of the People's Liberation Army (PLA) raised by the Maoists during their days in the insurgency into the Army.

Gen. Kul Bahadur Khadka, the No.2 in the Army, was asked by Prachanda to act as the Chief of the Army Staff (COAS) until further orders. Before announcing his decision, Prachanda met with Katawal and Khadka separately first, then jointly, before seeking the approval of the Cabinet for sacking the COAS. His decision was opposed by the Communist Party of Nepal (United Marxist-Leninist) with 108 members in the Constituent Assembly, which decided to quit the ruling coalition Government.

"We decided to withdraw our support to protest the Prime Minister's unilateral decision," CPN-UML General Secretary Ishwar Pokhrel said. While the Nepali Congress and the Madhesi Peoples Party joined 17 other parties in opposing the sacking of the General, the Madhesi People's Rights Forum (MPRF) with 51 members in the Assembly and some other smaller parties maintained an ambivalent attitude. The MPRF reportedly submitted a note of dissent disagreeing with Prachanda's decision, but did not leave the coalition. The CPN-Maoist with 229 seats in the Constituent Assembly needed the crucial support from MPRF and other small parties to continue to enjoy a majority in the 601-member Assembly tasked to frame a new constitution for the country after it abolished its unpopular 240-year-old monarchy last year.

Prachanda's action in unilaterally sacking the Army Chief despite strong opposition in the coalition Cabinet was nullified by the President Ram Baran Yadav, who faxed a special instruction to the Chief of the Army Staff "asking him to continue in his office in the capacity of COAS as per the Interim Constitution, 2007, and the existing law". The spokesman of the Maoists, Krishna Bahadur Mahara, who is the Minister for Information and Communication, told the media that the President's order to the COAS to continue in office was tantamount to a "constitutional coup" and said that the Maoists would fight back with street protests.

He said: "The President is violating constitutional norms. The President's move has put the peace process in peril. Our party has taken the President's step as a constitutional coup and we will fight against it. The executive power to sack and appoint an acting army chief lies with the government and not the President. We will stick to our decision. We don't have any plans to quit the Government."

Prachanda called the Attorney General Raghav Lal Baidya and senior Cabinet colleagues early on May 4 to discuss the constitutionality and consequences of the President's intervention. There was speculation that the Maoists might move for the impeachment of the President. After finding that they would not have the required support for such a move in the Constituent Assembly, he decided to resign.

It remains to be seen whether his resignation is a purely tactical move to confront the other members of the ruling coalition with the danger of serious political instability if they did not support his sacking of the Army chief or was forced by his realizing that there was no way he could have his way against the Army chief. Both the Army chief and Prajwal, the Commander of the seventh division of the PLA, were reported to have ordered the two forces under their respective command to remain in a state of alert to prevent any disturbance of law and order. The peace accord reached by various political parties before last year's election to the Constituent Assembly had provided for the rehabilitation and integration of the members of the PLA and other Maoist cadres, including members of the people's courts set up by the Maoists during their days in the insurgency.

After Prachanda assumed office in August last year as the Prime Minister, differences surfaced over the interpretation of this principle. The Maoists treated rehabilitation and integration as synonymous and insisted that the only of rehabilitating the 19,000 members of the PLA was by integrating them into the Army, barring those physically unfit or unwilling to serve in the Army. The Army and other political parties were strongly opposed to this. They held that rehabilitation and integration were two different processes. According to them, rehabilitation meant enabling the Maoist cadres to be gainfully employed, but not necessarily in the Army. While they were prepared to consider the integration of small numbers of the PLA into the Army if they were found to be professionally suitable, they were not prepared to agree to the wholesale merger of the PLA into the Army. Such an action would have resulted in about one-fourth of the Army consisting of indoctrinated Maoists, with their number steadily increasing with fresh recruitment.

Prachanda also wanted that the Maoists, who held officer-equivalent ranks in the PLA, should be given appropriate ranks in the Army. Thus, he reportedly wanted PLA commander Nanda Kishor Pun "Pasang" to be made a Major General and many others to get the rank of Brigadiers. He also reportedly wanted that there should be no new recruitment to the Army for some years.

Neil Horning, an American expert on the Maoist movement of Nepal, who is himself believed to be sympathetic to the Maoists, wrote: "The mainstream parties, as well as the elite in the army, view army integration in an apocalyptic light. While integrating the PLA into the NA was agreed upon time and again in the course of peace negotiations, the Non-Maoist parties made their agreements under the assumption that the Maoists could not possibly win electoral victory, and would not be in charge of implementing the integration. They counted on returning to the long standing Nepali political habit of agreeing to a demand in negotiation and then reneging on it later when the opponent is not in a position to make a challenge. They are trying to do the same now by continually insisting that Maoists combatants be "rehabilitated" rather than integrated, but it is they who have lost their bargaining position. Yet, why can't they let it happen in the first place? The Maoists don't have more than 20,000 troops to integrate into the more than 90,000 currently in the Army. This would hardly make the army into a force at the Maoists' beck and call. It's not that the army would become the private force of the Maoists, but that it would cease to be a check on them. With at least 25 per cent of troops and officers being former Maoist partisans, the possibility of a reactionary coup becomes impossible. The troops needed to suppress the public would simply turn their weapons on the command. Therefore, the army would cease to be a check and social change would continue unabated."

According to Kanak Mani Dixit, the Nepali political analyst, "At their large National Council conclave in the Kharipati outskirts of Kathmandu in late November 2008, the Maoists came to the conclusion that they were in government but did not control the state, for which the Nepal Army and the independent judiciary were found to be prime obstacles. It decided that the (Maoist) cantonments should not be disbanded until the new constitution is written."

When the Maoists found that whenever they had a dispute with the Army over issues such as the ban on new recruitment which was disregarded by the COAS the judiciary was taking up a position, which was unfavourable to the Maoists, they also started talking of integrating the members of the former Maoists' people's courts into the judiciary.

The COAS went ahead with the new recruitment recruiting nearly 2800 persons to fill up existing vacancies in the Army and the PLA retaliated by making fresh recruitment to the PLA in violation of the Comprehensive Peace Agreement. Thus, Nepal under Prachanda as the Prime Minister saw the spectre of two parallel armies—— the state Army and the non-State PLA— strengthening and preparing themselves for a future confrontation should the Maoists' demand for total integration be turned down.

While the Chinese closely monitored the situation by interacting intensely with various political formations, India and the US reportedly cautioned Prachanda against a confrontation on this issue. Prachanda increasingly became unresponsive to the advice for moderation from India and the US and insisted on having his way.

It is not clear why Prachanda decided to force a confrontation with the COAS at this stage instead of waiting till September, when Gen.Katawal is due to superannuate. One possible reason for his hasty action is that Gen.Khadka, who is believed to be not opposed to the integration of the PLA into the Army, is due to superannuate in June. It is suspected that Prachanda wanted to make him the chief before his superannuation and give him a two-year tenure so that the integration of the PLA into the Army could be brought about without any further opposition from the Army. His plans were thwarted by the President.

What could happen now? The following are the possible scenarios:

- A serious political crisis with violent demonstrations by the Maoists which results in one more compromise. The Chinese will try their best to see that the Maoist-led Government, which has effectively put down Tibetan activity in Nepali territory, remains in power.
- A violent confrontation between the PLA and the Army leading to an army coup.
- A new coalition without the Maoists, which will be unstable.

The holding of the elections to the Constituent Assembly before the ground rules for integration were agreed upon and the victory of the Maoists in the elections——significant, but not spectacular as projected by sections of the media— have led to a situation where the Maoists will be at the head of a Government which will take crucial decisions on the post-facto legitimisation of the terrorist infrastructure raised by the Maoists and on the ground rules for the integration of their ideologically motivated and well-trained cadres. The moment the Maoists assume leadership in the seats of power and decision-making, will it be possible to resist their demands? If the integration of over 3000 ideologically indoctrinated cadres of the insurgent army into the Nepal Army comes about, we will have to the west of us an army ideologically motivated by jihadi doctrines and to the east of us an army ideologically motivated by Marxism, Leninism and Mao's Thoughts. There are two possible scenarios— these fears turn out to be baseless and Prachanda turns out to be a genuine democrat and a genuine friend of India or Prachanda after the elections turns out to be different from Prachanda before the elections and takes Nepal on a road, which would be detrimental to our national interests. While hoping for the first scenario, we must be prepared for the second. "

As we try to move Eastwards to cultivate the countries of South-East Asia, it is trying to move southwards to outflank us. China is not a South Asian power, but it already has a growing South Asian strategic presence — in Pakistan, Sri Lanka and Bangladesh. It is hoping to acquire a similar presence in Nepal with the co-operation of a Maoist-dominated Government."

China would try its best to see that the Maoists stay in power. Their continuance in power in Kathmandu is important for stability in Tibet. In the past, we supported Maoists thinking that Prachanda would take a neutral line between India and China. These hopes are elusive. Should we facilitate the Chinese designs in Nepal by bringing about a political compromise which would enable the Maoists to continue in power or has the time come to work for a non-Maoist alternative? This requires serious examination in our policy-making circles.

CONSIDERATIONS CONNECTED TO THE THEORY OF CHINA AND NEPAL

In order to understand the relationship between China and Nepal, a close look at a number of factors is highly imperative for the understanding of this discussion. To understand the relationship between both the countries it's necessary for the understanding of this discussion and this has with the methodological approach. Under which different theories has been chosen for its justification and relevance to understand China and Nepal relationship. This chapter discusses the consideration made in the adopted methodology and the structure of the project. The methodology adopted in presented in terms of types of methods included and the way they are used in project. In order to understand one has to understand their historical perspective as well socio-economic relation between Nepal and China and India.

Nepal is in between two big Asian giant nations. In south world's biggest democratic country, India and in the north worlds biggest communist country, China. Between these two different political ideologies Nepal is having dilemma to walk in between. As India is always playing a vital role in Nepal's politics. And keep very close eyes in Nepal's politics. From the ancient times Nepal has good relationship with both the nations.

It portrays the survival of the state and the statemen. This theory is fit in the discussion. The core elements of the realism – statism, survival and self-help. Realism taught to focus on interest rather than ideology. Nepal is a small and weak in economic, weak in international politics. Due to the fact that India's influence is involved in Nepal's politics. Survival and security is considered the primary concern and objectives of the state which assume the supremacy of national interest. For the survival Nepal is fully dependent on India. Most of the foreign aid is coming from India and China. Without foreign aid Nepal is unable to manage the national's budget and other things. Due to dependent on other country and poor foreign policy national security is considered very weak. Nepal and India has open border in south, east and west. Due to poor security from Nepal's side and also due to poor national policy most of the time Indian security personnel entered to Nepal's earth and torture the local people and misbehave with them. Waltz states that states have security as their principal interest and therefore only seek the requisite amount of power to ensure their own survival. Nepal being small and weak states in front of India and China it has to make a good relation via diplomacy. Survival is important to both the country. For that clear and concrete policy has to make so that none of the country gets problem. To survive both the country need each others cooperation. To sell their goods Nepal is market and for that China needs energy and natural resources that Nepal has. Nepal is rich in water resources, natural herbs etc. Also Nepal could be the economic transit point for the China and India.

As Realism taught to focus on interest rather than ideology

Nepal is the country which never has been ruled by foreign country as other country has been ruled. So the Nepali citizen's interest is always Nepal has to remain sovereign country and do not want any other countries interfere.

Due to Nepal's geo- political structure and similarities between countries socio-economic, culture, language etc that makes Nepal and India relation closer than Nepal and China. When there was Rana rule in Nepal most of the Nepal's leaders were in India and started revolution from there. Beside that they also participated in the process of independence of the India. Due to the fact that Nepal's politician are very much influenced by the Indian political mentality. That is why Nepal's political leaders are influenced by Indian politics. Those things knowingly/unknowingly can be seen in the Nepal's politics. That is the reason also leaders are confused towards the national interest. National interest has always to be in the priority. Nepal's political leaders are traditional and influenced by the Indian political back ground that is why national interest is always in the shadow and in dilemma. While making the policy leaders has to give the prime focus on national interest. Policy has to be in the favour of the national interest and should not be influenced by foreign state.

After 1991 when kings regime was abolished and democracy has been established since then to till now many government has been formed and there has been lots of time political instability occurred. Always India's involvement has been seen while forming the new government in Nepal. Due to that in

1996 Maoist movement has been started in Nepal. Their focal point is to marginalise India's influence in Nepal and set the national interest in the primary focus. Due to open border between India and Nepal security problem is top priority. Nepal have open border with India from south, east and west. Nepal's sovereignty is in problem due to India's influence in Nepal's politics and being a powerful nation. Always Indian border security force enters to Nepal's territory and captures the Nepal's land. Sovereignty of Nepal is always in the problem. Nepal's citizen always raises their voice against of the anti Indian activities. The Nepali citizen's national interest is to build a sound and smooth foreign relation with their both north and south neighbour. Peace is in the prime concern too. There are no border disputes with China. It was in the past which was solved by both the country's joint border commission resolved in 1961.

Domestic and international order

Waltz argued that the key difference between domestic and international order lies in their structure. In domestic politics citizens do not have to defence themselves. Security can be realized through self-help. Providing one's security is fuelling the insecurity of others state. China is making their border high security alert because of the security purpose but India perceived it in another way. Like she feels insecure and takes it as a threat or China is preparing for the war. For example, in their border in Aruranchal Pradesh, Ladkah, Sikkim etc. Same way China's high authorities visits to Nepal and Nepal's high authorities visits to China also makes India insecure and vice versa. Like Nepal and China there is no border dispute. The same way Nepal's leader has to solve the border dispute between India and Nepal so that Nepal's citizen can feel secure and sovereignty remains sound.

Other theory that I am going to use in this discussion is World System Theory. The founder of intellectual school of world system theory, Immanuel Wallerstein describes that it is a set of mechanism which redistributed resources from periphery to core. According to him core denotes the country manufacturing and having industrialized. And periphery means the underdeveloped. Nepal lies in periphery and China is on the way to core. It supplies manufacturing goods to all over the world. It is industrialized and economically very strong.

This is a big lesson to Nepal that how China became able to shift from periphery to the core. Similarly other theory I am going to use is Three World Theory. Mao raised this idea publicly when he met the Zambian president. According to him USA and Soviet Union are the first world and Europe, Japan, Australia and Canada is second and rest is in third world country.

Aim of this theory is to strengthen the solidarity with third world country and strengthen the political situation in the world of international status, development foreign relations. Due to geopolitical structure of Nepal, it has to rely on India more than the China. Culturally and economically there is close similarity between India and Nepal. From the ancient time and its geopolitical structure Nepal and India has very close relation. India considers Nepal as a strategic partner. India from the history has huge influence in Nepal's politics. To marginalise its influence Nepal is showing interest with China. This will marginalise the India's influence and in long term will be beneficial for the Nepal. Also to make a balance bilateral relation it is necessary for Nepal. Third world was the main force to oppose the imperialism, colonialism, hegemony. Not directly but indirectly Nepal is imperialised by Indian hegemony.

Methodological Considerations Connection

In analysis it includes primarily of secondary data. Mostly books, articles, journal, magazine, internet sources. Data can be collected from so many sources which were not written particularly under this discussion but on similar historical circumstances and objectivity. Collected data from different sources as some of might be bias that might show different view and beliefs of the author. The use of the theories will clear the objectives of the analysis guided by scientific research and methodologies for a comprehensive understanding. The methodological considerations connection to gather empirical evidence and analysing these findings in connection to a theoretical framework can be done in various ways. I have decided to develop the empirical sections on an empirical analysis, where I don't only deliver as objective empirical evidence as possible but also will compare it with theoretical framework. Also deliver empirical evidence but also analyse and compare it in connection to the theoretical framework based upon the central question.

SCIENTIFIC PERSPECTIVES

In International Relation there are number to justify such relationships. The reasons and compatibilities of the choice of the theories to this essay will equally be justified in order to enhance clarity and better understanding of what this project is all about. In this regard I have chosen some of these theories-Three world theory, world system theory, realism and idealism.

According to Mao Zedong, Nepal falls under third world. The use of this third world theory has significant importance in understanding of this project as the theory that linked China and Nepal as having a sense of belonging in the third world. Therefore this theory is important for the understanding of relationship between China and Nepal. Similarly, the world system theory is also important to this project. How China has become successful to gear up from periphery to semi-periphery. This theory seems similar to the three world theory but different in the sense how China able to shift from periphery, semi-periphery and close to core and Nepal can also equally develop if it follows the same line of development.

Importance of Survival States and the Statemen

The reason behind choosing realism and idealism is it portrays the importance of survival states and the statemen. In terms of economy both the country needs each other. In Nepal china has been contributed significantly in the development sector. For China, Nepal could be an economic transit point as well strategic partner. The fact about Nepal, more than 15 years many governments have been changed and all the government keep promising about development, to minimize corruption but till now the citizens fail to feel any of the promises which they made. The fact is Nepal is governed by corrupt and power greed political leaders.

China's policy towards Nepal has driven by the need of curb the clandestine activities of some 20, 000 Tibetan refugees in Nepal. Consequently also playing significant role in determining the future shape Nepal's politics. Also other hand China's south Asia policy is to marginalise India's influence in Nepal.

Several Functions in the International Relation

Theory has several functions in the international relation, study. These functions throw more light to understanding the objectivity of the discussion in a justifiable way. The theory I am going to use here realism which helps to understand this collectively agreed phenomenon through systematically organizing the facts and evidences to support the arguments. International relation theory includes several different paradigms with a different world view. Focus will be on realism with its focus on the world as an anarchic place where survival, self-help and statism are the main centre point for the state.

REALISM

It's necessary to put the theoretical concepts in an historical context. Since in many cases the theory adopts and changes with historical events. Thus when explaining the theoretical school of realism several types of realism are touched and are a largely product of the historical period in which they appeared.

Realism is not a theory defined by an explicit set of assumptions and propositions. Rather, as many commentators have noted, it is a general orientation: 'a philosophical disposition'. 'A set of normative emphasis with shape theory'. Realism is an approach to international relations that has emerged gradually through the work of a series of analysts who have situated themselves with in and thus delimited a distinctive but still diverse style or tradition of analysis.

Realism emphasizes the constraints on politics imposed by human nature and the absence of international government. Together, they make international relations largely a realm of power and interest.

Human nature has not changed since the days of classical antiquity. According to realists, is at its core egoistic and thus inalterably inclined towards immortality. As Machiavelli puts in politics 'it must needs be taken for granted that all men are wicked and that they will always give vent to the malignity that is in their minds when opportunity offers'.

Since realists such as Reinhold Neibuhr and Hans Morgenthau, see Machiavelli's claim as largely descriptive, egoistic to make any other assumptions unduly risky. All, however, emphasize the egoistic passions and self interests in international politics. It's essential not to have faith in human nature. Such faith is very disastrous one'.

Most realists also recognize that men are motivated by other desires than the urge for power and that power is not only the aspect of international relations. Neibuhr couples his harsh doctrine of original sin with an insistence that 'individuals are not consistently egoistic. He even argues for an adequate view of human nature which does justice to both the heights and depth of human life. Morgenthau argues that 'to do justice and to receive it is an elemental aspiration of men. Realists also stress the political necessities that flow international anarchy. In the absence of international government, 'the law of jungle still prevails.

'The difference between civilization and barbarization is a revelation of what is essentially the same human nature when it works under different conditions'. Within states, human nature usually is tamed by hierarchical political authority and rule. In international relations anarchy not merely allows but encourages the worst aspects of human nature where to be expressed. 'Some human nature which in happy hideous'. According to Morgenthau the struggle of power is universal in time and space.

Classical Realism

In 21st centaury, classical realism was represented firstly by Hans Morgenthau in his work from 1947. His one of the primary claims and basis for his theory was that human nature is essentially aggressive and power seeking. Morgenthau also highlights some of the pivotal points of realism within international relation (IR) politics. That has persisted through the subsequent branches of realism.

According to him nation-state are considered to be the only actors in the world. The world is considered an anarchic place due to the lack of a world government. i.e. whereas in a state, individuals are liable to a government hierarchy than punish them in some way if they do not follow the laws of the state. Hence, states are all equal and no supranational instance exists above states to maintain international law, govern or punish the state.

The fact is that the realist world is anarchic and inhabited by sovereign states that due to human nature all seek power. International politics is an arena where states will focus on their own national interest, which ultimately is survival. This means not being the victims of other states power and states will use the means necessary to maintain their own sovereignty. These claims are often summarized in three words that is – statism, self-help, and survival.

The power struggle between states is continues and will be defined by differences in the amount of power between states. Therefore, in the theory the risk exists of one state becoming so powerful that it is able to dominate all other state a situation referred to as hegemony. However, in order to avoid such a situation, states are likely to pool their power against such a hegemonic state in order to create a situation of balance of power. In traditional and main stream international theory, realism is the main positivist theory, have a materialist view and theory use the state as the main unit of analysis. In addition realist theories assume the inherent sovereignty of the state. Realism is claim about what entities exist and claim about their independent nature. For the realist, the state is unitary and rational actors, whose interactions with other sates is primary interest and tend to be conflict because they occur under anarchic condition. The Stanford encyclopaedia of philosophy acknowledges that although the definition of sovereignty has varied across history, there is core meaning 'supreme authority within a territory'.

Realisms main assumption is that due to human nature international politics is driven by an eternal for power, often described as 'power politics'. The two general aspects of realism is claim about the existence and interdependence. The fact that in this universe moon exists and its shape is spherical and independent of anything anyone happens to say or think about the matter. According to R. Rothestein ' reality is complex and ambiguous that the policies which we choose to call 'realistic' any particular moment depend to a significant degree on personal predispositions. This is well and good in the world where things never change and everyone agrees on the meaning of 'reality'. Statism is the core of all realists thought and supports the notion of the sovereign state as the principal and most important actor, above all others, in the anarchic international system.

Prime Concern and Objectives of the State

Survival and security is the prime concern and objectives of the state which assumes the supremacy of national interest. New forms of realist theory actually provide insight to the current unipolar structure, with competitive political behaviour and violent conflict between nation state, which also lacks a strong supranational governing power with the authority to enforce collective rules/agreement and since realism helps explains the nature and role of coercive power, it can help to analyse and negative the dynamics of anarchic political system in order to successful implement humanitarian and relief tasks, which often also requires military support. Realist defines power in terms of military capabilities possessed by the states; State will wish to maximize their power relative to other states. Realism is state centric because realists view sovereign nation-states as the only legitimate monopolist over the use of force, which solely focus on state behaviour. Realist believes that states must fend for themselves and cannot rely on others for the protection and that statesman seek to preserve the existence of the state.

Struggle for power is the fundamental political fact which determines the foreign policy behaviour of all states (as they pursue their national interest defined as a power) in an anarchical system. Which means in international system objective of law is power. According to Morgenthau 'lust of desire' a desire for control over others; aggregated into states, humans behave as a function of this basic drive. The most famous realm in realism was Morgenthau's assertion that international politics is a 'struggle for power.......whenever (nation) strive to realize their goal by means of international politics, they do so by striving for power. Nations retain, increase or demonstrate their power, the first supporting the status quo, the second producing imperialism and the third involving displays of military force or other influence. Similarly Organski 'one of the most significant characteristics of a nation is power, for power is a major determinant of the part the nation will play in international relation. Deutch 'Who is stronger and who is weaker? Who will get his way leads to rank lists, such as the rankings of baseball clubs... of chicken in the pecking order and of great power in world politics.

Due to geographical location and the size, its capacity to sustain economically have brought the China into focus the potentiality not just economic competition terms but in political and strategic terms as well. Although China seeking greater involvement and influence in the region will be a cooperative international actor, is a matter of more immediate concern to China's regional neighbours. Its size and geographical position and the consequential implications for political and strategic influence, China's sustained economic growth has great significance in region and global. Other hand India also growing in the area of economic and trying to influence its power to the neighbouring country. As Nepal is in-between of both the Asian giant. China's position in the international system and its responses to the dynamics of that system can be expected to reflect not just domestic factors as well in international. China is seeking to good relation with economically strong country and with its neighbours in the region as an strong international economy. China and Nepal since the history have a good relation and always committed for none interference to any countries internal affair.

Geopolitically Nepal's Topography

Similarly, Nepal and India also have very good relation from the history. Due to culturally, linguistically, and geopolitically Nepal's topography is close to India than the China. India has a great influence in Nepal's politics and always considers Nepal as a strategic partner. Nepal and India has open border so that both countries people can travel easily. But Nepal and China does not have open border and one need to go to China has to take permission from the Chinese authority. The key point of Nepal and China policy was maintaining equal friendship with China and India while simultaneously seeking to lower down India's influence in Nepal and Nepal's dependence on India. Competition between two Asian giant would be beneficial its own economic development.

Both countries are trying to be super in south Asian region and for that the country Nepal plays a vital role. China wants to take a close look toward the India and vice versa. India and China have a border dispute in Aruranchal Pradesh, Sikkim, Laddhak etc. In recently Nepal's political situation has turned to other side. I mean to say Maoist party became the biggest party by electing in Constitution Assembly, since these party came into main political stream, Nepal and India's bilateral relation has been affected. India has a great fear if Nepal is going to be communist country then India will suffer from that. Because it's northern part and west Bengal is also affected by the communist naxalites.

The emergence of a strident India in the early 1970s introduced new dimensions in Nepal's China policy. King

Birendra did not abandon the policy of equal friendship between China and India but wanted to woo China to counter India's growing influence in the region. By realising this China was willing to oblige Nepal only to the extent of pledging support in safeguarding its national independence and preventing foreign interference. Nepal sovereignty is always in danger by the India. Nepal has open border in south, east and west. It has been always seen and news in the media that Indian police has entered to Nepal's territory and attack the local villagers. Similarly any political changes has to be done India's direct involvement has been seen.

Nepal's Sovereignty

There is always a question regarding the Nepal's sovereignty. Recently news published about some of the constituent assembly members and some journalist of Nepal met a religious leaders 'Dalai Lama' in India. When this has been heard by Chinese authority then Chinese embassy reacting very strictly towards the meeting with 'Dalai Lama' in India and also saying this is against of one China policy. China has been pressuring Nepal to adopt stringent measures on Tibetan refugees and raising strong objections against any activity that it thinks support the Free Tibet movement. The embassy had also raised serious objections when almost a dozen constituent assembly members met Dalai Lama last year. This means that Nepal does not have rights and freedom towards their own interest to meet religious leader 'Dalai Lama'. In China's perspective his ideology is anti China but on the other hand Nepal is a religious country and has rights to meet him. It does not necessarily means that meeting him is against the one China policy. It shows it's against of Nepal's sovereignty. One hand China says they will not interfere any countries internal affairs and other hand showing direct interference of Nepal's internal affairs. Nepal seems like poppet for India and China and they can use according to their interest.

Nepal's political leader's mentality has been affected by Indian politics since they were involved in India's independence and their education also done in India. Due to this fact Nepal's politics is much more influenced by India. That is why India has lot of influence in Nepal's politics and that affects while making policy. That statesman must adhere to in their foreign policies is that of national self interest and specifically national security- the latter being the foundational value that statesman duty is to bound to protect. This normative benchmark for evaluating foreign policies gives rise to Machiavellian precepts, such as: always put your nation and its citizens first; avoid taking unnecessary risks with their welfare; collaborate with other countries when it is beneficial or necessary but avoid needless foreign entanglements; avoid putting your own soldiers in harm's way if it is not absolutely necessary; make sure they are well trained and well equipped. These are the characteristics that statesman's responsibilities are determined by national interest and obligated to the citizens of their own country. I would like to mention here one of the politician of Nepal has mention Nepal have unwanted politician and but lack of statesman. According Ganesh Man Singh 'Political party are not qualified and having lack of statesman'. The state-whether it is formed by a social contract or by historically or by conquest or by any other method- is a self contained political community that is prior to any international associations it may subsequently join.

Nepal and India Treaty

Nepal and India have unequal treaty in 1950 and since then there was no significant changes occurred. That makes between two countries relation fluctuation. Due to imbalance of treaty Nepal has suffered a lot and India gets benefit more form the treaty. The treaty stated that 'neither government shall tolerate any threat to the security of the other by a foreign aggressor" and obligated both sides "to inform each other of any serious friction or misunderstanding with any neighbouring state likely to cause any breach in the friendly relations subsisting between the two governments." These accords cemented a "special relationship" between India and Nepal that granted Nepal preferential economic treatment and provided Nepalese in India the same economic and educational opportunities as Indian citizens'.

Friction has been seen when Nepal has criticized India's 1975 annexation of Sikkim as an Indian state. The same year late King Birendra proposed Nepal be recognized internationally as a peace zone and received the support from the China and Pakistan. Nepal repeated the same proposal and no reaction has been seen from India and in 1990 Nepal had received the support form 112 countries including China.

Nepal's refusal of accommodate India's wishes on the transit treaty caused India to call single transit and trade treaty. Then after Nepal took a hard line position that led to a serious impact between Nepal and India bilateral relations. In 1988 Nepal's acquisition of Chinese weaponry played a vital role for the India's dissatisfaction.

India government perceived this as an indication of Nepal intent to build the military relation with China and take it as a violation of the 1950 treaty. Due to unequal treaty Nepal has to make an approval while purchasing the arm from any other country. Which means Nepal' sovereignty is in India's hand that Nepalese citizen never tolerate. Due to this Nepal's political system has changed to parliamentary democracy system.

India's Dominance in Nepal

An open challenge to India's dominance in Nepal, Nepal negotiated a deal for the purchase of weapon from China in mid of 1988. This has been perceived by India the deal contravened an earlier agreement that obliged Nepal to secure all defence supplied from India.

Between Nepal and China there was no border dispute and no unequal treaty that is why there is sound relation from the 1955. In realistic view -state behaviour in terms of the fundamental difference between domestic and international forms of government. The realist paradigm, as conventionally understood, conjures up the grim view that beyond the borders of sovereign presence, politics is not about potential moral progress, but survival'.

NEPAL AND CHANGING RELATION BETWEEN TWO ASIAN GIANT INDIA AND CHINA

The two Asian giants have desire to become a super power in global perspective. Before that they have to take a leadership of region. India and China both are trying to get a regional leadership. Fresh long-winded visits of senior leaders from both neighbouring country emphasize Nepal's strategic importance for them. After nuclear deal was signed between India and America, America officially get a place in South Asia politics. The competition has got new dimension. After this nuclear deal the affect is observed between India and China relation have multidimensional effect in Nepal. Effect can be in the trilateral relation between India, China and Nepal. Nepal's political scenario has been changed after the constitutional assembly election. India and America never want to have a communist government in Nepal. For that this nuclear deal has greater importance in triangular relation. Hence, Nepal has to adopt the suitable foreign policy in changed circumstances.

We would like to mention the divine instruction given by Late king Prithwi Narayan Shah before he died 'Southern neighbour (India) as cunning and be aware about the national interest'. He had instructed to his successor to make a balance and try to remain close with northern neighbour (China) for national benefit. If one can analyse this statement then it gives very clear meaning. When Nepal and China established their bilateral relationship since then to until now there is neither border dispute nor other problem. Never trying to hurt the nation's sovereignty and as it promised follows too. China has clear policy towards that never intend to involve country's internal affairs. And if there somewhere dispute then in friendly environment with positive attitude wants to solve. As Chinese authority has clearly gives the statements regarding the matter of 'Kalapani' issue. It says its matter between India and Nepal and both countries' official has to solve this matter. North neighbour always shows its friendly, cordial image towards Nepal. One can not deny the fact that the topography, language and culture of Nepal makes to become closer to India. He was a real state man and has clear vision about the nation. He dares to give this clear statement before his death. After his death Nepal has got other leader and signed the most unequal treaty in 1950. Because of this treaty Nepal is suffering since then to now. This treaty gives the authority to India political and economical dominance over the sovereign Himalayan country. Prachnada on his first visit to India has expressed 'I think due to our historical, cultural and geographical relation and also due to our whole tradition of interdependence the relation with India is crucial and vital although we also want to develop a relation with China'. This statement shows in competencies of the leadership. Not having sufficient homework on it. Nepal definitely needs both south and north neighbour due to its geographical structure. But first Nepal's leadership have to have clear mindset and lots of homework before visiting any neighbouring country.

During each democratic regime, Nepal's relation with India and China remained inconsistent. Where as China's non intervention policy to other countries internal affairs fuelling and giving opportunity to India to play active role in Nepal's politics. In other hand China want to show that against of their policy to take part in other country's internal affairs. However, India's excessive influence in Nepali Politics makes Chinese involvement in Nepal's politics weaker.

After coming to the government unified communist party of Nepal (Maoist) an immature foreign policy adopted by Nepal regarding India and China has made its foreign policy weak. Lack of confidence and hesitation or excessive India's involvement in Nepal's politics whatever to maintain political as well as economies ties with China. Nepal needs to perform excessive homework to cooperate with difficult and changing scenario to formulate appropriate policy.

Power greedy countries are eager to exploit resources of their periphery countries for their economic prosperity. Bangladesh and Burma contains huge amount of natural resources (gas). Similarly Nepal is reach in water resources.

Around 83000 mega watt hydropower energy can be generated in Nepal. Such aggression and hunger towards natural resources could be the cause to invite the conflict between them in future.

After the Beijing Olympics strategically Nepal's importance for both India and China became immense importance in the region. After the game held in Beijing, vast interest exhibited by the Chinese authority towards Nepal and exhibits strategic importance. Other hand India is intending to show the Nepal has become a safe place for criminal activities in the international arena. For example, India airlines IC-814 had hijacked from Nepal in 1999, recent Mumbai blast and Indian media had alleged that Nepal is safe place for the terrorist group. This can be seen as revenge showing by India. Because China have good relation with its periphery countries (Pakistan, Nepal, and Burma). India and China both can be seen as major opponent and trying take a leadership in South Asia Regarding water resources issues 'Kalapani' is well known issue between India and Nepal. This is about the belongingness. Nepal had raised the voice of necessity of triangular consensus between Nepal, India and China for solution of this issue. China has clearly says on this issue in may 10, 2010 'Government of China has informed the ministry of foreign affairs that there is not concern belonging to Kalapani among the documents signed between China and India during visits of Chinese Premier Wen Jiabao to India'. India needs huge amount of water for the irrigation purpose as well as electricity. Due to lack of homework and negligence of Nepali authority from the past time to until now this issue has not been solved. These shows the roles of Nepal on its resources and raise question about the sovereign country and national interest.

NEW EMERGING RELATION BETWEEN NEPAL AND CHINA, INDIA'S WORRY

Nepal's political scenario has been totally changed after the resignation of Prachanda. His resignation only pushes the Nepal towards the political crisis but also affects the geopolitical vulnerability of the country as it is in between two big Asian giant India and China. India always considers Nepal as a part of its influence which is challenged by China inroads to Nepal. If Nepal will become the communist country then it would be biggest threats as well as challenge to India. That is why India always wants to influence and involve in Nepal's internal affairs directly/indirectly. India perceives Nepal is facilitating China's security interest in the South Asian region. The statement given by the Chinese ambassador in 2008 makes India to think in that way. The statement was given at council of world affairs by the Chinese ambassador Zheng Xianglin- 'Nepal is situated in a favourable geographical position in South Asia and a passage linking China and South Asia.'

Nepali print media says more than 60 years ago India was playing such game with Nepal. The first elected Prime minister of Nepal and founder member of Nepali Congress Mr. Bisheshwor Prasad Koirala was thrown and with the help of India Late king Mahendra reformed again the king rule in Nepal. It was written in the article that after being elected as first prime minister of Nepal it was fixed his first official foreign visit to China.

But India's Prime Minister Jawahar Lal Nehru had forced him (Bisheshwor Prasad Koirala) to make his first visit to India and not to visit China. This shows India's cunning behaviour as well as clearly seen that India thinks Nepal is literally its sphere of influence. India has feared that if his first visit would be China, it means to India that Nepal wants to build its bilateral relation stronger with China rather than India. And if it goes like that then India's influence to Nepal would be less and can not use Nepal in monopoly way.

At the time when Bisheshwor Prasad was Prime Minister Jawahar Lal Nehru gave the statement that 'India's border will starts from the Himalaya.' India did it intentionally because when India forced him not to visit China. He refused the proposal. It's other way to make a Nepal's political situation unstable. It seems very well planned game to put Bisheshwor Prasad in Jail and after that in Nepal there will not be any more democracy.

It happened and again king rule has been reformed. Further more articles say that Chief of the Indian army came to Nepal and met late king Mahendra and advised him to do so. Nepal seems like independent and sovereign country but in reality not like that. Nepal's national interest is in always in the shadow. What India or other foreign country says the political leaders are following. It means leaders are not capable or if someone wants to follow the national interest then foreign power forced not to do so or otherwise he/she can get death penalty.

For example of Leaders from Nepal communist name as Madan Bhandari. His death still mystery. Nepali citizens are not ready to accept as just a car accident. But investigating committees report says it's just an accident. Similarly the case of late king Birendra, he was trying to make sound bilateral relation with both the neighbouring country and he seems nationalistic and always thinking about the national interest that is why he easily transform the 237 long king rule history into the democracy in 1991.

To neutralise India's influence he was trying to increase the relation with China which India does not like. In 2001 in Nepal royal massacre occurred and the mystery until now has not been solved. Late king Birendra was proposed the proposal about Nepal has to be recognized as peace country in the world. Except India, Nepal got 112 countries support including China and Pakistan.

Similarly Maoist led government only was in the government for 9 months and after that their government also fell down due to their advocacy on integration of Maoist rebel army into Nepal army. There has few official visits been done to India from the Nepal's side and India was against of this. China is always in favour of integration rebel army to Nepal army. Indian Army chief also advised to Nepal's army Chief it should not be happened. Due to this there was huge politics was going and finally Maoist led government fell down. Since then Maoist are trying to be in the government again but could not succeed.

According to Abanti Bhattacharya, China has laid down a four folded policy with the aim to strength its bilateral relations with Nepal. First accommodate each others political concern, second is enhance the economic cooperation on the basis of mutual benefits third is boos people to people culture exchange and last one is strength the cooperation and coordination in international and regional affairs. China wants to develop the relation with Nepal in a way that it would serve as a model for bilateral ties between small and big countries. Normally there is saying that big fish eats small one but China wants to prove this proverb not always. China in one hand wants to show that Nepal's is independent and sovereign country and will be. Also other hand to get Asia's powers its necessary to marginalise the growing India's involvement in Nepal and other periphery country.

According to Bhim Prasad Bhurtel, executive director of the Nepal South Asia Centre, Kathmandu, there are 33 China study centres have already been established adjoining to India border in the south. Further more he concluded with the aim of close contact with Nepal, China has launched a local FM radio station in Kathmandu. With the aim to strengthen the diplomatic relations between both countries in 2005 Nepal-China Mutual Cooperation Society (NCMCS) has been established which is funded by Chinese embassy, Nepal. So due to Nepal's geopolitical structure and culturally and linguistically also Nepal is very close to India. That is why also what ever is going India always keep its eyes on it. Especially after Maoist Rebel came to the political main stream.

7

Economic Interests in Nepal and China

As described above, Nepal and China have substantially boosted economic ties in recent years. This is evident from the increase of the trade volume by 80 percent in a single year from 2009–10 (US$744 million). This reflects China's 'Going Out' policy, which aims to sustain high levels of domestic economic growth through external economic engagement.

Since the CPC's domestic legitimacy is based heavily on continuing the country's high rates of growth, economic motives play a central role in Beijing's foreign policy, including its increased engagement in Nepal. Economic engagement in Nepal facilitates the entry of Chinese firms into new markets. Nepal represents one such market, but beyond lie the larger markets of South Asia.

Improving its economic relations with Nepal – as well as the local infrastructure – could potentially enable China to use Nepal as a transit country for trade with the whole of South Asia. China's growing engagement in Nepal can, therefore, be seen to be motivated in part by its strategy of economic expansion. This is further illustrated by the close link between Chinese aid and Chinese business interests. A large proportion of Chinese aid to Nepal is provided as 'aid in kind', often the construction of infrastructure by a Chinese contractor. China's White Paper on Foreign Aid explains how in such cases "the Chinese side is responsible for the whole or part of the process...

After a scheme is completed, China hands it over to the recipient country". According to the White Paper, such schemes account for 40 percent of total Chinese aid.

The rapidly increasing economic engagement between China and Nepal – in terms of aid, trade and investment – illustrates an important new dimension of China's interest in Nepal. While Nepal's significance for stability in Tibet has underpinned China's relations with the country since the 1950s – and this remains Beijing's predominant concern – it also offers substantial potential to fuel China's economic development. Nepal is a market for Chinese goods in its own right, but more importantly it could also be a gateway to the markets of South Asia. A senior Chinese official spoke of "developing Nepal as a transit hub between China and the larger sub-continent". This demonstrates the synergy between China's security interests in Nepal *vis-à-vis* Tibet and China's economic interests. A stable Nepal is in China's interests as far as Tibet is concerned, while it also presents a more attractive opportunity for Chinese trade, investment and other forms of economic engagement.

Geopolitics

China and India have the two largest populations and fastest growing economies in the world. Relations between these two rising powers have been characterised by a "persistent mutual trust deficit". At present, China is the more powerful of the two in economic and diplomatic terms at the global level, while it also threatens India's predominance in South Asia. Since 2004, China has improved trade relations with a number of India's neighbours and the volume of trade with Pakistan, Bangladesh and Sri Lanka has grown rapidly. Strengthened bilateral relations between China and India's neighbours are complemented by China's admission into the South Asian Association for Regional Cooperation (SAARC), which enables China to engage in South Asia through a multilateral mechanism.

These developments have prompted references to "China's growing dominance of the South Asian landscape... and the rapidity with which New Delhi is ceding strategic space to Beijing on the sub-continent". While this may be overstating the case, there is certainly an asymmetric relation between China and India, despite both being economic powerhouses. And it follows that India may be concerned about further expansion of Chinese influence into what has historically been regarded as New Delhi's sphere of influence.

Nepal's position has turn out to be more strategically significant with the rise of China. Situated between the two regional powers, it can be seen as a prize to be captured and could become the locus of geopolitical competition between an expanding China and a defensive India. This possibility is increased by the fact that Nepal is weak and internally vulnerable, and thus less able to resist foreign interference. According to some, "the ongoing political paralysis in Nepal... [has] created the ideal conditions for Beijing to increase its leverage and influence over Nepal". Others foresee that "the weakness and collapse of Nepal would offer an opportunity for China to engage directly in South Asia".

There is a counter-argument based on the fact that China and India share a strong interest in their own economic development and do not wish to jeopardise current growth trajectories, nor undermine their lucrative bilateral trade. China was India's largest trading partner in 2008, and trade between the two countries has risen dramatically from US$1.0 billion in 1994 to US$61 billion in 2010.82 According to this view, the main driver of China – India relations is a mutual interest in economic growth and this will safeguard the region against a confrontation between the two powers. Nevertheless, the unprecedented economic growth of both powers does not yet seem to have had the effect of cementing stability in the political relationship. Nepal's role is also related to wider geopolitical dynamics, both within the Asian region and globally. There are many and diverse perspectives on these dynamics. Some contend that the US seeks to strengthen its alliance with India in order to contain China, a goal whicn underlies its engagement in Pakistan and Afghanistan and also informs US policy towards

Nepal. Others hold that China is supporting Pakistan to keep India tied down in South Asia, leaving Beijing free to expand its access and influence more broadly across the Asian continent, including in Nepal. However, the significance of Nepal for either China or India should not be over-stated. It is questionable to what extent Nepal is regarded as a foreign policy priority in New Delhi, while equally it does not feature much in foreign policy debates in China. According to one analyst "both countries have bigger fish to fry", and more dispassionate analysis suggests that both countries will prioritise their relationship with the other over their relationship with Kathmandu.

In this regard, it is distinguished that both China and India are increasingly using multilateral structures to facilitate bilateral relations. Both have an interest in reforming the international diplomatic architecture, which they consider to be Western-led. Hence the emergence of new configurations of 'rising powers', including the China-India- Russia strategic triangle and the BRICS (Brazil, Russia, India, China and South Africa) grouping. China is also increasingly engaged in the South Asian regional structure SAARC, where India has the main voice, while India has observer status in the Shanghai Cooperation Organisation, which China dominates. These various multilateral frameworks may provide a framework for strengthening understanding and mutual trust, including in respect of Nepal. What is clear is that Sino-Indian relations have a significant effect upon geopolitics in the South Asia region, and thus upon peace and stability in Nepal. Some degree of competition between the two rising powers seems inevitable; yet historical rivalries have been managed thus far, and the hope is that shared economic interests will outweigh geopolitical rivalry.

POLITICAL AND SECURITY SITUATION

Nepal's role as a bridge between China and India for Tibetan refugees highlights the country's strategic location between its two giant neighbours. The political and security situation within Nepal cannot be understood without reference to the relationship between India and China. There is an oft-quoted metaphor attributed to an 18th Century Nepali king that describes Nepal as "a delicate yam between two boulders". This aptly describes the country's potentially vulnerable position between the two great regional, and increasingly global, powers of India and China.

Given Nepal's size and land-locked location, the fact that its powerful neighbours have a major interest in its affairs – potentially squeezing it between them – is no great surprise. However, the country also has geostrategic significance as a buffer between the two main power-brokers in the region. For India, the Himalayan mountains represent the principal land barrier between China and the resource-rich Ganges plain. After the Chinese profession of Tibet, Nepal became the main Himalayan buffer-state for India. Thus New Delhi has long regarded Nepal as an integral part of India's sphere of influence, and developments in Nepal are seen as closely linked to India's own security.

Indian policy towards Nepal has focused on forging strong links in the security, political and economic arenas. This 'special relationship' was enshrined in the 1950 'Treaty of Peace and Friendship' between the two countries. This granted Nepal a range of preferential economic agreements with India in return for New Delhi achieving its security objectives, including control over Nepali arms acquisitions. The Treaty also granted nationals of both countries reciprocal rights with regard to residence, property and trade. Today people and goods are able to flow relatively freely across the India- Nepal border, and generations of the Nepali elite have been educated in India. These connections have sustained the close historical links between the people of India and Nepal, based on a shared religion, as well as ethnic, linguistic and cultural affinity. Despite the predominant role played by India, China too has a long history of engagement with Nepal. It has been providing some degree of economic aid to Nepal since the 1950s, and in 1960 Beijing and Kathmandu signed their own 'Treaty of Peace and Friendship'. For the most part Beijing appears to have accepted that Nepal is within India's sphere of influence and has respected New Delhi's primacy. However, when tensions between the two regional powers came to the fore in the Sino-Indian war of 1962, Nepal was caught in the middle. China presented itself as a benevolent power in contrast to the superior attitude of India towards its smaller neighbours. Beijing subsequently supported Kathmandu in disputes with New Delhi on trade issues, using propaganda in Nepal to fuel nationalist feeling and anti-India sentiments. The limitations of China's ability to support Nepal were exposed in 1988 when the Nepali king signed an agreement for the supply of anti-aircraft guns from Beijing. This provoked a fierce response from New Delhi, which imposed an economic blockade on Nepal from 1989 to 1990 and closed down most of the transit points on the border, with devastating consequences for Nepal's economy. This highlighted the link between India's security interests and its economic relations with Nepal, as well as demonstrating that China was not then in a position to supplant India from its dominant role *vis-à-vis* Nepal.

The above episode also illustrates Kathmandu's limited room for manoeuvre in designing its foreign policy. It realised it could not afford to antagonise New Delhi by too close a friendship with Beijing, but equally to go too far the other way could jeopardise its relations with China. Hence Nepal's foreign policy has been characterised by the attempt to balance its association with both sides. As long as India and China are locked in competition to extend their power and influence in South Asia, Kathmandu will have to tread carefully. Thus the geopolitical competition between India and China and its implications for regional security loom over Nepal.

From this rundown of the post-conflict context, current conflict issues and the wider regional dynamics, it is clear that peace in Nepal cannot yet be considered as secure and sustainable. Since the end of the war in 2006, there has been considerable progress in certain areas of political development, but some key issues remain unresolved. As a consequence, the conditions for a return to violent conflict remain. It is against this backdrop that we next consider the nature and extent of China's engagement in Nepal.

CONTACT ON PEACE AND ARGUMENT

How does China's increasing engagement in Nepal relate to issues of peace and argument? Clearly, different actors will view this differently, depending upon their underlying assumptions about what causes argument and builds peace. From a Chinese perspective, the presumption is that economic development leads to peace. The general opinion is that the root cause of argument is underdevelopment, and so by providing resources for infrastructure and economic development in Nepal, China's engagement will have a positive long-term impact on peacebuilding and argument prevention. This contrasts with the dominant view among Western donors that, in simple terms, arguments arise from a variety of sources, including underdevelopment but also encompassing issues to do with identity, inequality and governance. It is based on a model of peacebuilding developed in the post-Cold War period referred to as a 'liberal peace'. This model includes an emphasis on political solutions; human security; the rights of minorities to self-determination; the universal significance of human rights; freedom of speech and free and fair elections; and a definition of state sovereignty that, in extreme circumstances, legitimates humanitarian intervention by external actors. As recent events in Libya illustrate, the liberal peace model is far from being universally accepted.

In Western discourse around peace and argument, there is also increasing recognition that any external engagement in a argument-prone context, such as Nepal, will inevitably have an impact upon the peace and argument environment – whether directly or indirectly – and China's engagement is no exception. The consensus from a range of interviews in Kathmandu was that China's primary concern in Nepal is stability so that it can contain the threat from Tibetan dissidents; and that this desire for stability is reinforced by China's economic interests and geopolitical strategy. Based on this view, there is little to suggest that China's increasing engagement will have a directly negative impact upon the argument drivers and risks identified in the earlier part of the paper. Interlocutors in Nepal did however identify a number of ways in which China's increasing role and influence could potentially affect, or indirectly impact upon, argument issues and dynamics. In the next section we consider each of these issues in turn and assess to what extent they can be considered significant threats to peace and stability in Nepal.

Governance Engagement

Another way in which China's engagement may affect peace in Nepal relates to governance. A common criticism in the West of China's engagement in developing countries is that its policy of non-interference undermines good governance and democratisation. This is especially the case in China's relations with regimes that are isolated by the West (such as Burma/Myanmar and Zimbabwe), but it also applies in countries going through a post-argument transition, such as Nepal, where Western donors seek to promote 'progressive' reforms in governance and related areas. China's position on this issue is that "standards, rights and rules ... need to be worked out by [national stakeholders] and not imposed by outsiders".

In other words, it is not for China to determine what it regards as the political choices of sovereign states. In the case of Nepal, Beijing wants stability and is pragmatic about the means used to achieve this. As argued above, it appears to have little concern about what the governance system that delivers stability looks like, but will back the perceived favourite. Hence Beijing's previous support for Nepal's monarchy, while currently it regards the Maoists as the best bet – or the least worst – for achieving stability. However, some foresee that China will lose patience with the current peace process, predicated on multi-party politics and a democratic model of governance, as it is taking so long to deliver stability. A fear was expressed that in this case Beijing may support an alternative, more authoritarian system in Nepal, which would not reflect the governance values (e.g. representation and legitimacy) that are associated with Western concepts of peace and stability.

This scenario may be possible but it seems unlikely. A return to monarchy, although it has its proponents, is highly improbable; while residual fears that Beijing would automatically favour a Maoist form of authoritarianism have little ground. Despite the apparent ideological kinship with Nepal's Maoists, Beijing has been careful not to be seen to favour one Nepali political party over another.

As described above, it has reached out – not always successfully – to political actors on all sides and in 2011 invited all four of Nepal's major parties to visit Beijing. Thus China has sought to present itself as an impartial and apolitical presence in Nepal. Some consider that Beijing is simply 'hedging its bets' in light of Nepal's chronic political instability and volatility. Nevertheless, its repeated exhortations to Nepal's politicians to resolve their differences through dialogue and to complete the peace and constitutional process seem to reflect a judgement in Beijing that fulfilling the existing peace process currently offers the best prospect for stability in Nepal.

POLITICAL DIMENSION OF NEPAL'S ECONOMIC POLICY

Diplomacy is the power game. It is a game to control others, neutralize them or use them to one's advantage. It is a new form of war. Although economic diplomacy is being understood as the mobilization of foreign policy for creating opportunities of economic growth and prosperity, the birth of nations, wars, imperialism, colonialism, international organizations, treaties and conventions are basically reflection of the same interest. Agreements and treaties are also influenced by balance of power. According to Adam Smith:

"Exportation was encouraged by drawback, sometimes by bounties, sometimes by advantageous treaties of commerce with foreign states, and sometimes by the establishment of colonies in distant countries"

The first and second points referred to by Smith relate to enhancing competitiveness of goods while the last two points help develop friendly market. Taking advantage of external markets without the need for indentifying areas of comparative advantage is a far more pragmatic course.

According to Khanal (2059 BS), developed countries tend to mobilize unlimited resources for the promotion of their global interests which are preserved through technical, strategic, military, political and economic organizations at the national, regional and international levels. This shows that no assistance, loan and grant provided by multi-lateral, regional or international NGOs are free from strategic and political interests of major powers. This perspective has been formulated even more forcefully by Fukuyama, who argues for the use of American soft power for promoting the emergence of middle class attuned to the American value system and its global interest and the establishment of democratic regimes He also describes the sponsored propaganda of vote rigging in Ukraine, Serbia arid Georgia, mobilization of the, popular revolt and the establishment of regimes suited to the American interests, and named several persons who led the civil society at the time (Fukuyama 2007: 136-8).

Fukuyama also refers to several world organizations like the United Nations, which are either incapable of taking quick decisions favoring American national interest or are dominated by countries whose interests clash with those of the United States and recommends creation of global organizations that endorses the American decisions or give legitimacy to American interventions.

According to Khanal, there is a general tendency in Nepal to link a particular policy to an individual. For example, China's domestic modernization and the liberalization of her foreign policy is linked to the policy of Deng Xioping. This could be true to a certain extent....However, we must understand that serious strategic and economic interests (rather than individuals) have governed the policy changes in China and the United States. What are involved are national interests of each countries involved, and the individuals are superfluous (Khanal 2059 BS). The perspectives of someone recognized as the architect of Nepal's modern diplomacy indicates that national interests are at the core of foreign policy of a country..

The government has been providing a grant of Rs.1 million to each of the village development committees. However, the Indian Embassy can provide lump sum Rs.50 million to any VDC without even asking any agency of the Nepal government.

A former member of the National Planning Commission told an interaction that once the Indian Embassy wrote a letter to the Nepal government, asking to raise the ceiling of amount it could provide to any one in Nepal from Rs.30 million to Rs.50 million. As required, the approval of the NPC was sought. The NPC formally discussed the proposal but rejected on the grounds that the loyalty of the party leaders or workers negotiating such assistance between the recipient and the Indian government would be towards the Indian government. However, the very next day the news by the official media said the Indian proposal has been accepted and approved. The major beneficiaries of such assistance have been the leaders and workers of all political parties.

It is true that Nepali bureaucrats, security officials, traders, businessmen and leaders and workers of the political parties thus favoured by India have invested their income in India. Even today, the sons and other relatives of most Nepalis including the Prime Minister and political leaders are studying in India under Indian scholarships. Most scholarships are provided at the recommendation of the political leaders. This is the spider web of Indian diplomacy, which is one of the several reasons why the growing trade deficit between Nepal and India has not been able to be narrowed down.

On the other hand, the legitimacy of any state power or government is measured in terms of the country's economic prosperity and the opportunities available to the people. Most of the third world countries had survived on the goodwill of superpowers in the post-colonial period when the world was bipolar led respectively by the United States and the Soviet Union. The demand for rights and prosperity of the people were suppressed with the help of the masters. This situation changed dramatically following the end of the Cold War in 1990s. The legitimacy of the regimes now depends on the popular support, thus the emphasis on economic development.

Economic policy of any country is no more a matter of independent choice. Global integration of the economies is the reality. Countries such as North Korea and to some extent Myanmar that have failed to march with global economy are sick and fragile. Independent policies without adjusting to the policies of the World Trade Organization, World Bank and International Monetary Fund are next to impossible. Those with power and money dominate such multilateral organizations. It is for this reason also that the representation of developing countries has shrunk in the structures of these organizations.

The world economy is being managed on the basis of Washington consensus. However, the consensus has weakened gradually. As a consequence, efforts are. being' made for creating the Beijing Consensus as an alternative and make structural changes in the World Bank on the basis of the changing balance of power in order to enhance the roles of emerging powers such as China, Russia, India, South Africa and Brazil.

The Beijing Consensus has two important aspects. The first aspect is to end the dominance of dollar in the world market and create an alternative world currency. This is primarily aimed at reflecting the reduced economic influence of the United States and its developed capitalist allies. It takes into account a number of factors including the origin of the global economic meltdown in 2008 and the Chinese investment of US$150 billion in US bonds (Stiglitz 2010). The second aspect is the kind of challenge it poses to the US political value sc,,stem on which its foreign policy is based (Subedi 2010).

Only recently, China has overtaken Japan as the world's second largest economy. China is the emerging world power. Emerging powers like China and others exert pressures on the US dominated institutions to open up for democratic reforms.

Until 10 years ago, the trade between China and India was to the tune of $1 billion. That was the time when it was said that Chinese goods had swamped India. Today the total volume of trade between the two countries has swelled to $50 billion, and the balance of trade is favourable to India. The growing trade would have impact on their relations. Nepal should take the advantage out of this flourishing trade at least as a transit country as the travel distance between India's Siliguri and Delhi via Nepal is much shorter by hundreds of kilometers.

The changing nature of the global balance of power will certainly leave an impact on Nepal. The tourism market dominated by the arrivals from European countries, United States and Japan so far will see growing impact from fresh arrivals from China and India. Our tourism policy must focus on these traditional but emerging markets. The pashmina, carpet and garment export needs to be diversified to cater to the Chinese markets. In order to be able to do so, we must get out of the South Asian level of human resources and products (Pyakuryal 2067 BS). The country must get ready for the changes in the global economy in order to identify areas of advantage and make commensurate policy changes. It is clear that we may not move forward at the current pace and style.

NEPAL-CHINA ECONOMIC COOPERATION NEPAL-TIBET RELATIONS

Political Relations

Relations between Nepal and China, date back to ancient times. There have been frequent exchanges of visits at popular levels for over 1500 years. Fashien, a Buddhist monk and

scholar from China visited Lumbini in 406 AD in pursuit of knowledge and peace. Almost around the same time, a Nepalese monk named Buddhavadra visited China to preach teachings of Buddha. The visit to Lumbini and Kathmandu by Xuan Zhang, Chinese traveler in the 7th century and his travel writings have been one of the main sources of Nepalese history of pre-medieval time. Princess Bhrikuti, daughter of King

Amshuvarma, was given in marriage to King Srong Tsangampo. She, along with the Chinese Princess, was instrumental in converting Tibet into a Buddhist State. Later, Arniko accompanied by his followers visited Tibet and then to China to build monasteries and temples. The White Pagoda, which still exists in Beijing, is an immortal witness and testimony to the antiquity of Nepal-China relations.

Modern Development

Nepal-China relations entered a new epoch after the establishment of formal diplomatic relations on August 1, 1955. The five principles of peaceful co-existence, which constitute the basis of peace and friendship, have nurtured our relations. Regular exchange of highlevel visits has played an important role in further consolidating our mutually beneficial relations. The successful conclusion of boundary agreement in 1978, Chinese assistance in Nepal's economic and technical development and mutual cooperation in international fora including the United Nations have greatly increased mutual understanding leading to still closer cooperation between the two countries.

Nepal has been consistently pursuing 'One China' policy. Nepal was among the first group of countries to recognize and establish diplomatic relations with the People's Republic of China. Nepal had taken a leading role in sponsoring China's admission to the United Nations and all other international agencies. In the UN Human Rights Commission sessions, Nepal has consistently voted in favour of China. China has deeply appreciated Nepal's stand in this respect.

China has appreciated the stand of His Majesty's Government that Nepal will never allow her territory to be used for anti-China activities and that Nepal has recognized Tibet as an autonomous region of the People's Republic of China. China has supported the measures taken recently by His Majesty's Government of Nepal in containing terrorism in Nepal. Nepal and China have, during the last few years, liberalized their economies and are engaged in a process aimed at achieving higher standards of living for their peoples. As a more developed economy with rich resource endowments and technical know-how, China is placed in a very advantageous position to extend economic and technical assistance to Nepal in her development endeavors.

China has been earmarking a certain amount for economic assistance to Nepal each year. The two governments prioritize the projects to be run under the Chinese assistance. At present, the amount has been fixed at 80 million RMB per year.

The Chinese government has encouraged its viable enterprises to invest in friendly countries. Possibilities of developing bilateral co-operation through large-scale induction of Chinese technology and capital in the form of joint ventures, do indeed, exist. During the visit of Prime Minister Sher Bahadur Deuba in April 1996, Nepal and China signed two separate agreements-on the Consultation Mechanism between the Foreign Ministries of the two countries and on the Establishment of Nepal-China Non-governmental Cooperation Forum (between Federation of Nepal Chambers of Commerce and Industry and All China Federation of Industry and Commerce). These two joint bodies have met regularly and have proved to be useful tools of interaction with each other.

Nepal-China relations have been nurtured by the exchange of high level visits between the two countries. His Late Majesty King Mahendra Bir Bikram Shah paid a State Visit to the People's Republic of China in 1961, which was the first ever visit to China by Nepal's Head of State. His Late Majesty King Birendra Bir Bikram Shah visited China ten times, the last being from 26 February to 04 March 2001. The state visit of His Majesty King Gyanendra Bir Bikram Shah Dev to China at the invitation of President Jiang Zemin in Junly 2002 is expected to further strengthen the relations between the two countries. Former Nepalese Prime Ministers Mr.Tanka Prasad Acharya, Mr. Bishweshwar Prasad Koirala, Mr. Kirtinidhi Bishta, Mr. Girija Prasad Koirala, and Mr. Manmohan Adhikari paid their official visits to the People's Republic of China. The Rt. Hon. Prime Minister Mr. Sher Bahadur Deuba also paid an official visit to China in 1996. Premier Zhou Enlai from the People's Republic of China visited Nepal two times in 1957 and 1960. Similarly, Premier Zhou Ziyang, President Li Xiannian, Premier Li Peng, President Jiang Zemin and Premier Zhu Rongji visited Nepal over the years. The paramount leader of China, late Deng Xiaoping also visited Nepal in 1978 in his capacity as Vice Premier.

Prospects for Future Co-operation

During the visit of Chinese Premier Zhu Rongji to Kathmandu in May 2001, Nepal and China signed important agreements namely the construction of Syaprubesi-Rasuwa road, establishment of a poly-technique institute and construction of a civil service hospital in Kathmandu among others. The construction of the road connecting Syaprubesi of Nepal to Kerung of Tibet Autonomous Region of China will help boost the bilateral trade, people to people contact and tourism between the two countries.

Since Nepal is the first South Asian country included by the Chinese Government in its outbound tourist destination list in 2001, there is a great potential for Nepal to attract many tourists from China. In order to facilitate the prospective visitors in obtaining Nepalese visas, His Majesty's Government of Nepal is going to open an Honorary Consulate in Shanghai. Nepal and China have signed an agreement on June 17, 2002 in Kathmandu making Chinese currency convertible into Nepalese Rupees. These will immensely help promote tourism from China in the days ahead.

China has recently hammered out strategy to develop her Western region. This includes her plan to link Lhasa with major Chinese cities through railway and express highway. Similarly, the plan will also bring an increased amount of investment in the region. The enhanced Chinese economic activities in the region will positively influence the economic activities in Nepal's bordering region. With the increased development activities in Tibet, there seems great potential for supplying construction materials and foodstuffs to Tibet.

CHINESE ECONOMIC AND MILITARY ENGAGEMENT

The increase in Chinese economic and military engagement in Nepal has its corollary in the upgrading of diplomatic relations between the two countries. The appointment in June 2011 of Yang Houlan as Ambassador to Nepal, a high-profile regional security expert and former Ambassador to Afghanistan, was widely viewed as a sign of Nepal's growing strategic significance for China. Further evidence can be seen in the proliferation of diplomatic exchanges between the two countries. In 2011, a series of delegations of senior Nepali officials from the Ministries of Home Affairs and of Defence, from the Nepal Police and the Army all visited China for consultations and training. In August 2011 it was reported that there were three different delegations in China from the Home Ministry alone, amounting to a total of 50 officials on a so-called "China junket".

As well as government officials, Beijing has invited delegations from all of Nepal's major political parties to visit China. In June 2011, a delegation of leaders of the Maoist and the CPN-UML parties visited Beijing at the invitation of the Communist Party of China (CPC). The leadership of the Nepali Congress party was also invited to Beijing but declined the offer, claiming that it was not appropriate to leave the country at the time. More recently, Beijing has been trying to extend its reach to the political parties representing the Madhesi communities of the Terai.

In return, there have been an increasing number of visits by senior Chinese officials to Kathmandu. In August 2011 Zhou Yongkang travelled to Nepal at the head of a 60-strong delegation from Beijing. Zhou is a high-ranking member of the powerful Politburo Standing Committee of the CPC and is the most senior Chinese official to visit Nepal since 2006. Zhou put forward a five-point proposal to enhance ties between the two countries, which included: more high-level exchange visits; Chinese investment in a variety of sectors, including business, infrastructure, tourism and water resources; Chinese support for security in Nepal; people-to-people contacts and cultural exchanges; co-operation between political parties; and joint efforts to tackle food insecurity, climate change and the global economic recession.

Soft Power and Aspects of China

As mentioned in Zhou Yongkang's five-point suggestion, there are also less tangible aspects of China's engagement in Nepal, such as cultural and educational exchanges. These aspects of China's engagement are often referred to as 'soft power' in contrast to the economic assistance, infrastructure and hardware that Beijing also provides. The significance of this aspect of China's engagement was explicitly recognised in Zhou Yongkang's proposal to boost people-to-people exchanges between the two countries in order to reinforce the foundation for bilateral friendship.

Beijing is well-aware of the deep-rooted Indian cultural influence in Nepal and it is widely perceived to be deploying soft power in an attempt to counter-balance and dilute India's influence. There are various vehicles for this sort of people-to-people exchange. A number of China Study Centres (CSCs) have been established in Nepal in order to promote cultural and language exchange with the Nepali people. Reportedly, "thirty-three CSCs have been established in southern Nepal adjoining the Indian border". In 2007 a Confucius Institute was established at Kathmandu University, where nearly 1,000 Nepali students now learn Chinese. Meanwhile, Beijing also provides scholarships to Nepalis to study in China, where there are a growing number of Nepali students.

Another facet of China's soft power is radio broadcasting, with a branch of China Radio International set up in Kathmandu in 2010, including a Nepali service to teach the Chinese language. A further dimension of soft power is tourism. China and Nepal's tourism ministries have been working together to increase tourist numbers to Nepal; for instance by Beijing designating Nepal an authorised tourist destination (the ninth country to be thus recognised), and by Kathmandu waiving visa fees for Chinese visitors. This has contributed to a rapid growth in the number of Chinese tourists, so that by 2010 there were almost as many tourists coming from China as from the US or United Kingdom (UK) (who have the second and third highest number of tourists); though it is still a long way behind the number of visitors from India. With increasing Chinese investment in infrastructure and construction, there is also potential for Chinese investors to make inroads into Nepal's tourism market, which is yet to be fully tapped by the Nepali government.

There are limits to the efficiency of soft power however, and the controversy over the Lumbini development scheme may serve as a cautionary tale for Beijing. This was a vast scheme worth US$3.0 billion aimed at transforming the town of Lumbini, the Buddha's birth-place, into a key pilgrimage destination for Buddhists from around the world. It was proposed to build an airport, a highway, hotels, a convention centre, temples and a Buddhist university. However, the initiative also appeared to be strategically aimed at reducing the influence of the Dalai Lama and his followers by creating a focal point for Buddhism that was free from Tibetan influence.

The Lumbini scheme involved a diverse cast of characters, including Prachanda and the former Crown Prince of Nepal, and it was supposedly a partnership between the Hong Kong-based Asia Pacific Exchange and Cooperation Foundation (APECF) and the United Nations Industrial Development Organization (UNIDO). It collapsed however after UNIDO and others reported to be backing the scheme made clear that they had no involvement.

The official word from Beijing was that the Chinese Government had no hand in the initiative. However, APECF is based in China and regarded as a quasiofficial NGO, which suggests that the Lumbini scheme was at least endorsed by Beijing. As The Economist concludes, "If this was an exercise in Chinese 'soft power' it was a disaster". Nevertheless, while this particular initiative foundered, it may signal the shape of things to come. Prachanda was due to meet with UN Secretary-General, Ban Ki-Moon, in New York regarding the development of Lumbini, and plans to develop the site as the "Buddhist equivalent to the Vatican" continue.

CHINA'S MILITARY MODERNIZATION: ITS IMPLICATION

The People's Liberation Army (PLA) is on course to become the most significant military force in East Asia after the United States within the next decade, by modernizing to create a military capable of defeating regional forces and credible enough to deter intervention by outside forces. As China expands its area of operations, U.S. and PLA forces will come into contact with increasing frequency, which makes continued U.S.-China strategic consultation critical to avoid accidental confrontations. Larry Wortzel of the U.S.-China Economic and Security Review Commission and David Finkelstien, Director of the Chinese Studies Centre at the CNA Corporation, offered their assessments of China's military modernization and the threat it poses to the United States and Asia in the third of Carnegie's China policy debates. Carnegie senior associate Michael Swaine moderated the event.

Contingencies and Capabilities

The first Gulf War "shocked the PLA into confronting the stark reality that it was incapable of fighting twentieth-century warfare," according to Finkelstein. In 1993 the PLA embarked on a holistic modernization program designed to develop the capabilities necessary for the small, high-technology conflicts typical of the latest generation of warfare. The PLA also designed its modernization program to prepare for several contingencies. Open-source data indicate that China is preparing for possible conflict with the United States, potentially over Taiwan, and is also focused on being able to defeat Taiwan.

Wortzel argued that China is close to achieving that goal and is capable of dominating the militaries of other Asian powers (excepting Japan). The fact that the United States treats China as an enemy in its strategic planning is a driver of Chinese military planning, according to Wortzel.

Implications for the United States

The potential for miscalculation and misreading of intent are the biggest threats to the PLA and the U.S. armed forces, and as the PLA expands its area of control into parts of the Pacific to which the U.S. has traditionally had unfettered access the potential will increase. Confidence-building measures and regular defence consultations are the best way to reduce the threat posed by the PLA.

However, Wortzel and Finkelstein agreed that as long as China's decision-making process remains opaque the United States must maintain a sufficient deterrent. The U.S. should also ensure that allies are not selling sensitive military technology to the PLA. Both participants stressed that while the PLA is preparing for scenarios in which they could engage with the U.S. military, conflict is far from inevitable, given the deep economic and strengthening political ties between the two countries. Continued military-to-military exchange is crucial to preventing an arms race and to reduce the likelihood of unintentionally igniting a security crisis. Each side should make clear what actions will lead to conflict.

IMPLICATIONS OF CHINA'S FINANCIAL POWER

China's economic growth and liberalization has affected India in significant ways. China set a positive example for India in the 1980s by liberalizing its economic system and transforming China into an economic success story. However, the lessons of China's modernizations were implemented by its neighbour a decade later, after an economic crisis forced India to reform its bureaucratic economic system. China's economic growth and wealth has also decreased the incentives for it to engage in conflict with its neighbours, increasing its initiatives to make peace with India. Similarly, India's liberalization and growth has led its leaders to accept the same conclusion.

China and India are currently addressing their challenges with very similar programs that are meant to propel their economies and strengthen their militaries. Both countries face the threat of growing income disparity, ethnic unrest, and separatism and both China and India are focused on modernizing and developing their economies to integrate more closely with the rest of the world. Minor disputes over territory do not further this agenda well. For China, high tensions with Taiwan provide a good reason to resolve old quarrels with India. In addition, China has concerns with internal security. Separatist movements in Xinjiang and Tibet continue to absorb much of its attention, and reflect problems that China is facing regarding its ethnic composition. Rising unrest from unemployment and gaping inequalities in income distribution between regions are exacerbating these ethnic divides. Securing its external borders and relations with neighboring countries allows China to focus on these growing internal problems.

Indian policy makers are more confident than their Chinese counterparts regarding their ability to deal effectively with domestic ethnic and economic forces. In fact, they overwhelmingly state in interviews that the unity of the Indian state does not hinge upon keeping Kashmir, whereas in the view of most Chinese policy makers, a separation from Taiwan could mean the end of China as we know it. Rather than worrying about the country disintegrating, India is trying to refocus its national efforts on economic growth in order to match China's success. Indian growth rates have averaged 6% in the past decade, but growth needs to be even faster to eradicate poverty and raise living standards. Conflict and tensions with neighboring China and Pakistan have posed a large economic hurdle for India in the past, impeding foreign investment and absorbing critical budgetary resources. Moves by Vajpayee's government to foster ties with Pakistan complement the recent initiatives in China, and could eventually lead to a significant demilitarization of India's northern borders.

A breakthrough in relations with China is also likely to mean a tremendous growth in trade between the two countries in coming years. Whereas a decade ago, trade volume was a paltry $300 million per year, it has now increased to $5 billion, and growing. Trade estimates for 2004-2005 are closer to $7 billion, and trade is expected to reach $10 billion by 2005-2006. These changes mean a boost to the Indian economy, and greater interdependence between the two economies. Of course, the field for competition has also shifted to economic interests. India eyes with envy China's rapid growth rates and competitiveness in the consumer goods sector. For years, Indians were worried that cheap Chinese goods were flooding the Indian market and threatening domestic manufacturing. In the past few years, however, businesses are looking to China more as a model for attracting foreign investment. The difference in FDI to the two countries is stark, China drew an estimated $52.7 billion in FDI in 2002, whereas India attracted only $5.5 billion. Indian businesses realize that much effort is needed to match China's performance in this arena, including added attention to education, infrastructure, and less bureaucratic entry and exit procedures for businesses.

China, for its part, is hoping to emulate India's success in the information technology arena. In China, recent media reports indicate that concerns are rising regarding India's increasing competitiveness in microchip manufacturing. Chinese analysts argue that because India's salaries are lower, costs are cheaper, thereby making Indian products more competitive. Language is also a factor in China's concerns. Businesses in China fear that U.S. businesses will prefer Indian products because of the Indian facility with English relative to their Chinese counterparts. In a strange turn of events, the Chinese population is now asking whether their market is likely to be flooded with cheap Indian goods. With common strengths and export markets, trade competition is inevitable. But competition on economic terms is beneficial for both countries.

Safety Relations

Both countries fought a border war in 1962, leaving a sense of suspicion and tension between the two countries in the following years. Diplomatic relations were reinstated in 1976, but both sides have retained thousands of troops along their disputed borders for years. Complicating matters further, India's 1998 nuclear tests were initially interpreted as a hostile manoeuvre aimed at China. The situation was exacerbated by the Indian Defence Minister's statement claiming that China was India's main threat. Since then, both countries have slowly come to the understanding that their national interests can be compatible. When asked, leading officials and scholars in both countries state that remaining disputes on borders are not worth a war. As the populations of these two countries comprise a total of a third of the world, this is no small achievement. Furthermore, India's decision to formally accept Tibet as a part of China, and China's decision to show flexibility on the issue of Sikkim in recent discussions has helped to ameliorate relations.

The U.S. role in Asia is undoubtedly a significant factor in China's strategic calculus with regard to India. Calls within the U.S. to work with India to contain China have provided Chinese strategists with a reason to warm relations with India. A closer relationship with India is beneficial to China in that it precludes the U.S. from being able to co-opt India into a containment strategy, whereas the existence of tensions between China and India would provide an ideal opportunity for both the U.S. and India to work together in containment. China and India's growing economies and trade ties have also had considerable influence on improving their security relationship. Both countries have come to the understanding that economic cooperation is the key to the future, and closer diplomatic and security relations must follow.

The shift in relations has been manifested most recently in the first bilateral military exercises between China and India that took place in November 2003. Both countries engaged in a joint naval search and rescue exercise off the coast of Shanghai, a significant move in their relationship, though limited in its military significance. Working together in the military arena will undoubtedly decrease the possibility of miscommunication and misunderstanding, making conflict less and less probable. The joint exercises also serve as confidence building measures between the two countries militaries. However, the exercises do not mark the beginning of a security alliance by any means. China and India will take time in deepening their security ties. Trust will need to be built through expanding economic interdependence, political agreements, and further military cooperation to create a mature and stable relationship.

China and Pakistan

China's relationship with Pakistan has also been shifting in recent years. During the Cold War and the 1990s, China maintained a close relationship with Pakistan, to India's disadvantage. China's military assistance, including the possible transfer of nuclear and missile technology, to Pakistan has been a persistent irritant in Sino-Indian relations. However, China has in recent years emphasized its intent to pursue a balanced foreign policy towards India and Pakistan, a change from the past policy that was markedly in Pakistan's favour.

This shift is likely a result of India's growing significance as an economic and military power in Asia. However, other issues are increasingly affecting China's relations with Pakistan. Revelations of Pakistan's transfer of nuclear technology to North Korea have placed China in a difficult position vis-a-vis the international community and North Korea. China finds that it must now scramble to defuse the situation in Northeast Asia created by North Korea's nuclearization.

In addition, whereas Pakistan's support for fundamentalist groups was previously not a priority to China, reports now indicate that the numbers of Uighur separatists trained by Pakistan has created problems for China in Xinjiang. As a result, the issue has become a liability for Pakistan in the bilateral relationship.

Nonetheless, the strong historical relationship between the two countries is unlikely to disappear. Military cooperation continues, and China may want to maintain close ties with Pakistan as a hedge against being surrounded by a hostile U.S., Japan, and India in an unknown future. However, cooperation with Pakistan will increasingly be tempered by the current trend of warming ties with India.

SOCIAL AND ECONOMIC DEVELOPMENT INDICATORS

With about 23.9 million population and having a per capita income of US$ 210, Nepal remains one of the poorest countries of the world. It ranks 144th position in UN Human Development Index out of 174 countries listed in the Human Development Report. Nepal's Human Poverty Index is 51.3 percent. More than fifty percent of its population live on less than a dollar a day. Over 80 percent of population live in rural areas, pursuing agriculture as a source of livelihood, most on small plots that produce insufficient food for survival.

If the current growth rate (2.4 percent) of population continues, the population of Nepal will reach 40 million by the year 2020. The Human Development Report concludes that in Nepal the rich are getting richer and the poor are getting poorer. While the richest 20 percent of the population earn 44.8 percent of income, the poorest 20 percent earn 7.6 percent of the income only. Adult literacy is 39.2 percent and school enrolment ratio is 61 percent. The social sector still receives a low priority in budgetary allocation. At present, the human expenditure ratio in Nepal is less than 3 per cent of GNP that is very low as compared to the internationally recommended ratio of 5 per cent.

The average annual Gross National Product (GNP) growth rate of 3.4 percent roughly balances the population growth. The population growth is higher than food grain production (2.2 percent). Until 1975, Nepal used to be a major food grain exporting country. Despite heavy investment and top priority given to the agriculture sector, the country now imports food grain every year from abroad. Ironically, this sector still dominates the economy viewed from the share in GDP contribution. More than 60 percent of its development budget comes from foreign aid and aid constitutes a major instrument for Nepal to escape from poor income, low saving (about 10 percent) and low investment trap. The growing fiscal deficit gap in the economy indicates a trend towards debt spiral. Debt is so huge that even four years of revenue collection cannot pay back the debt. About 90 percent of population do not have access to adequate health services, 29 percent do not have safe drinking water and 85 percent of population do not have access to sanitation. The infant mortality rate is 83 per thousand, and the average life expectancy of male is 57.6 and that of women 57.1. Nepal is the only country in the world in which life expectancy for women is lower than for men. The literacy rate for women is 28 percent and for men 62 percent. Only 23 percent of women above 15 years of age in Nepal are literate, as against 58 percent of males.

The Ninth Five-Year Plan Document (1998-2002) defines three broad objectives of the state: poverty alleviation, employment generation and promotion of balanced development in the country. The Report of Nepal Development Forum 2000 reports that "fiscal management has been poor; and the budget has been balanced largely at the expense of development activities. And, there has been little tangible progress in reducing widespread poverty—Nepal's principal development challenge—as well as in addressing structural problems which are hampering Nepal's longer term development."

The statistics in Nepal are very confusing. The data produced by Central Bureau of Statistics, National Planning Commission and Nepal Rartriya Bank are not consistent to each other. On September 5 Nepal Rastra Bank claimed that Fiscal Year 1999-2000 marked acceleration in economic growth and a sharp deceleration in inflation rate. The real economic growth stood at 6 percent due mainly to improvement in the agriculture sector followed my marked growth in the manufacturing, trade and electricity sectors. Broad money registered a decelerating growth of 19.2 percent amounting to Rs. 182,211.6 million compared with the growth of 20.8 percent during the previous year. The growth of time deposits decelerated from 25.1 percent in the previous year to 20. 6 percent during the review period. Narrow money growth accelerated from 13.1 percent in 1998-99 to 16. 6 percent during the review year. Total domestic credit of the banking system decelerated slightly to 16.1 percent from 16.4 percent in the preceding year. The flow of bank credit in the private sector increased by 20.1 percent compared with 18.9 percent in the preceding year.

The government expenditure increased by 9.9 percent, against 8.8 percent in the preceding year. Of the total expenditure, regular expenditure increased by 10.4 percent, development expenditure by 7.8 percent, and freeze expenditure by 43.1 percent. Resource mobilization marked a growth of 9.1 percent, against 18.1 percent in the preceding year. Revenue mobilization stood at Rs. 42,870.0 million, marking a 15.1 percent growth against 13.1 percent in the preceding year. Budget deficit amounted to Rs. 10,214.3 million, which is 13. 5 percent higher than during the preceding year. The government issued treasury bills worth Rs. 2,510.0 million, national saving certificates worth Rs. 2,200.0 million and development bonds worth Rs. 790.0 million during the review period. The annual average National Urban Consumer Price Index recorded a rise of 3.3 percent, against 11.3 percent in the preceding year. A fall in the prices of food and beverages helped lower the annual average inflation rate to a single digit. The annual average price index of Kathmandu, hills and Terai increased by 3.6 percent, 3.7 percent, and 3.0 percent respectively. Exports increased by 44.7 percent and imports by 22.2 percent. Exports of pasmina increased significantly while the exports of pulses, tanned skin and nigerseed declined. The export-import ratio, which was 40.8 percent in the preceding year, improved to 48.3 percent. Trade deficit, which had declined in the previous year, increased by 6.7 percent. The overall balance of payment recorded a surplus of Rs. 14,047.6 million. As a result, foreign exchange holdings of the banking system increased by 22.6 percent as of mid-July 2000.

BUDGET AT A GLANCE

On May 30 Finance Minister Mahesh Acharya announced a package of 91.62 billion rupees annual budget for the Fiscal Year 2000/2001. The new budget identifies poverty alleviation as its prime objective. To achieve this goal, the budget aims at enhancing public expenditure management, continuing financial sector reform and improving institutional efficiency. The new budget, up by35.6 percent from the revised estimates of the current fiscal year ending mid-July, would launch various pro-poor programs in the spirit of "Income to the Poor and Justice to the Downtrodden". 48.10 billion rupees had been allocated for development and 43.51 billion rupees for regular expenditure.

The share of the development and regular expenditure is 52.5 percent and 47. 5 percent respectively. Out of 43.51 billion rupees allocated for regular expenditure, a major chunk (12.76 billion) will go for debt servicing, 3.89 billion rupees for defense and security, 5.27 billion for police force, 8.20 billion rupees for education and 1.66 billion rupees for health. On the development side, 35.1 percent will go for the social service, 7.1 percent for education, 6.3 percent for health, 8.0 percent for drinking water and 10.7 percent for local development.

The economic service sector constitutes 63.4 percent of the total development fund, 13.8 percent for transportation, 22.0 percent for hydropower development and 19.6 percent for agriculture, irrigation, land reform and forest sector. As the sources of financing, revenue mobilization projection stands at 47.92 billion rupees, while the contribution of foreign grants and bilateral and multilateral debts would be 11.84 billion and 19.79 billion respectively. Twelve and a half billion rupees would remain as deficit. Critics blame that the whole budget is like a subsidy, given importance to defense spending rather than poverty alleviation, regionally unbalanced and unrealistic. It will widen the gap between the rich and the poor. The general expenditure is higher than development expenditure—the latter is purely based on foreign aid.

WEAPONS DEVELOPMENT AND THE NATIONAL DEFENCE ECONOMY

It is common knowledge that modern warfare is not only the competition of weapons on the battlefield but is also, at the same time, an all-out competition of the total strength of the opposing side's politics, economics, military, and science and technology. During the development of weaponry, the four aspects of politics, economics, military and science and technology are completely brought into play. In today's climate of rapid development of national defence science and technology and the daily emergence of new weapons, the material base of the actual national defence economy should be not only strong but also exceptional.

- With the upgrade in the tactical and technical performances of weapons, manufacturing costs would correspondingly be also more expensive. Since the end of WWII, science and technology development has flourished. There has been a multitude of achievements in science and technology that have continuously increased weapon precision, its powers to cause casualties, and its military effectiveness. The explosive power of a small atomic bomb has the same effectiveness as 100 bombers from WWII. The fire power of today's tank is tenfold greater than that of WWII. A mission to destroy 60 percent of the equipment of a tank division would today require only 1 percent of the aircraft used 40 years ago. During the Falklands War between England and Argentina, the EXOCET missile, which cost only $200,000, fired by the Argentinean Air Force was able to sink a British SHEPHARD missile destroyer that costs $200 million. The ratio of the two costs effectiveness is 1:1,000. The precision of precision-guided bombs and artillery shells is 2 to 3 times better than that of non-guided bombs and artillery shells. However, the upgrading of weapons performance has also brought with it the consequence of more expensive manufacturing costs. The cost of scientific research and technical components compared to the cost of a system with microcomputer technology, new materials, and new techniques imported in great quantities would appear to be prominently greater. Each of the U.S.'s HELLFIRE antitank missile costs about $28,100 to buy, but the scientific research to produce it costs $310 million. Each of the LEOPARD-II tanks of the Federal Republic of Germany costs $3.58 million to buy, yet the scientific research cost was $360 million. The research cost of Japan's MODEL 61 tanks cost ▯500 million to research and develop in the 1950s, its MODEL 74 tanks cost ▯2.5 billion to develop in the 1960s, and the MODEL 88 tanks that currently are under research and development have a budgeted cost that could reach ▯25 billion. The research and development expenditures of three generations of tanks seem to have increased geometrically. According to statistics, the costs of fighters and tanks increase about tenfold every 20 years and the costs of aircraft carriers increase by tenfold every 30 years. Weapons development has come to rely more and more on the national defence economy, causing great burdens for many countries.

- The increase in weapon power has also created battlefield situations where the consumption of battlefield material and economic losses are immense. It requires a huge quantity of material reserves. The 4th Middle East War lasted only 18 days and both sides, Egypt and Israel, suffered economic losses of over $5 billion. The loss of aircraft by both sides was comparable to the combined loss in aircraft in a year by all of the participant countries during WWII. In the first 3 days after the war started, the total number of tactical missiles launched by both sides was equivalent to the combined total of all the reserves of the countries in NATO. The loss of tanks was equal to one-third the number of those in the possession of NATO countries at that time. Both sides strategic reserves and materials were exhausted a week into the war. We can infer the amount of economic loss that could be created by modern warfare from this. In the Falklands War, the English spent a total of $2.16 billion, about $1.2 million every hour. This kind of consumption, to fight one mid-size modern war, is difficult for even an economically great power to support.

In addition to the above, research and production of weapons, ammunition, technical facilities and engineering equipment all consume large amounts of metal and various kinds of nonferrous metals. They also need the support of the chemical industry and energy resources, as well as military industrial products. According to the statistics from affiliated departments at the United Nations, 15 to 16 percent of the world's copper output and 10 percent of it tin, nickel, lead, and zinc outputs are used for weapons production and toward the building of other national defence installations. The consumption of energy resources is even greater. During WWI, the consumption of fuel by each soldier for each day averaged about 6 kg. During WWII, it was increased to 20 kg for each person each day. In the several local area wars fought in recent years, the fuel consumption of each man each day increased to 90 kg. The consumption level is shocking! This not only raises problems for logistics support, it also increases the economic and energy resources burden.

- The rapid increase and shorter intervals in the updating and replacement of weaponry have sharply increased military expenditures and expenses. The advancements of science and technology have caused new weapons to emerge in an endless stream and greatly accelerated replacement and updating of weaponry. Before and after WWI, the time period for a weapons system to go from research and design, through trial tests and production to its deployment within the service required about 20 to 30 years. At present, this procedure requires only 10 to 15 years or an even shorter period. According to the analysis of a Soviet economist, Maj. Gen. Guluofu, a new weapons system for the Soviet military from research to its deployment in the services requires 10-15 years. Since the 1960s, Soviet missiles have already been updated three generations. The majority of its aircraft, submarines, and surface ships underwent updating long ago. Its anti-air defence missiles, radar, command equipment, communications equipment, and other equipment have also been through several generations of updating. The research of new weapons and the updating of existing weapons have greatly increased the military expenditures and expenses of every country. According to an analysis by western observers, "The world economy is already shouldering a burden of massive destructive weapons, poverty, and debt. Militarization will further sap its strength." Since the 1960s, the global expenditure for weapons has been about $14 trillion. In 1985 it was about $800 billion, in 1986 about $900 billion. Every second of every year about $1.7 million are spent. Immense military expenditures have become serious economic problems for each of the world's countries.

- The research and production of modern weapons have made even greater demands on the national defence economy and national defence industries. Since WWII, especially during the 1960s and 1970s, the unceasing discovery of new technology has led to a great revolution in weapons and military-use equipment.

In 1945, the atomic bomb appeared. The research of computers for weapons use came in 1946. In 1952, the first transistorized computer was developed. In 1953, the world's first hydrogen bomb was exploded. In 1955, the first nuclear-powered submarine was launched. In August 1957, the first intercontinental ballistic missile was fired, and in October of that same year, the first manmade satellite was orbited. In 1960, mankind recovered its first satellite. In 1961, the world's first manned satellite did an orbit around the earth and returned to the surface. In 1967, the first integrated circuit was successfully developed. In 1969, man had his first landing on the moon. In 1977, the neutron bomb was researched and developed. In April 1981, the world's first spacecraft flew. The research and production of all these new weapons and equipment and a large portion of the new technology that entered into the sphere of the national defence economy not only greatly changed the production and industrial structure of the national defence economy, it also added a series of new production and industrial sectors. These changes helped to restructure the traditional national defence industries, moving them in the direction of technological improvement, and development of a technological reserve. The diffusion of a large quantity of high technology made it possible to turn a consuming national defence economy into a propagating field of national defence economy.

Weapons development is reliant on the development of the national economy. It also encourages the growth of national defence science and technology. Military high-technology also gave impetus to the development of the economy. Looking at this from two-dimensional space, this big "O" cycle could possibly expand further. Analysing it from a three-dimensional space, this kind of spiraling trend is perfectly suited to the objective laws of material development.

Weapons and Equipment Development and Military Scientific Theory

"Technology determines the tactics." The appearance of large quantities of technical equipment inevitably brings about great transformations in military theory and tactics; this in turn leads to great changes in strategic thinking, patterns of combat, combat style, and military structures:

Weapons development enhances man's strategic consciousness, deepens his strategic reflections, and increases the emphasis on strategic projections. In today's world, strategic research is extremely dynamic. With the development of strategic rockets and various spacecrafts, as well as the gradual development of energy beam weapons, kinetic energy weapons, and other space weapons systems, war has extended from the surface, air, and sea toward outer space. The areas of man's activities have already extended beyond the earth and moved into space.

This has opened up man's field of vision and expanded his modes of thinking. In the wideness of space, the earth is no longer "boundless and limitless," but has become one of the "global villages" in the universe. In the eyes of the strategist, the earth has become small and man's strategic reflection is becoming more profound and his strategic consciousness has been greatly enhanced. Man's heart embraces the whole of the universe. The development of strategic research is even more important than at any time in history and has become an especially important issue for all countries globally. What is coming will be conflicts in space. One of the conflicts will be the military struggle for "control of the high ground in space." The other will be exploitation and use of space, the struggle for the resources of space.

For this reason, every country in the world is busily formulating and developing strategic plans. In March 1983, the United States became the first to formulate a "Star Wars Plan." This caused global commotion in strategy research. The Soviet Union responded with "defensive measures" to the "Star Wars Plan." Western Europe came up with the "Eureka Plan." Each of the COMECON countries announced a "Plan for the integrated advancement of science and technology by the year 2000."

Japan had its "Policy outline for science and technology;" China had a "Policy for a new technological revolution;" India came out with "Policy statements for new technology;" South Korea had its "Conceptions for long range national growth;" and Yugoslavia had its "National science and technology development strategy." To rank within the world's family of nations, to live and survive in the "global village" in this universe, each nation must come up with ideas for a "grand strategy." "To stand shoulder to shoulder with the giants" one must intensely fix one's eye on the growth of national defence construction and weapons in the next century.

Modern weapons are not only direct combat strengths between opposing combat opponents, they are also strategic deterrents and tools for international political struggles. The appearance of offensive strategic weapons like missiles, atomic bombs, nuclear-powered submarines, and long-range bombers has caused great changes in military strategy. The research, production, and large stockpiles of strategic weapons are already more than needed to seek out and kill an enemy. It has turned into a tool for political and diplomatic struggle. The large-scale arms race have caused the United States to stockpile over 9,400 nuclear warheads with a total nuclear weight equivalent of over 4 billion tons. The Soviet Union's stockpile of over 8,000 nuclear warheads has a total nuclear weight equivalent of over 5 billion tons. The quantity of nuclear warheads possessed by these two nuclear powers comprises above 97 percent of the global total.

Both have the capacity to destroy the other several times over. Living under these conditions, the military strategy of both sides has gone through many changes; strategic ideologies have been revised about every 10 years. However, pressure from the threat that "destroying the enemy doesn't necessarily mean one's own survival" has kept them from crossing the "nuclear threshold" and taking the next step of pressing the button to launch those nuclear missiles. England, France, and China have independently and on their own developed into national nuclear powers. The limited power of these countries is not enough to compete with the capabilities of the United States and the Soviet Union, but they do play a role in the even development of political, economical, and military affairs within the world. This power is entirely a symbol of a country's independence and its existence within the world of politics, economics, military affairs, and science and technology.

Bibliography

Adhikari, Krishna Kant. *Nepal under Jang Bahadur, 1846-1877*. Kathmandu: Buku, 1984.

Ashok K. : *The Royal Nepal Army : Meeting the Maoist Challenge*, Rupa, Delhi, 2005.

Cheek, Timothy: *Mao Zedong and China's Revolutions: A Brief History with Documents*. Boston: Bedford/St. Martin's, 2002.

Debray, Regis. *Revolution in the Revolution*. New York: Grove Press, Inc., 1993.

Dhanalaxmi, Ravuri. *British Attitude to Nepal's Relations with Tibet and China, 1814-1914*. Chandigarh, India: Bahri, 1981.

Digumarti Bhaskara Rao: *Military Conversion : Impact on Science and Technology*, Discovery, Delhi, 2003.

Ellis, F. 2000. *Rural Livelihoods and Diversity in Developing Countries*. New York: Oxford University Press.

Evelyn Goh, *Meeting the China Challenge: The U.S. in Southeast Asian Regional Security Strategies*, DC: East-West Center, 2005.

Gaige, Frederick H. *Regionalism and National Unity in Nepal*. Berkeley: University of California Press, 1975.

Gao, Mobo: *The Battle for China's Past: Mao and the Cultural Revolution*, London, Pluto Press, 2008.

Huntington, S.P.: *The China Modernisation Military and the State*, N.Y., Vintage Books, 1964.

Jagannath P. Panda: *China's Path to Power : Party, Military and the Politics of State Transition*, Pentagon, Delhi, 2010.

Jain, M.S. *Emergence of a New Aristocracy in Nepal, 1837-58*. Agra, India: Sri Ram Mehar, 1972.

Kant, Adhikari, Krishna. *Nepal under Jang Bahadur, 1846-1877*. Kathmandu: Buku, 1984.

Keane J.: *Democracy and Civil Liberty*, London, Verso, 1988.

Kumar, Satish. *Rana Polity in Nepal: Origin and Growth*. New York: Asia, 1967.

Misra, Shashi P. *B.P. Koirala: A Case Study in Third World Democratic Leadership*. Bhubaneswar, India: Konark, 1985.

Parmanand. *The Nepali Congress since Its Inception: A Critical Assessment*. Delhi: B.R. Publishing, 1982.

Pemble, John. *The Invasion of Nepal: John Company at War*. Oxford: Oxford University Press, 1971.

Rose, Leo E., and Margaret W. Fisher. *The Politics of Nepal: Persistence and Change in an Asian Monarchy*. Ithaca: Cornell University Press, 1970.

Stuart R. Schram: *The Political Thought of Mao Tse-Tung*. New York: Praeger, 1969.

Thapa, Deepak : *Understanding the Maoist Movement of Nepal*, Centre for Social Research and Development, Delhi, 2003.

Tse-tung Mao: *Mao and the Nepali Revolution*. London: Oxford University Press, 1965.

Tyagi, Sushila. *Indo-Nepalese Relations, 1858-1914*. Delhi: D.K. Publishing, 1974.

Uddhab P : *Maoist Movement in Nepal: A Sociological Perspective*, Adroit, Delhi, 2007.

Upreti, B C : *Maoists in Nepal : From Insurgency to Political Mainstream*, Kalpaz Pub, Delhi, 2008.

Index

R

S

T

W